Praise for

ONLY THE RICH CAN PLAY

"In *Only the Rich Can Play*, David Wessel masterfully makes policy wonkery into a riveting story. A cautionary tale of good intentions gone bad, it is a must read, from Wall Street to Main Street."

—Arthur C. Brooks, professor, Harvard Kennedy
School and Harvard Business School, and
New York Times–bestselling author

"David Wessel is a Washington treasure, and anything he writes is a must-read as far as I'm concerned. In *Only the Rich Can Play*, Wessel marries the depth of his understanding of economics with his years of experience as a Washington reporter and his skill at storytelling. He traces the origins of the Opportunity Zone tax break from conception to birth and then shows how it actually works (or not) on the ground. This is both a great read and an important one because it shows those of us outside Washington how things really work there."

—Bryan Burrough, coauthor of *Barbarians
at the Gate* and *Forget the Alamo*

"David Wessel has long been one of the keenest observers of the American economy. This book shows his remarkable ability to combine intellectual meat with compelling narrative. Many Silicon Valley moguls are politically clueless, but Sean Parker of Napster and Facebook managed to slip his real estate investment scheme—Opportunity Zones—into law, despite almost no support from traditional thought leaders. You should read this book if you want to understand how to get things done in Washington. You should read this book if you want to understand the most important new urban policy in a generation. You should read this book if you just want to be entertained by a terrific political yarn."

—Edward Glaeser, Fred and Eleanor Glimp
Professor of Economics, Harvard University

"Vegas, opulent parties, wine-filled dinners.... Not since the classic *Showdown at Gucci Gulch* has tax policy making been this much fun. But look beyond the vivid anecdotes and there's an important and underappreciated story about a program that will cost the federal treasury billions while helping a fraction of the people Congress intended. Wessel weaves together on-the-ground reporting, the best data and evidence, and deep knowledge of the policy process to show how strong moral convictions, vast wealth, and a turbocharged media presence can run up against entrenched special interests and inadequate vetting. The result, as one interviewee says, is a missed opportunity indeed."   —Tracy Gordon, Urban Institute

"A fascinating and entertaining—albeit at times depressing and infuriating—story of how a major policy initiative came to be....A lesson in how social policy in America should not be made, but too often is, and an explanation of why the rich always seem to win."
                  —Melissa Kearney, Neil Moskowitz Professor
                  of Economics, University of Maryland

"If you want to understand how the US has ended up with a tax code that on paper is progressive but in practice is so regressive that the very wealthy pay virtually no tax, *Only the Rich Can Play* is the place to start. In his wry style, Wessel uses the story of a tax provision dreamed up by a tech billionaire to show what happens when good intentions and arrogance collide with our tax-avoidance-industrial complex."
                  —Paul Romer, New York University,
                  Nobel laureate in Economics

"A must-read for anyone who wants to really understand how an idea can in time become a law—with the help of a large budget, skilled lobbying, and the support of a few key members of Congress. I thought I knew a bit about how Washington works, but I learned an enormous amount from David Wessel's very carefully researched and extremely well written book."

—David M. Rubenstein, cofounder and co-executive chairman of The Carlyle Group and author of *How to Lead*

"The real story of the Trump years is one you have never heard. Beneath all the outrage and the hysteria, the same old depressing familiar was chugging along all the time: billionaires designing innovative tax breaks for other billionaires, poor people being used as a moral excuse to cut the taxes of the rich. David Wessel tells us the story in its every glittering detail, and his title might well be the catch-phrase for our era: *Only the Rich Can Play*."

—Thomas Frank, author of *What's the Matter with Kansas?* and *The People, No*

ONLY
THE RICH
CAN PLAY

ONLY
THE RICH
CAN PLAY

How Washington Works in the New Gilded Age

David Wessel

PUBLICAFFAIRS

NEW YORK

PublicAffairs
Hachette Book Group
1290 Avenue of the Americas, New York, NY 10104
www.publicaffairsbooks.com
@Public_Affairs

Printed in the United States of America

First Edition: October 2021

Published by PublicAffairs, an imprint of Perseus Books, LLC, a subsidiary of Hachette Book Group, Inc. The PublicAffairs name and logo is a trademark of the Hachette Book Group.

The Hachette Speakers Bureau provides a wide range of authors for speaking events. To find out more, go to www.hachettespeakersbureau.com or call (866) 376-6591.

The publisher is not responsible for websites (or their content) that are not owned by the publisher.

Library of Congress Cataloging-in-Publication Data
Names: Wessel, David, author.
Title: Only the rich can play : how Washington works in the new gilded age / David Wessel.
Description: First edition. | New York : PublicAffairs, 2021. | Includes bibliographical references and index.
Identifiers: LCCN 2021005455 | ISBN 9781541757196 (hardcover) | ISBN 9781541757202 (ebook)
Subjects: LCSH: Parker, Sean, 1979- | United States. Tax Cuts and Jobs Act. | Enterprise zones—United States. | Business enterprises—Taxation—Law and legislation—United States. | Rich people—Taxation—United States. | Tax havens—United States. | Economic development—Corrupt practices—United States.
Classification: LCC HD257.5 .W47 2021 | DDC 338.8/7—dc23
LC record available at https://lccn.loc.gov/2021005455

ISBNs: 9781541757196 (hardcover); 9781541757202 (ebook)

LSC-C

Printing 1, 2021

To Bruce, Paul, and Lois, my inspiring siblings

Contents

Introduction

B LUE DUCK TAVERN IS ADJACENT TO THE LOBBY OF A PARK
Hyatt hotel, which sits alongside other luxury hotels, pricey
condos, and fine dining restaurants in Washington's West End
neighborhood, between the White House and Georgetown. The
tavern is the sort of place that has a nineteen-page wine list, boasts
of its humidity-controlled tea cellar, had a Michelin star for a couple of years (it lost it in 2019), and draws the likes of Barack and
Michelle Obama, who celebrated their seventeenth wedding anni-
versary there. Its open-plan kitchen allows diners a view of chefs
working over a Molteni range that was custom made in France at a
cost in the high five figures.

One evening in September 2013, four Washington insiders and
one Silicon Valley billionaire wunderkind met for dinner at Blue
Duck. The host—and star—was thirty-five-year-old Sean Parker,
founder of Napster and first president of Facebook. He was in town
to shop one of his many really big ideas over a long, boozy meal.

"It's hard to remember because so much wine was flowing," says
Jared Bernstein, a left-leaning economist (and now a member of

President Biden's Council of Economic Advisers) who was at the table. Change-the-world banter was flowing freely, too. At one point, Bernstein remembers Parker telling him he'd cured cancer. "I said, 'What the fuck are you talking about?' He said, 'I have this regime. It costs $50 million. There's a 50 percent chance you are cured and a 50 percent chance it kills you.' That's what it was like." (Parker's spokesperson denies he said that.)

But Sean Parker hadn't come to the nation's capital with a cure for cancer. He was pushing another audacious idea: to convince Congress to embrace a scheme that would encourage very rich people to invest in left-behind parts of the country in exchange for a generous tax break.

Also at the table that night was the *yin* to Bernstein's *yang*: Kevin Hassett, a conservative economist (and later chair of President Trump's Council of Economic Advisers). The other co-conspirators were two young Washington up-and-comers hired by Parker to accomplish his improbable goal of building a bipartisan coalition in Congress to write his idea into law: Steve Glickman, a Democrat who had left the Obama White House, and John Lettieri, a Republican who had quit a job helping to lobby on behalf of US subsidiaries of foreign corporations to join Parker's crusade.

Big-time Silicon Valley entrepreneurs and investors like Parker style themselves as visionary, risk-taking disrupters. They swing hard and miss more often than not, but sometimes they hit. And when they do, they exit with a couple of billion dollars, as Parker did at Facebook.

Parker's latest bet—still short on details—had three basic premises.

One, the existing, bureaucratic ways of boosting Rust Belt cities, shrinking rural towns, and deteriorating pockets in otherwise prosperous urban areas were failing. They weren't bold enough.

Two, there was a lot of money in the portfolios of people like Parker—including fellow billionaires Mike Milken, the onetime junk bond king; Jim Sorenson, a very successful serial entrepreneur from Utah; and Dan Gilbert, the cofounder of Quicken Loans. These emblems of the new Gilded Age, Parker surmised, would readily flood capital-starved neighborhoods with money if doing so offered tax savings free of nettlesome rules.

Three, market forces work better than government rules or programs. They can and should be harnessed to bring private money to downtrodden communities.

The odds were decidedly against Parker. Other very rich, very smart people have seen their big ideas make headlines but never make it through Congress. Washington's reporters and pundits ooze cynicism about start-up billionaires attempting big social change. Underscoring the skepticism of his peers, Parker once joked publicly that his friend and onetime business partner, Peter Thiel (founder of PayPal and Palantir Technologies, and the first outside investor in Facebook) bet him $1 million he couldn't get the bill passed.[1] (Parker tells me that as he was brainstorming about the concept, he asked Thiel if he would be tempted to put some of his profits from selling stock into businesses located in economically distressed neighborhoods, if by so doing he could avoid paying taxes. Thiel said, sure, but you'll never get that through Congress, and facetiously offered to bet that Parker would fail. Parker didn't take the $1 million wager seriously and, in any event, Thiel never sent a check.)

But Parker succeeded. His idea became law in late 2017, creating 8,764 Opportunity Zones across the United States and its territories.

In Baltimore, about fifty miles north of Blue Duck Tavern, Rev. Donté Hickman, a locally prominent pastor and economic-development advocate, has soured on Parker's idea. In 2018, Hickman stood next to President Trump and celebrated Opportunity Zones as a key to economic revitalization. Two years later, still waiting for the first Opportunity Zone dollar to arrive in his East Baltimore neighborhood, which is scarred by vacant lots and empty brick row houses, Hickman has become a critic. Investors are taking advantage of the tax break, he says, but the money is going into already gentrifying places. "It's all about the money," he says. Giving wealthy investors a tax break is no substitute for simply investing public money into rebuilding neighborhoods like his.

Parker's Opportunity Zone law has one element in common with the $50 million cancer cure he breezily described to Bernstein: only the rich can play. But in contrast to his cancer cure's risky fifty-fifty survival rate, the odds of winning from the tax break are distinctly higher for investors. Indeed, one reason Hickman isn't seeing investment pour into East Baltimore is because other cities offer safer investments. And that's where the bulk of the money seems to have gone: to pricey condos in Portland, Oregon; to luxury student housing in Louisville, Kentucky; to a boutique hotel in New Orleans; to self-storage units in San Antonio. Not exactly left-behind places or downtrodden communities.

Opportunity Zones got traction in part because they were styled as a solution to twenty-first-century America's increasingly severe problem of economic inequality, a phenomenon exacerbated by the uneven recovery from the 2008 global financial crisis and by the COVID-19 pandemic. Some people and places are doing very well, but many are not, and the gulf between them is growing. Opportunity Zones are a peculiarly American solution to the problem, one that reflects an antipathy toward raising taxes to support big government investment. In the United States, taxes at all levels of government account for about 24 percent of gross domestic product (GDP), well below the 34 percent average of developed countries, according to the Organisation for Economic Co-operation and Development.[2]

The go-to solution for every economic problem when Republicans are in power is a tax cut. Tax cuts are essentially attempts to bribe the richest Americans to move their money to whatever place, business, activity, or charity is popular with politicians at the time. They allow politicians to brag they've done something worthwhile and simultaneously win the gratitude of the (almost always) rich constituents who enjoy the savings. And because many Americans think a tax cut costs the government less than an equivalent expenditure, elected officials usually avoid political fallout. The problem is that tax savings for the rich always materialize; the promised benefits to the left-behind don't always show up.

When I first heard about Opportunity Zones—or OZs, often pronounced Oh-ZEEs, sometimes pronounced Oz, like the Wizard, and occasionally called OH-zones—I was intrigued. OZs were stealthily inserted in six pages of the 185-page Tax Cuts and Jobs Act of 2017, largely thanks to the determination of Sean Parker's chief congressional ally, Republican Tim Scott of South Carolina, the first Black man to be elected to the US Senate from the South since Reconstruction.

I wondered how a political novice like Parker had taken his dream from conception to Donald Trump's signature in less than five years, without a single congressional hearing or significant public scrutiny. And how had he done it with a campaign that cost a relatively modest, by Washington lobbying standards, $11 million? What did his success reveal about how Washington works in this new Gilded Age? And who was playing the OZ game now that it was law? Would Parker's brainchild disrupt old notions about fighting poverty and really lift up left-behind communities? Or was it fatally warped by aversion to government oversight and excessive faith in unfettered markets as the best way to achieve social good? Opportunity Zones were clearly a big tax win for the wealthy, but did they also do some good for the poor folks and neighborhoods in whose name they were sold?

I wanted to know more about Parker's gamble. So I went to Vegas.

CHAPTER ONE

And You Don't Have to Die...

Mandalay Bay Resort and Casino sits at the south end of the Las Vegas strip. It has 3,209 hotel rooms on forty-three floors (five set aside as the upscale Four Seasons Hotel Las Vegas), twenty-four elevators, and 135,000 square feet of casinos. Gold leaf lines the windows, giving the building a gleaming sheen in the desert sun. The floors have been renumbered to eliminate "32" from the elevator buttons: the floor from which Stephen Paddock opened fire in October 2017, killing fifty-eight outdoor concertgoers below.

On a sunny day in May 2019, before the COVID-19 pandemic, the hotel is packed, mostly with gamblers, tourists, and showgoers. The check-in line is long despite largely unused automated check-in kiosks nearby. I walk along the lobby's garish, boldly geometric rugs, the kind one sees only in big hotels, through the noisy, purple-lit casinos, past Fleur by Hubert Keller, Aureole, Libertine Social, Lupo by Wolfgang Puck, and a dozen other restaurants, and past an eleven-acre water park called Mandalay Bay Beach. I eventually reach the hotel's adjacent convention center and the foyer outside the South Pacific—each ballroom's name echoes the hotel's theme—to register for the Opportunity Zone Expo.[1]

I know the basics of the OZ game, but not much more.

Rule number one is that, unlike the hundreds of slot machines I just passed, this game can't be played by most Americans. Players must have a capital gain: a profit from the sale of stock, real estate, art, or some other asset. Fewer than one in five American households has *any* unrealized (that is, unsold and untaxed) capital gains from financial assets, excluding equity in their homes. And couples with 2019 taxable incomes (that is, after all deductions) under $78,750 are already exempt from capital gains taxes, should they be lucky enough to have any gains at all. This OZ convention targets a select crowd.

Two, if you put capital gains in a Qualified Opportunity Zone Fund—more than a thousand have appeared in the past couple of years—and that fund invests in one of the 8,764 census tracts across the country designated as OZs (more on that later), you can defer tax on those capital gains until 2026. Paying taxes later is always better than sooner: you get to use the money in the interim. Deferred taxes on capital gains are essentially interest-free loans from the government to investors.

Three, if you get in early and stay in for seven years, you not only defer your payments but also shave 15 percent off the capital gains tax you'll owe in 2026.

Four, and this is the big carrot, if you hold onto your Opportunity Zone investment for at least ten years, you won't pay any capital gains taxes—zero—on profits made from that investment.

Here's how it works: Say you sell some stock and turn a $1 million profit. Ordinarily you'd owe the federal government $238,000 in taxes (the 20 percent capital gains rate plus the 3.8 percent net investment income tax) when you file your tax return. Put that $1 million into an OZ fund, though, and you defer those taxes until

2026. If you put the money in a fund before the end of 2019, you'll owe only $202,000 instead of $238,000. Hold onto that $1 million OZ investment for ten years, get an annual return of, say, 8 percent (most real estate deals promise a lot more than that), and you'll have an asset worth $2.2 million. And you won't have to pay any capital gains tax on your $1.2 million profit.

Americans, mostly wealthy Americans, pay a lot to the federal government in capital gains taxes: more than $130 billion in 2017, the year OZs became law.[2] It's no wonder that so many people have flocked to an OZ convention, including the well-off who want to learn how to cut their own taxes and the hundreds of promoters and middlemen who want to help them.

Rule number five: unlike nearly every other federal program aimed at luring private money to poor neighborhoods, there is currently no limit to how many people can play the OZ game, or how much in taxes they can avoid.

And, six, there's no application process and no government official certifying that projects fit the law, although the IRS can audit you later to confirm you followed the rules—rules that, in May 2019, the Treasury and IRS have yet to publish to clarify precisely what steps investors need to take to qualify for the tax break, to define terms such as "substantially all," and to detail how the IRS interprets the bare-bones language of the law. But one thing is clear: the statute has no requirement that an OZ investment create jobs or help people who live in the designated zone, or that the local community even be consulted. And there's no authoritative data yet on how much has been invested in Opportunity Zones or where the money has gone or for what purpose.

It's clear why the OZ tax break unleashed a flurry of interest from the wealthy, investment funds, real estate developers, and conference organizers. I'm here to witness tax-avoidance capitalism firsthand.

THE NEW GOLD RUSH

Outside the South Pacific ballroom, I get a badge to hang around my neck from a lanyard, and a small, silver foil-lined shopping bag with "OZ" printed in blue and white letters. Inside the bag is a six-by-eight-inch, 188-page book printed on high-grade, glossy paper. The book features bios and photos of speakers, from Derek Armstrong of the Nevada Governor's Office of Economic Development (a lawyer who spent five years in the Marine Corps) to Johnney Zhang, a Los Angeles developer. It also lists sponsors in order of generosity, from LA hotel and multifamily housing developer Relevant Group (the sole "Diamond & Lanyard Sponsor") to Mainstream Group Holdings Limited, an Australian firm that provides administrative services to asset managers (a mere "Panel Sponsor").

I'm not used to attending conferences where I don't know anyone, so I scan the people milling around as I wait for the first session to begin. They are mostly, though not all, white and male. The tax lawyers and accountants wear ties. The real estate men wear sports jackets, no ties.

One man stands out. Robert Whyte is wearing a cowboy hat wrapped with a piece of white paper that says, in large black letters, "Looking for OZ Funds. Operating business looking to expand and acquire a building." He is very pleased with the attention he is getting, and with the number of people taking his one-page leaflet.

Whyte has a factory that does contract packaging for wine and liquor—legally known as a distilled spirits plant—that has outgrown its facility in Downey, California, south of Los Angeles. He is looking for $3 million to relocate to an OZ in Southern California. Besides putting liquor in pouches and bottles, Whyte's company also makes vitamin water designed for dogs, which he insists is the next big thing. On his LinkedIn page, Whyte claims to have earned an MBA at the School of Hard Knocks, "learning how to deal with unethical people and survive."

Before starting his contract packaging business, Whyte spent about twenty years as a low-profile investment banker. He tells me he previously raised $1 billion in EB-5 funds, through a US government program that offers visas to foreigners who invest in US businesses.[3] I listen to Whyte skeptically, but as I scribble notes I think, this could be a fun few days.

This is what a modern-day gold rush looks like. Few people noticed the Opportunity Zone provision when the tax bill went through Congress just before Christmas 2017. There were too many bigger tax breaks to ponder. It took several weeks for most tax lawyers and accountants, wealth advisers, real estate developers, and reporters to discover it. The first *New York Times* story didn't appear until the end of January 2018. The first *Wall Street Journal* story ran in July of that year. But by May 2019, around one thousand extroverts are at Mandalay Bay to talk, listen, and learn about OZs, and—if they're lucky—to make a deal.

There are all sorts of people at this convention, drawn together by the possibility of making money and reducing their taxes. But given that Opportunity Zones were sold as a way to steer investment toward left-behind communities, there are notable absences. I don't come across, say, many heads of local economic-development groups or capital-starved entrepreneurs based in poor neighborhoods.

Instead, I meet proselytizers and the DC insiders who wrote the bill; they know what OZs are meant to do and want them to be a success. There are investors with money—capital gains, to be precise—who are intrigued by the possibility of reducing their tax bill and interested in influencing the rules the Treasury and IRS will write to administer the law. There are business owners, like Whyte, looking for investors, and real estate developers eager to boast about the money they've already raised. There are people who've discovered they own property in an Opportunity Zone and are hoping to cash in. And then there are the middlemen—legions of lawyers and accountants, financial advisers and wealth managers, consultants and service providers, podcasters and website operators—panning for their share of the gold as money flows from rich people to buildings and businesses in Opportunity Zones.

THE PROSELYTIZERS

Steve Glickman is one reason OZs exist, so he gets star billing on day two of the OZ Expo: a one-on-one interview at the opening plenary with Ali Jahangiri, whose company organized the conference. After a few years in the Obama administration, Glickman accepted Sean Parker's offer to run the Economic Innovation Group (EIG), a think tank Parker created to promote OZs and which ultimately made them a reality.

About eight months before the OZ Expo, and five and a half years after launching EIG, Glickman cashed in: he quit EIG to form his own company, Develop LLC, to consult for OZ investors and developers or, as he puts it, to be a consigliere for big OZ funds. Glickman, in suit and tie, sits on stage in a big, boxy armchair. Jahangiri, suit but no tie, sits in a matching chair. Behind them is an American flag and "OZ" in big blue and white letters.

Glickman explains how OZs went from an idea on the back of an envelope to a white paper to legislation, describing the 2017 Tax Cuts and Jobs Act as "a ship for our little stowaway of legislation to latch onto" while "not too many people were paying attention." OZs, he says, are "a Marshall Plan for the heartland."

Shay Hawkins, another player in the OZ origin story, is also in Las Vegas. The agenda lists him as an aide to Tim Scott, the chief Senate backer of OZs. Hawkins, a lawyer and investment banker, was a key behind-the-scenes agent for Scott as he maneuvered to get OZs included in the 2017 tax bill. But the agenda is out of date: Hawkins has just quit the Senate job to become founding president and chief executive of the newly formed Opportunity Funds Association, a trade association that promotes OZs.

Hawkins speaks very briefly at the opening of a panel, emphasizing that OZs have bipartisan support ("which has implications for us going forward") and prescribing a strategy for pressing the Treasury for investor friendly regulations. "We don't need 150 letters asking for 150 things," he says. "We need 150 letters asking for three things." (He doesn't say what those three things are.) Hawkins is silent for the rest of the panel, and no one directs a question to him. Afterward, though, he draws a small crowd of people around his wheelchair—he was injured in a car accident in 2009—who want the latest gossip from Washington.

THE INVESTORS

In a wide ballroom set with classroom-style rows of narrow tables, a stage at the front, big video screens at either end, and more people than chairs, I snag a seat next to a slim, sixtyish woman with closely cropped gray hair. Cindy Leuty Jones, from Los Angeles, was a respiratory therapist and model when she was young and, later, a real estate investor and developer.

Her friend is starting an Opportunity Zone fund and wants her to help run it, but Jones isn't interested. How come? "I already have a boatload of money, and my husband has a bigger boatload of money," she says matter-of-factly.

The couple lives in a ten-thousand-square-foot house on seven acres, in a gated community on Moraga Drive in Bel Air and has substantial real estate holdings in Southern California. "But it's hard to be Type-A retired," she says. She has lots of interests—posting videos of her exercise routines on Facebook, fundraising for the Jack and Cindy Jones Youth Center and other charities, and self-publishing self-help books, the latest of which is titled, *DOABLE: Little Decisions That Will Transform Your Life.*

So, if she's not getting into the OZ business, why come to the OZ Expo? Well, she owns an Andy Warhol painting that she bought for $35,000 shortly after he died, thirty years ago. It's worth millions now, and she's thinking of selling it and investing the substantial capital gain in an Opportunity Zone fund. The painting is small—ten inches by twenty inches—and isn't prominently placed in her house; it's in her second-floor study. She's not emotionally attached to it, she says.

What is it a painting of? Three dollar signs: $ $ $.

Later, in another ballroom, this one with round, banquet-style tables, I meet Jim Goldfarb. He has been a McKinsey consultant, an associate at Bain Capital, a principal at a private investment company backed by the Milken family and Larry Ellison, a vice president of MP3.com and, since 2001, founder and managing partner of Broadstream Capital, a Los Angeles merchant bank.

Goldfarb tells me he sold Antares (maker of Auto-Tune software for vocal musicians), a company he'd owned since 2016, to a New York family office two weeks prior. He's looking for some place to put his capital gains, and he wants to diversify into real estate. His accountant alerted him to OZs; he's interested in learning more and scouting possible deals. This is his second OZ conference. "If I am going to invest in real estate," he tells me, "I might as well do it in a tax-advantaged way. I want my investment to be passive. I don't want to be a developer. I don't want to be an owner."

THE REAL ESTATE PROS

During a panel at which different flavors of real estate developers (multifamily, big-city, small-scale) describe the potential for OZs in their niches, Mohi Monem from Atlanta-based Arcis Real Estate Capital (known as ArcisRE) talks about the attractiveness of OZs as a way to invest in apartment buildings aimed exclusively at college students. These tenants may be rough on apartments, but they are reliable rent payers, they have parents willing to cosign a lease, and landlords can raise their rent every year. It's a market in which his company was active before OZs. Monem reports that more than eighty colleges have OZs adjacent to their campuses.

ArcisRE was spun off in 2019 from a private-equity firm that advises and manages money for foreign investors—Monem once worked with wealthy folks from Dubai—to concentrate on connecting OZ investors with developers of student housing, apartment buildings, and hotels. The spin-off's press release oozed enthusiasm: "The Opportunity Zone program could prove to be a windfall for both investors and low-income census tract communities. Having been involved in Opportunity Zones since early 2018, ArcisRE has built a network of capital relationships looking to invest in Opportunity Zone deals within its specified sectors of focus."[4]

Monem is sober, calm, and measured compared to another panelist, Jimmy Rose, who sports a look-at-me powder-blue suit. Rose is from Saint George, a rapidly growing city of about 87,000 in the southwesternmost corner of Utah, a small section of which qualified for OZ status partly because it is home to Dixie State University; students show up as poor in census data. Settled in the 1850s, Saint George is reputedly named for Mormon apostle George A. Smith (known as the "Potato Saint" because he urged early settlers to eat raw potatoes as a cure for scurvy).

A developer and contractor, Rose discovered OZs in June 2018, when a state official showed him a letter from the governor designating Utah's forty-six zones. Much to his chagrin, Rose and his wife had purchased five properties in Saint George's compact downtown Opportunity Zone on December 7, 2017—twenty-four days too early to qualify for the OZ tax break. Nevertheless, Rose found a way to exploit the benefit, turning his real estate company into a Qualified Opportunity Zone Business, which will allow him to escape capital gains taxes if the value of the business grows.

Because Rose doesn't like learning about things secondhand, he flew to Washington for the first IRS hearing on OZ regulations, which was postponed when a congressional budget dispute caused a government shutdown. Rose went back for the rescheduled hearing on February 14, 2019. There is a lot of misinformation about OZs, he says. He holds up two pink folders. One contains the first set of OZ regulations (73 pages, he says); the other, the second set (168 pages). "Read it yourself. Don't rely on your accountant and attorney to tell you what it says. When an attorney or CPA says, 'you can't do that,' ask for the citation." A New York tax lawyer on the same panel looks on incredulously.

THE MONEY SEEKERS

An early afternoon panel, "Investor Types 101: Learning more about individual investors, family offices, investments banks," draws a standing-room crowd. At Q and A time, Susan Iwamoto, in the back of the room, has a question. She stands out in her geometrically patterned, indigo-blue cotton poncho; she definitely isn't a tax lawyer or developer. Iwamoto's family owns a boatyard on just over an acre of land in Costa Mesa, in Orange County, California, a couple of miles from the Newport Beach harbor. Together with neighboring landowners, they have fifteen acres available for OZ investment.

"I don't know how we got an OZ," she admits. "We live in one of the most affluent zip codes in the world." I, too, wonder why her neighborhood made the OZ cut. It turns out census data show that one in three residents in Iwamoto's census tract, many of them migrant workers, live below the poverty line.[5] But Costa Mesa is adjacent to Newport Beach, home to more than a few of the billionaires on the Forbes 400 list.

The local government is anti-growth, she complains, and offers her no help. "So I thought I could come here and make something happen." Much to their frustration, people like Iwamoto who owned land in an OZ before the law was created can't easily take advantage of the tax break. Selling their land at a premium price is the best way to cash in (even though they'll pay capital gains taxes).

From the podium, a panelist from a real estate investment trust says, "I want an exclusive on your property." But he is joking. He suggests she find a local developer to partner with. Even before the session ends, she is surrounded by folks offering counsel and business cards. She smiles at the attention and is optimistic the trip to Las Vegas will pay off.

Also in Las Vegas looking for money is Pitichoke Chulapamornsri, whose business card identifies him as VP of International Business Development and Strategic Projects for two affiliated California-based firms, Crop One Holdings and its retail brand, FreshBox Farms. Crop One is growing leafy greens in energy-efficient, indoor vertical farms. Chulapamornsri has placed tiny lettuce plants on his exhibit hall table, distinguishing his display from the brochures, giveaway pens, and computer monitors on the others. His company has one farm in Boston and another underway in the Emirates, which he tells me will be the world's largest vertical farm. They are soliciting OZ fund investors to raise money for a vertical farm in an OZ in the Austin–San Antonio corridor.

I ask him when he launched the fund.

"Yesterday," he says.

THE MIDDLEMEN

Opportunity Zones will eventually save wealthy people money on their taxes, they will help real estate developers raise capital for future projects, and they may someday help people who live in needy neighborhoods. But the very first people winning at the OZ game are the middlemen.

OZ Expo organizer Ali Jahangiri has long made a living as a middleman, initially building online platforms to link doctors and patients, lawyers and clients. He currently runs a website on which experts answer questions about OZs, a slick OZ-focused magazine with ads, and (pre-COVID-19) $500-a-ticket OZ conferences. Before OZs appeared, he was running a website and overseas conferences for prospective EB-5 applicants: foreigners trying to obtain green cards by investing $1.8 million (or $900,000 in a Targeted Employment Area) in US commercial ventures, often real estate, that promise to create at least ten jobs.

It turns out a lot of the Las Vegas OZ Expo attendees—like Jahangiri and the cowboy-hat-wearing Robert Whyte—are veterans of the EB-5 business. They've made careers of selling dealmaking, paperwork-processing, or legal and accounting expertise, connecting foreigners seeking EB-5 visas with American developers seeking foreign money. The EB-5 program, now thirty years old, highlights the shortcomings of government attempts to drive private capital to socially beneficial ends. EB-5 has come under criticism for everything from national security dangers (Iranian and Chinese intel operatives buying green cards) to fraud (prosecutors have brought charges involving tens of millions of dollars).

Many middlemen at the conference are also well versed in a much older capital gains tax break known as 1031 like-kind exchanges.[6] This one allows people to avoid paying capital gains taxes on the sale of an asset as long as the sale's proceeds are used within 180 days to buy an asset of the same kind—trading, for example, an older apartment building for a newer one. Like-kind exchanges were first added to the tax code in 1921, to make it easier for property owners to sell to someone who would put the holdings to better use, and to reduce the hassle to farmers of replacing a horse or a plot of land with another. Over the decades, an industry grew up around arranging 1031 exchanges for all sorts of properties, even baseball players' contracts.[7] The 2017 tax bill banned 1031 exchanges for all assets except real estate.

The legacy of these two programs pops up everywhere at the conference. "When 1031 met EB-5 they had a love child—Opportunity Zones," Jill Jones from NES Financial, a company that provides third-party administrative services for financial firms, says to me, smiling broadly. (OK, it's an insider joke.)

A few speakers, like Steve Glickman, talk in lofty terms about the potential for Opportunity Zones to attract money to distressed communities and bring prosperity to the downtrodden, but not very many. People who come to an OZ Expo are interested in, well, making money and cutting their taxes.

Brad Cohen—a burly, balding Los Angeles business, real estate, and estate planning lawyer who doesn't look like the Ironman triathlete the moderator mentions in his introduction—can barely contain his surprise at how generous the OZ tax break is. "They went overboard, in my opinion, to create benefits for people who have capital gains," he says. He marvels at the already gentrifying census tracts designated as OZs: "Is there any place in Oakland that is *not* an Opportunity Zone?"

Cohen walks the crowd through the benefits of the tax break, including the provision that exempts all profits made on an OZ investment from capital gains if the asset is kept for ten years. The only other way to escape capital gains taxes, he notes, is to hold onto assets for your whole life and then pass them to your heirs, who won't have to pay capital gains when they inherit the property.

This is better, he says: "You don't have to die."

In this crowd, that one-liner draws a lot of laughs.

Susan Rounds, a tax lawyer who advises wealthy clients of Deutsche Bank, sounds a more sober note: "You can't let the tax tail wag the dog. You have to look at the investment itself." This or a variant—OZs can't make a bad investment good; they can make a good investment better—is like the chorus of a long song. Everyone knows the words and repeats them to me. But the focus at the OZ Expo is not on the quality of the underlying investments, it's on the lust for tax breaks.

NEVADA CENSUS TRACT 68

The exhibit space at the OZ Expo is lame. There are none of the cool giveaways I recall from the pediatricians' conferences my dad took me to when I was a kid. Inexplicably, one booth offers ways to remove wrinkles without surgery. I skip that one.

At a table with nothing but a laptop, a radio mic, and a one-page leaflet, I find Jimmy Atkinson from Fort Worth, Texas. He launched an online OZ directory and podcast at his ad-supported site, Opportunitydb.com, in August 2018, almost immediately after hearing Glickman tout OZs on an investment-advice podcast. "It's kind of hard not to be excited about eliminating capital gains taxes forever," Atkinson says. Well, it's certainly hard not to be excited about that in *this* crowd.

Atkinson shows me an app on his phone that instantly maps OZs. The app opens to Las Vegas, and I see a little pulsing blue dot that indicates where we're standing. Wait a minute, I say, we're in an OZ now? Looks like it, he says.

I am sure this is a mistake. Mandalay Bay is in an OZ? I walk over to a booth where CoStar, a big-time commercial real estate information provider, is demonstrating its software on several big iMacs. Show me how it works, I say to the guy. Someone told me we are in OZ right now, I tell him. Can't be, he says. He types a few strokes on the keyboard, clicks the mouse, and, looking surprised, tells me: Yes, we are.

Mandalay Bay and the Four Seasons are in Nevada census tract 68—along with the sphinx and pyramids of the four-star Luxor and the fairytale turrets of Excalibur Hotel & Casino. Much of the rest of the tract is consumed by the Las Vegas Airport, which makes this an unlikely, to put it mildly, Opportunity Zone. But the rules don't care about how many people live in a tract, just the demographics of those who do. At the far northeastern corner of Nevada census tract 68, the Census Bureau finds about 1,700 households, many of them identified as Hispanic. About a third of the people living inside the boundaries of the tract are below the poverty line, and that's enough to make the tract eligible for OZ designation. In an adjacent census tract, just to the west of Mandalay Bay, a $2 billion, sixty-five-thousand-seat football stadium is rising for the Las Vegas Raiders. The county planning office, more focused on local economic development than on the lofty goals expressed by OZ proponents, successfully lobbied the governor to designate both tracts as Opportunity Zones.

Back in my room in Mandalay Bay (I've opted not to splurge for the Four Seasons), with its view of the Las Vegas strip, I'm hooked. I need to know how Washington ended up offering the same tax break to Las Vegas real estate developers and entrepreneurs as it offers to those in South Central LA or impoverished communities in Appalachia. The story begins around 2013, with Sean Parker.

CHAPTER TWO

Wizards of OZ: Sean Parker and the EIG Boys

S EAN PARKER IS NOT THE FIRST GUY YOU'D EXPECT TO LEAD A successful effort to make a big change in the tax code, but he's been surprising people since he was a kid. His dad taught him to program on an Atari 800 when he was seven. When Parker was fifteen, he was caught hacking into corporate and military computer networks; the FBI raided his family's suburban Virginia house. He was sentenced to community service at a library with other teenage offenders. At nineteen, he shunned college and, with buddy Shawn Fanning, founded Napster, the peer-to-peer music file–sharing service that blew up the music industry, until the courts shut it down for copyright infringement. After that, he raised venture capital for Plaxo, a service that automatically updated users' electronic address books; the board threw him out in 2004.

That same year, when Parker was twenty-four, he spotted an early version of Facebook on the computer of a roommate's girlfriend. He tracked down Mark Zuckerberg, then a sophomore at Harvard, and, on a whim, flew to the East Coast to meet him at a Chinese restaurant. A few months later, the two ran into each other on the streets of Palo Alto. Zuckerberg invited Parker, who was jobless but driving a BMW, to move into a summer house Facebook had rented. Over the next few months, Parker talked Zuckerberg out of returning to Harvard, helped him raise money from Peter Thiel, and became Facebook's first president. Parker's impact at Facebook was huge, but his tenure was short. The next year, police in North Carolina found cocaine after raiding Parker's beach house. He was forced to leave the company, walking away with Facebook shares that would be worth around $2 billion when the company went public.[1]

In October 2010, a movie about the founding of Facebook, *The Social Network*, raised Parker's already significant public profile, but not in a good way. Justin Timberlake plays the young Parker as a conniving opportunist who pushed out and ripped off one of the other founders. It's a portrayal that neither Parker nor those who know him find accurate. He is more frequently described as brilliant, charismatic, egotistical, flaky, and loyal. Start-ups love his visionary big ideas. Venture capitalists hate his unpredictability. In his younger years, Parker was known for working hard, partying hard, and sleeping until early afternoon. Whatever the inaccuracy of the on-screen portrayal, Parker says he had "a hard time psychologically dealing with it."[2] It was released at a time when he was already down—he'd just ended a four-year relationship and was gaining thirty pounds while holed up in a hotel, recovering from knee surgery.

But Parker is resilient. In 2011, the thirty-one-year-old legend posed for the cover of *Forbes*, having made his debut on the list of America's 400 wealthiest. He came in at number 200 with an estimated wealth of $2.1 billion. (On the 2020 list, he slipped to number 319, but his estimated net worth was up to $2.7 billion.)

Forbes reporter Steven Bertoni, who labeled Parker the "Picasso of business," described the photo shoot, which took place at Parker's lavish Greenwich Village townhouse (one sign of opulence: a mowed lawn on a third-story patio), with great gusto in a video interview with his editor.[3]

"He had a stylist come out from LA and they lined up all the clothes," Bertoni said. "In the living room of his $20 million townhouse he had three racks full of Italian suits. There were twenty dress shirts still in the wrapping.... There were suspenders. There were his ties. There were twenty pairs of eyeglasses to choose from. So he had the stylist picking out what, together, what he wanted to wear. He had hair. He had makeup. He had catering. He had his publicist, and he had his fiancée, and he had a friend there, too." (Bertoni called it "the Seantourage.") "He's extremely obsessive about design.... If he's doing a photo shoot, he's going to have ten people there to make sure it's perfect for him, up to his standards."

But obsession with appearances didn't stop Parker from continuing to come up with—and invest in—new ideas. After joining Peter Thiel's venture capital outfit, Founders Fund, Parker became the first American investor in Spotify, the Swedish music site that was Napster's legal offspring; it was a huge hit. He and Shawn Fanning of Napster launched Airtime, a video chat site, in 2012; it was not a hit.

It was around this time that Parker turned his attention to politics. "Politics for me," he said at a 2011 conference, "is the most obvious area [to be disrupted by the Internet]."[4]

The West Coast is packed with people who have made a fortune in some high-tech venture and are convinced that success means they can change the world, or at least solve social problems better than politicians and bureaucrats can. Bill and Melinda Gates have their foundation, which tried to reinvent the American high school, among other things, before turning to public health. Tom Steyer organized an impeachment campaign and spent $345 million of his own money in a quixotic run for president in 2020.[5]

Mark Zuckerberg famously, and largely unsuccessfully, gave $100 million to fix Newark's public schools.[6] Most of these initiatives fail, overwhelmed by the scale and intractability of social problems or drowned in the swamp of politics.

Parker would ultimately prove an exception, but not before a few disappointments. One example is an app called Brigade, which Parker hoped would become a social network for organizing political activity, connecting people with similar views, and increasing voter participation.[7] It drew hundreds of thousands of users, raised millions of dollars, and Parker himself invested tens of millions before he sold it to Pinterest in 2019. (The Brigade.com brand is currently listed for sale.)

At Parker's side for his business and philanthropic ventures has been Michael Polansky, a 2006 Harvard grad who was working at Bridgewater Associates, the hedge fund, when a friend—a childhood neighbor who was working as Parker's assistant—insisted he meet Parker. It took about a year for her to arrange, but the two men finally met at Parker's Greenwich Village townhouse in 2009. "We talked about all the things he wanted to accomplish. He had so many ideas, so many resonated with me," Polansky says.

He quit his job and went to work for Parker, initially spending time at Peter Thiel's venture capital fund. Today he describes his job as running Parker's family office. (If Polansky's name rings a bell, it's probably because of his highly publicized romance with Lady Gaga.)[8]

THE BIG IDEA

After his forced departure from Facebook, but before *The Social Network*, the *Forbes* magazine cover, and Spotify, Parker had a revelation. During a trip to check out United Nations work on malaria prevention and economic development in western Tanzania (where

Stanley met Livingstone), Parker saw a problem—and an opportunity. The daunting problem was that poverty in desperately poor regions would never be eradicated with foreign aid. Private investment was essential. And the opportunity was to tap people, like him, with large, unrealized capital gains—that is, investments in companies or property that had risen in value substantially since the initial investment.

"There was all this money sitting on the sidelines," said Parker, who was guarding an enormous as-yet-untaxed capital gain himself. "I started thinking: How do we get investors to put money into places where they wouldn't normally invest?"[9]

Back in the United States, he witnessed the same problem in the distressed neighborhoods of San Francisco. The financial meltdown that began later that year only exacerbated the inequality. Parker saw not just poverty, but systemic poverty related to certain places. It wasn't only in Tanzania, but also in San Francisco's Tenderloin or in Toledo, Ohio.

"You could see that the financial crisis disproportionately affected certain communities, and that when the recovery happened, it really only happened in certain major cities," Parker recalled in an interview with *Fortune*. He added: "People in these economic deserts were stuck there because of their mortgages or their community. We talk a lot about economic mobility, but there are all these reasons why people can't move."[10]

The idea of developing a mechanism for getting entrepreneurial money invested in struggling communities gestated in Parker's head for several years. He and Polansky talked about creating what they called "D Corps": corporations that would be certified for meeting certain conditions that offered their investors a tax advantage. This would have been a variant on the B Corp concept, which under law in most states certifies that a for-profit company—Patagonia and Allbirds are examples—agrees to take into account not only the interests of its shareholders, but also the interests of workers, the community, and the environment (or some other public benefit) as well.

"The thinking really had nothing to do with real estate," Parker says today. "It had everything to do with new-company creation. The inspiration came from wanting to democratize access to capital and use that as a mechanism to help entrepreneurial people all over the country."

The D Corp idea was an example of Parker's spitballing before his concept was moored to a location-specific tax break, but it didn't stick.

The first time he recalls floating the rudiments of Opportunity Zones in public was in January 2013 at the World Economic Forum in Davos, the high-profile annual gathering of the rich, the powerful, and the famous. He says he and Marc Benioff, founder of Salesforce, hosted a "Future of Philanthropy" forum that featured presentations on various novel philanthropic ideas. When the audience was asked to vote, his concept came in second to last, he says. "They were more interested in things like maybe the US should roll out a national gross domestic happiness index or do more free therapy and psychoanalysis for people because that would make the world a better place," he told me. "So the early learning from that was that this is a super-unglamorous, very long-term, and ultimately difficult thing to try to achieve."

The forum itself got no attention from the press and left no tracks on the Davos website. The "Future of Philanthropy Nightcap" party did, however. Parker spent a reported $1 million to transform a bar into what one attendee, businessman-blogger Henry Blodget, dubbed "a one-of-a-kind 'taxidermy' emporium" with stuffed animal heads on the walls that had red and green laser beams shooting from their eyes.[11] Musicians John Legend and Mark Ronson performed. "It felt like a piece of obscenely expensive performance art, sending up the way in which conspicuous consumption gets rebounded as 'philanthropy' in order to give it a veneer of sophistication," Reuters columnist Felix Salmon wrote.[12]

Undaunted by the reception in Davos, Parker later that year took a tangible step toward what would eventually become Opportunity Zones by consulting Ro Khanna, one of the many nodes in his policy and politics network. Unlike Parker, Khanna had gone to college, graduating from the University of Chicago and then getting a law degree at Yale. Khanna walked comfortably with both the Silicon Valley crowd, some of whom had been his law clients, and Democratic politicians. He had been a deputy assistant secretary in the Obama Commerce Department for a couple of years, a post he left in 2011 to join a prominent Silicon Valley law firm. Khanna got onto Parker's radar after writing a book, *Entrepreneurial Nation: Why Manufacturing Is Still Key to America's Future.*

Parker invited Khanna to New York to sketch out his idea over a four-hour meeting—a short get-together by Parker's standards. At that stage, Parker wasn't thinking about starting a long-lived think tank with a brand, but rather a one-off campaign to push his pet project. Parker asked Khanna to lead the effort. Khanna said no. He was contemplating a run for Congress from a California district that encompasses much of Silicon Valley.

The meeting proved fruitful for both, though. In 2014, Parker supported Khanna's bid for Congress. At a fundraiser for him, Parker talked about what the Silicon Valley ethos could bring to national politics. "We feel for a long time that Silicon Valley just hasn't been properly represented at a federal level," Parker said, adding: "We're starting to come into a realization of our own power and our own capability, not just as innovators and technology pioneers, but also in a political sense."[13]

With Parker's help, Khanna raised as much money as the incumbent, $3.4 million, much of that from high-tech executives. He made it to the two-person runoff but lost to another Democrat. In 2016, he ran again and won, ousting the eight-term incumbent. (He has been in Congress ever since, trouncing his 2020 opponent 71 percent to 29 percent.)

Khanna suggested Parker consider hiring a former colleague of his at the Commerce Department, Steve Glickman. Glickman is a low-profile Washington insider and skilled networker. After growing up in Los Angeles, where his dad started a long-term care insurance company, Glickman earned both a bachelor's and a master's degree at Georgetown—a useful network node in Washington. In college, he was president of the senior class and won various leadership prizes, including a $4,500 community service award for his work with Habitat for Humanity and his travel to Ukraine to lead Passover seders. And he worked part-time in Democratic politics.

After finishing Columbia Law School, Glickman returned to Washington in 2005, where he worked as a federal prosecutor and, subsequently, as an investigator for Representative Henry Waxman's aggressive oversight committee on issues ranging from the wars in Iraq and Afghanistan to abuse of steroids in baseball. Through his connection with Phil Schiliro, who was Waxman's chief of staff and then a high-up in the 2008 Obama campaign—networking comes naturally to him—Glickman got a job doing opposition research on John McCain and Sarah Palin for the Democratic National Committee.

When Obama won, Glickman first volunteered and then was hired by the transition team. "I did seating charts. Really low-level stuff," he says. "But the thing about transition teams is there are no gatekeepers. All the lawyers from the Obama campaign were tired of being lawyers and went to various agencies. I became senior vetting attorney for the White House Counsel's Office. There was a lot of 'last man standing,'" he says. He was twenty-eight years old.

After a two-year stint at the Commerce Department, Glickman returned to the White House to work on international trade issues. There, he was surprised to encounter so much hostility toward international trade emanating from factory towns. Glickman believed there was no alternative to trade in a globalizing economy, but people who lived in those towns didn't see it that way. They didn't think trade was working for them, and they weren't interested in moving somewhere else.

"Most people don't leave," he says. "The only people who leave are the economic futures of the communities." The experience—chronic, place-based poverty—would later influence his interest in Opportunity Zones.

At the end of Obama's first term in 2012, Glickman was ready to leave the White House. He wanted to spend more time with his fiancée, a lawyer from Texas named Christen Krzywonski, whom he'd met at a Capitol Hill reception when she was an aide to a Democratic senator. He had grown weary of a job that required he surrender his cell phone and avoid Gmail while at his office in the National Security Council suite in the Eisenhower Executive Office Building next door to the White House. He had an offer from the consulting firm headed by former secretary of state Madeleine Albright and Sandy Berger, a former national security adviser.

Then Khanna called and connected Glickman with Polansky, Parker's right-hand man. Early in 2013, Glickman went to New York to meet in person with Parker and Polansky at Parker's suite at the Plaza Hotel. All meetings with Parker are long, and this one was no exception. It lasted several hours. Parker had what Glickman calls "a kernel of an idea," but he was still thinking internationally—how to use the tax code to reinvent aid to developing countries.

Glickman told him that approach wasn't politically viable, but, recalling his experience in the White House, talked up the idea of

giving dying factory towns a lift. Interested, Parker suggested Glickman take on the project as a part-time job.

"I told him this is a long-term commitment—five or ten years.
If you think you're going to get it done in the first year, let's not
waste our time," Glickman recalls. He knew Parker had interest and
money but wondered if the start-up wizard was patient enough to
get something done in DC. Parker was reassuring.

For his part, Polansky wanted to be sure this wasn't seen solely as a
Sean Parker project. He wanted at least one other prominent Silicon
Valley person to be part of the founding narrative. So he shopped the
OZ idea to Ron Conway, a prominent Silicon Valley "super angel"
investor who had been in on the ground floor at Napster, as well as
at ventures like Google and Facebook. Conway tells me he "loved it
from the start." Polansky was pleased: "It was a good moment for me
to realize, 'Cool. This can be something that has heft behind it.'"

Parker had Silicon Valley arrogance about his ability to get things
done in Washington that partisan politicians couldn't. "Nobody
thought it could get done," Glickman says. "Sean Parker thought it
would be easy."

In fact, Opportunity Zones would combine several of the key
ingredients that do make things happen in Washington: Every state
and nearly every city would get a piece of it. It would be wrapped
in do-good-for-the-poor packaging. Wealthy, tax-averse, campaign-
contributing constituents would benefit. Ribbon cuttings and press
releases for politicians would proliferate. And because of the way
Congress keeps its books, it wouldn't appear to cost as much as it
truly did.

After the meeting with Parker, Glickman and Polansky sketched
out an initial budget for the project—about $2 million to start.
They picked an anodyne name: Economic Innovation Group. Who
could be against that? EIG was created in April 2013 as a 501(c)(4),
a nonprofit organization that can legally lobby; donations to it are

not tax-deductible. Parker, Polansky, and Khanna were the original board of directors. Khanna wasn't paid anything in 2013, though he earned $36,000 as a consultant in 2014. Glickman went on the payroll in August 2013, earning $250,000 in total compensation for that first partial year.

IN SEARCH OF A REPUBLICAN

At that point, EIG was looking distinctly partisan. Parker's campaign contributions had been exclusively to Democrats; Glickman had worked in the Obama White House. To make their effort overtly bipartisan, Parker and Polansky wanted Glickman to find a Republican partner. For months, Glickman had been talking about the Parker approach with a small group of friends, only one of whom was a Republican: John Lettieri.

Lettieri grew up in Spartanburg, South Carolina, an old textile mill town whose economy was revived when carmaker BMW put a big factory there. His hometown's turnaround is proof, Lettieri says, that a community's past does not have to be its prologue. He attended a Christian prep school and, in 2004, graduated from Wake Forest University in North Carolina with a major in political science. Right out of college he landed a job with Chuck Hagel, the Republican senator from Nebraska who was later torn apart by his own party when Obama nominated him to be secretary of defense. Lettieri worked at Hagel's office for three years before going to head government and public affairs in Washington for a European helicopter maker. He later volunteered to help with Hagel's stressful confirmation. (Hagel was confirmed by the Senate in February 2014, fifty-eight to forty-one, with only four of his fellow Republicans voting for him.) Like Glickman, Lettieri is married to a former Senate aide, D'Ann Grady; unlike Glickman, he met his wife in college, not in DC.

At the time EIG was coming together, Lettieri was number two at the Organization for International Investment (OFII, pronounced OH-fee), a Washington trade association of US subsidiaries of foreign companies. One of OFII's reasons for being is to press Congress and the Treasury to avoid raising taxes on US units of foreign multinational corporations. (Amid political hostility to international trade, and weary of calls from people looking for stock market advice or funding for overseas projects, OFII changed its name to the Global Business Alliance in early 2020.)

After Glickman enlisted in the Parker project, he talked frequently with Lettieri over drinks and by email about how to assemble EIG from scratch and how to develop a political strategy that had a chance of success in gridlocked, hyperpartisan Washington. Glickman talked about hiring consultants. Lettieri warned against that, saying Glickman needed in-house expertise. The two began trading ideas about how to build an organization as well as a campaign to turn Parker's idea into legislation.

One spring day, outside a bar on bustling 18th Street in Dupont Circle, Glickman said to Lettieri, "We should do this together." It made sense. They were both interested in pushing cross-party initiatives. They were both DC insiders, always adding to their network of contacts on Capitol Hill and cultivating Washington reporters.

Lettieri initially wasn't interested. He had a good job and a shot at becoming head of OFII someday. When he consulted others in DC, they reinforced his wariness, almost unanimously telling him not to enlist in the campaign. The conventional wisdom was that the Opportunity Zones concept was somewhere between a long shot and hopeless. Why get involved in something everyone knew was not going to work?

The Sean Parker connection intrigued Lettieri, though. "Sean helped me share a lot of music with my friends in college," he says with a smile.

He and Glickman did a lot of brainstorming about how to go back to Parker and give him the SWOT analysis—strengths, weaknesses, opportunities, and threats. "It was during that process," Lettieri says, "that I started to think, gosh, this would be fun."

He jokes that he helped Glickman craft a plan that would demand so much of Parker he'd reject it, and then Lettieri could say he would have enlisted if only it had been done the right way. As Lettieri recalls thinking: "If Sean balks, or if when I talk with him, I don't hear what I need to hear about his level of commitment, I'll be able to walk away without any regrets. But if he agrees, I'm in."

Lettieri had a couple of phone calls with Polansky before talking to Parker by phone. He was wowed: "If your bar for Sean is you saw Justin Timberlake play him in the movie, you're shocked. The reality is very different. His depth and intellectual curiosity did not fit the media stereotype."

Lettieri was sold. The day before he formally accepted the EIG job in August 2013, he and his wife learned she was pregnant with their second child, not the best moment to make a risky career move. But he was thirty-one years old, ready to chuck the security of OFII for an adventure, and his wife didn't try to talk him out of it. And no one was asking him to take much of a pay cut: his total compensation for his first year at EIG was $281,000.[14] The new organization would never have to scramble for money as long as Parker was engaged. That left Glickman and Lettieri free to create a credible, bipartisan outfit that could style itself as something different from just another lobbying organization.

The pair worked out of Glickman's apartment in Washington's Shaw neighborhood for the first six months. Then the fledgling organization moved to an office shared with a manufacturing lobby shop run by one of Glickman's friends in Washington's Chinatown. Lettieri recalls assembling office furniture they bought at Ikea. It wasn't glamorous, but it was the perfect place to launch a low-profile mission with ambitious goals.

The objectives of the campaign were beginning to become clear.

First, they wanted to build an image for EIG that ensured it was seen neither as partisan nor as a special-interest lobby. This would be no small task, given the increasingly partisan nature of Washington, DC.

Second, before even considering legislation, the EIG boys wanted to develop credibility for the idea of steering unrealized capital gains into struggling communities. That meant getting a certain number of decision makers and influencers to convincingly argue that *geographic* inequality was at least as important as *income* inequality. With academic validation for the idea that geographic inequality was a problem, it would be much easier to push the solution of place-based policies—as opposed to policies targeted at individuals.

Finally, they would start crafting legislation that met Parker's basic premise: a juicy enough tax break to lure people sitting on huge unrealized capital gains to put their money into neighborhoods that desperately needed investment.

STEALTH MODE

Washington think tanks come in several strains. Some are distinctly partisan or ideological, partly because that's often the best way to raise money, partly because that's often the best way to influence the party in power. The Center for American Progress is a refuge for out-of-office Democrats that crafts talking points and policy ideas for Democratic candidates and—when they're elected—officials. The Heritage Foundation is aggressively conservative. The Cato Institute is distinctly libertarian. The American Enterprise Institute is a collection of conservative scholars, nearly all of them Republicans.

The Brookings Institution, where I work, resembles a university with a collection of scholars with different viewpoints, most of them Democrats.

Regardless of political affiliation, all these think tanks seek to influence policy through advancing narratives, floating ideas, using their "convening power" to promote their scholars and allies, and reaching out to like-minded members of Congress. They usually don't have a well-articulated political strategy to get a particular bill passed. Other organizations do commission papers and research, but they basically represent the interests of the industries that fund them, like Lettieri's old employer, OFII, or the National Association of Manufacturers or the US Chamber of Commerce.

Glickman and Lettieri agreed that EIG would be different. Some think tanks are nonpartisan, but very few are explicitly *bipartisan*. The vast majority of think tanks don't embrace a single, clear objective (in this case, Opportunity Zones) or tie their economic research so tightly to a legislative strategy for getting a particular proposal enacted. From the start, EIG would marry a well-crafted political strategy with white papers, data, talking points, and graphics, the tools most often wielded by agile DC think tanks.

EIG would be distinctive in another way. For the first two years, the EIG boys relied on a tactic common among Silicon Valley start-ups but rare in Washington: they went into stealth mode while they developed their product.

This low-profile approach was alien to Washington. It was harder than Glickman anticipated to duck the incessant DC cocktail party question: What do *you* do? His November 2013 wedding announcement in the *New York Times* described him as "a lawyer in private practice in Washington."[15] Lettieri felt like he was in the witness protection program. They did hire a communications director, Mark Paustenbach, who had handled press for Joe Biden's 2008 presidential campaign and later worked in the Obama Treasury. He lasted only nine months; developing OZs was taking longer than initially anticipated, so there wasn't much need for PR.

There were very good reasons to stay out of sight, though. Among them was avoiding the public stumbles of a political initiative launched by another Silicon Valley big shot, Facebook CEO Mark Zuckerberg. In April 2013, Zuckerberg, whose net worth dwarfed Parker's (thanks, in part, to Parker), launched an effort called FWD.us. Like EIG, FWD.us attempted to be seen as bipartisan. Its main goal was to pressure Congress into passing comprehensive immigration reform. This was already a massive undertaking: immigration is complex, emotionally fraught, and deeply politicized. But FWD.us also became linked to unrelated issues. Its support for the Keystone XL pipeline, for example, brought criticism from progressive and environmental groups.[16] Meanwhile, conservatives perceived the group as a naked power play by wealthy, liberal elites from Silicon Valley who wanted to employ more immigrants.

FWD.us's media campaign was messy. The group went public before developing a clear strategy, and then triggered unfavorable press when unartfully worded internal memos leaked. The media pounced. As one headline writer put it: "Zuckerberg's Lobby Is Collapsing like a 'House of Cards,'" a reference to the dark Netflix series about Washington.[17]

It didn't end there. One of the cofounders of Twitter tweeted a link to a May 2013 BuzzFeed piece by Josh Miller, who had dropped out of Princeton to start a company called Branch Media, which accused Zuckerberg of "employing questionable lobbying techniques, misleading supporters and not being transparent about the underlying values and long-term intentions of the organization."[18] Miller described the political effort as intelligent, well-funded, and fatally poisoned by Silicon Valley hubris. "You put money and support behind a smart team tackling massive problems, with the faith that they will figure out the details along the way. However, that lack of introspection is ultimately harmful in the world of public policy," Miller wrote. (Eight months after that post, Miller sold Branch to Facebook for a reported $15 million and went to work in the Obama White House. Facebook shut the site in 2015.)[19]

Out in California, EIG's patron was busy with his personal life, which attracted its own negative coverage. Parker and singer and actress Alexandra Lenas were married in June in a multimillion-dollar wedding at a hotel campground under the redwoods at Big Sur. It was a you-can't-make-this-up moment of nerdy-billionaire excess. Each of the 364 guests (including then California attorney general Kamala Harris) was outfitted in a *Lord of the Rings* costume made by the designer who won an Oscar for the movie.

According to Ro Khanna—he attended, along with Glickman and his fiancé; Lettieri wasn't yet on the team so he wasn't invited—there was some sort of jamming technology that barred guests from taking photos, though other accounts challenge that. In any event, thirty-eight photos by two big-name professional photographers illustrated a detailed account in *Vanity Fair* a few months later. A taste:

> San Francisco design eminence Ken Fulk was put in charge of the setting's visual elements. Everyone entered through a 20-foot-high gate, with the couple's initials intertwined in wrought iron, before descending a path lined with imported evergreens. People literally gasped as they emerged into a glade in which planted flowers and hanging garlands conferred a riot of color and a sense of undulation.... Set designers had constructed faux bridges, a ruined stone castle, a 10-foot Celtic cross, and two broken Roman columns that straddled the altar, beneath the largest tree in the grove. A pen of bunnies was nearby for anyone who needed a cuddle. Says Fulk: "It was Citizen Kane meets Gatsby–like in its scale—but beautiful, not gross or overwhelming."[20]

The wedding itself went smoothly, but press accounts were vitriolic: "Sean Parker Wedding Is the Perfect Parable for Silicon Valley Excess"..."Eco-Wrecked Wedding"..."Ecological Wedding Disaster"..."$10 Million Destruction of a Park"..."Tasteless Eco-trashing Wedding."

The wedding was beyond opulent, but its negative environmental impact was overstated. Although Parker and Lenas picked the site with help from the Save the Redwoods League, the California Coastal Commission ordered the venue shut twenty days before the wedding—over an old dispute with the hotel and adjacent campground. Two days before the ceremony, Parker met with the commission, startling them, in classic Parker fashion, by displaying an extensive knowledge of the state's Coastal Act. (He had read it the night before.) Parker agreed to pay $1 million on behalf of the hotel, chipped in another $1.5 million to facilitate camping for underprivileged kids, and helped the state develop a mobile phone app, YourCoast, that shows the locations of 1,563 public beaches in California.[21]

The commission was satisfied, but not everyone else was. Parker claims that, following the wedding, he and Lenas were spat at on the street and sworn at by a waiter in a restaurant. They cancelled their honeymoon to deal with the public backlash.[22]

"Nothing is sacred on the Internet, not even a wedding," Parker wrote in a nine-thousand-word rebuttal on TechCrunch.com—without apparent irony given that he was one of the founders of Facebook. "We were charged and convicted, by the Internet press and the court of public opinion, with every imaginable environmental crime....Never mind that none of the accusations were actually true. Truth has a funny way of getting in the way of a great story."[23]

Parker had other preoccupations as well: in July 2014, he and his wife spent $55 million to buy a nine-bedroom Los Angeles mansion from Ellen DeGeneres. The residence houses the couple's modern art collection and is the venue for Parker-hosted salon dinners. "I had never heard peacocks before. They crow in the middle of the night," says a guest at one of those dinners, John Persinger, who is currently spearheading OZ-fueled urban renewal in Erie, Pennsylvania. "They were next door at the Playboy Mansion. And I had never seen a Picasso in person. So two items off my bucket list."

Parker was also pursuing his philanthropic interests. He started a foundation with a $600 million gift. Frustrated that promising research into cancer immunology wasn't getting enough support, and that there was too little cooperation among leading research institutions, Parker initially earmarked $250 million of that gift to form an institute on cancer immunotherapy. Another $24 million went to an allergy research center at Stanford University. Parker is still a night owl, but, now a forty-one-year-old father of two, his late nights are more often spent reading medical journals than partying, his associates say.

Parker was not publicly engaged in EIG during its first two years of existence, a situation that suited everyone. The very public controversy over the wedding and news reports about the $55 million house reinforced the EIG boys' decision to stay in stealth mode for now. Glickman and Lettieri were playing the long game. They didn't need to make a media splash right away. They needed to assemble a team.

CHAPTER THREE

The Brains

WASHINGTON HAS HUNDREDS OF ECONOMISTS—THE FEDeral Reserve alone has more than four hundred PhDs—but only a handful are capable of talking in short sentences on TV news shows or on public panels in ways that the press, politicians, and folks who read the *New York Times* or watch the *PBS NewsHour* can understand. To build the credibility of their idea, EIG needed to recruit a couple from this handful.

Very early in the evolution of OZs, Parker had consulted Kevin Hassett, a Republican economist. Hassett, who has a round face and reddish hair, grew up in Greenfield, Massachusetts, played minor league baseball, and got a PhD in economics at the University of Pennsylvania. He spent five years on the staff of the Federal Reserve Board (a credibility-enhancing line on the resume of any economist practicing public policy), published academic work on taxes (almost always making the case for cutting them), advised several Republican candidates, and had a couple of hundred-thousand-dollar-plus consulting gigs.

In 1999, just before the dot-com crash, he coauthored a book that would forever make him the butt of ridicule: *Dow 36,000: The*

New Strategy for Profiting from the Coming Rise in the Stock Market.
But Hassett has an affable, disarming manner and—though he had
been at the American Enterprise Institute, a conservative think tank,
since 1997—he had shown a willingness to team up with liberal
economists when their views overlapped.

To maintain the political balance, with Hassett's encouragement the EIG boys recruited Jared Bernstein. In contrast to Hassett, Bernstein has a long, narrow face, short white hair, and strong
Democratic credentials. He had been chief economist to then vice
president Joe Biden in the first couple of years of the Obama administration. A Connecticut native, Bernstein went to college in New
York City to study music—he played the double bass—and got a
master's in social work. He played in jazz bands and did bar mitz-
vahs and weddings for a decade while counseling the city's troubled.
He then got a PhD in social welfare with a focus on economics at
Columbia and came to Washington in the early 1990s to work at
the left-leaning Economic Policy Institute (EPI). He has bounced
around DC ever since—from the Clinton Labor Department, back
to EPI, then to Biden's office, and on to another left-leaning think
tank, the Center on Budget and Policy Priorities.

Although they often differed on both diagnosis and solution,
Hassett and Bernstein got along well and were always available for
CNBC (where Bernstein had a paid gig) and for the never-ending
parade of Washington think tank convenings. In fact, the two sometimes were paired on the ubiquitous Washington panels and talk
shows that sought to demonstrate political balance.

Glickman and Lettieri met with the two economists in November 2013 at Art and Soul, a Capitol Hill restaurant that features
Southern cuisine, to firm up plans for their work on the OZ concept and strategy. With Hassett and Bernstein on board, EIG could
check off a key item on their to-do list: namely, to sell OZs as an

idea that both right and left, Republican and Democrat, could support.

But the EIG boys wanted even more brainpower, and Parker enjoys talking with smart people. So on the afternoon of March 21, 2014, they convened a three-plus-hour session at Parker's suite at the Plaza Hotel on Central Park. Parker was staying there during renovations to the Greenwich Village townhouse he bought in 2011 for a reported $20 million.[1] The meeting at the Plaza began with lunch, served by waiters. Steve Glickman, John Lettieri, and Kevin Hassett were there. So was Matthew Slaughter, an international economist from Dartmouth's Tuck School of Business who had been on George W. Bush's Council of Economic Advisers. Slaughter knew Lettieri because of work he'd done with OFII. Polansky joined by phone. Parker did most of the talking, much of which wasn't even about EIG but about his quest to find a cure for cancer, one of his long-standing interests.

Around three o'clock, the meeting moved to the living room of the Plaza Hotel suite and the group expanded to include Ken Rogoff from Harvard, who'd been chief economist at the International Monetary Fund, and Steven Davis, from the University of Chicago Booth School of Business, an expert on business dynamics. Jared Bernstein joined by phone. The EIG boys and the PhD economists discussed what EIG should be, and how it might promote policies to encourage innovation and economic growth and to reduce inequality. They also talked about a white paper that Hassett and Bernstein were drafting. They were all big names, but none had particular expertise in the long history of crafting government policies to lift people out of poverty, or in resuscitating economically distressed communities.

From a tactical standpoint, one of the most important players in the room was a lower-profile Harvard PhD economist named Peter Merrill. He worked in the economics group of the accounting-consulting firm PricewaterhouseCoopers (PwC), helping corporate clients (such as Lettieri's OFII) understand what Congress and the IRS were doing to their tax bills and offering tips on ways to nudge tax policy in their direction.

Of everyone in the room, Merrill had the most extensive knowledge of the arcane way Congress vets tax bills. One of the critical numbers in any bill is the cost analysis—a score—crafted by the nonpartisan Joint Committee on Taxation. Before joining PwC in 1989, Merrill spent six years as chief economist of the committee. He knew the ins and outs of creating an official cost analysis. Part of Merrill's assignment was to help the EIG boys design a tax break that wouldn't cost too much—at least by the official score—so it would have a better chance of passing. The committee estimates the costs of a proposed tax cut over a ten-year period. So, from a political standpoint, any tax cut created by Opportunity Zones needed to carry a small price tag within that window. A larger revenue loss that happens, say, twelve years out isn't nearly as important, at least politically.

The early version of OZs outlined at the meeting was less generous than the one I later saw being celebrated by lawyers, accountants, and real estate developers at the Mandalay Bay conference. Not all the economists in the room were fans of tax incentives that are limited to particular geographies, but that didn't discourage Parker or the EIG boys.

Slaughter, Rogoff, and Davis would later be named to an EIG board of advisers along with another high-profile economist, Austan Goolsbee, who'd chaired Obama's Council of Economic Advisers. They didn't do much work—indeed, Rogoff insists to me that he had nothing to do with "developing, writing, assessing, or researching" OZs—but they did add luster to the enterprise.

POLITICAL DIVERSIFICATION

While Glickman and Lettieri worked to get EIG off the ground, Parker made a significant change in his personal political investment strategy: he began contributing to Republicans. In 2013, campaign finance records show he contributed $571,000 to Democrats and only $10,200 to Republicans, all of that to Senator Marco Rubio of Florida. The next year, he again gave $571,000 to Democrats, but also $409,000 to Republicans, including $350,000 to a super PAC supporting Mississippi Republican senator Thad Cochran, who had been in Congress since before Parker was born and was facing a stiff Tea Party challenge.[2]

In what reads like an authorized leak, Parker's moves were noted by *Politico*, a news site widely read by Washington insiders. Parker was meeting quietly with Republican politicians and strategists, and his "associates" whispered to *Politico* that the billionaire planned to contribute to those he considered credible dealmakers.[3] A subsequent story in *Politico* noted, but only in passing, that Parker had been talking about ways to drive investment dollars to distressed parts of the country.

Among the politicians with whom Parker met was Representative Pat Tiberi, a Republican from Columbus, Ohio. First elected to the House in 2000, Tiberi had risen in seniority and influence as an ally of John Boehner, also from Ohio and at the time Speaker of the House. As a senior member of the House Ways and Means Committee, the committee that writes the tax laws, Tiberi was precisely the kind of congressman EIG needed if it was to have a chance of getting anything through Congress. Educating Parker to the way Washington works, Glickman and Lettieri told him that, just as the most prominent venture capitalists get first peek at the hottest start-ups, the most important members of Congress get first look at promising proposals. And if they sign on, other members of Congress figure the idea must be a winner and sign on as well.

Tiberi didn't need much convincing. The son of a steelworker and the first in his family to go to college, he had been frustrated that existing tax breaks meant to encourage investment in poor neighborhoods simply weren't getting the job done—either in the pockets of poverty in urban Columbus or the rural Appalachian communities he visited after his congressional district was redrawn to include them.

"I was just blown away. He had two interests: How to cure cancer. How do we stop generational poverty," Tiberi recalls about meeting Parker. "He said the recovery hadn't hit every community, especially in the Midwest. That was music to my ears." Tiberi would later be the lead Republican sponsor of OZs in the House.

Tiberi's Democratic counterpart was Ron Kind, who'd been in Congress since 1997 representing a largely agricultural district in southwestern Wisconsin. Kind, also a member of the Ways and Means Committee, was among the House's self-styled New Democrats, business-friendly centrists who court and are courted by Silicon Valley entrepreneurs. Frustrated that America's bountiful venture capital was concentrated on the East and West Coasts, Kind and like-minded members of Congress made occasional pilgrimages to Silicon Valley and New York City—where Kind first met Sean Parker.

"The rest of the country seemed to be left behind," Kind recalls. "We were looking for policy ideas and how we could incentivize capital to come to flyover country. Sean had this idea and was thrilled that someone was interested."

Unlike some other Silicon Valley billionaires, whose palpable arrogance hampers their ability to influence members of Congress, Parker's limitless curiosity and engaging manner proved effective. The chief executives whom Lettieri brought to Capitol Hill while he was at OFII understood why visiting with senators and representatives was important, but they didn't enjoy doing it. Parker did.

At one point, he asked Lettieri how the roles of chiefs of staff in the House and Senate differed. No corporate executive had ever asked Lettieri a question like that.

Parker approached Washington with the mindset of a Silicon Valley entrepreneur. He told me that dealing with members of Congress reminded him of talking to record label executives when he was building Napster and Spotify. "You have a lot of people you have to convince at the staff level, and you have to convince the people you think are the decision makers, and it turns out that there's a whole leadership structure... that you also need to convince."

"And," he added, "just when you think you've convinced the key decision maker, you find out that, like a 1980s video game, you beat the boss only to find out that there's a big boss, only to beat the big boss, to find out that there's an even bigger boss and you're kind of just like, 'I thought I won this thing. Why is there another level?'"

TWO SHAVED SENATE HEADS

In the Senate, the EIG boys targeted two newcomers who would prove to be crucial allies: Republican Tim Scott, a conservative from South Carolina, and Democrat Cory Booker, a liberal but business-friendly former mayor of Newark, New Jersey.

The EIG boys couldn't have found better public faces for their initiative. Both were African American. Both were charismatic and passionate speakers about the struggles of the poor folks in their states. As former local elected officials—Booker as a mayor and Scott as a member of the Charleston County Council—both knew something about the challenges local governments face in fighting poverty, violence, and despair. Both were rising stars in their forties looking for ways to make a mark in the Senate.

Booker, with his shaved head and expressive face, talks almost incessantly about his neighbors in the poor Newark neighborhood he moved to in the 1990s, although he grew up in a wealthy New Jersey suburb, the son of a couple of the first African American executives at IBM. He went to Stanford as an undergrad, was a Rhodes Scholar, got a law degree from Yale, and became an instant celebrity. When he was elected mayor of Newark in 2006, the opening sentences of a *New York Times* profile compared him to Barack Obama, who was then merely "the charismatic United States senator from Illinois."[4] Booker, of course, aspires to be one of Obama's successors in the White House, but his 2020 attempt fizzled.

Booker can't recall when he first met Sean Parker. He met lots of future Silicon Valley stars while he was at Stanford in the late eighties and early nineties. "Sean's a guy I feel like I've known for years," he says. Booker and Parker are both insomniacs; sometimes when Booker would arrive in San Francisco at midnight, he'd call Parker to see if he was free for a drink or dinner. When Booker became mayor, he decided to make his city a national cause and sell philanthropists, big corporations, and investors on helping him make Newark "an incubator for great ideas."

During his time as mayor, Booker successfully lobbied the state legislature for a new tax credit that had some resemblance to Opportunity Zones. Enacted in 2007 with the support of a Democratic governor and revised with the support of a Republican, the Urban Transit Hub Tax Credit offered to reduce state taxes by one dollar for every dollar invested in Newark and one of eight other cities designated as Urban Transit Hubs—provided the project's price tag was at least $50 million and employed 250 people. Prudential and Panasonic, among others, took advantage of the credit to build in Newark. Booker says he was determined to save his city from the gentrification Harlem was experiencing. The municipal government owned a lot of the land available for development and exercised substantial control, including requiring residential developers to set aside units for low-income tenants (a feature that is not included in the OZ law or regulations).

"We really loved this idea of getting incentives to draw in capital that hadn't moved before," Booker says. Indeed, he and his aides tried, without success, to talk the Obama White House into embracing such incentives nationally. So Booker didn't need much persuading when Parker pitched the idea that eventually became Opportunity Zones. "Sean is one of these guys that if you talk to him, it's about a big idea, a change-the-world idea. That's the frequency on which he thinks," Booker says. "Like 'let's cure cancer' or 'let's look at the United States as the home of dozens of emerging markets.'"

Parker contributed $10,400 to Booker's 2013 special election campaign and, when Booker ran for a full term the following year, he gave another $15,000 to Booker and the New Jersey Democratic State Committee.[5] Even the most idealistic members of Congress need money for their campaigns; the average winning Senate candidate in 2014 spent $8.6 million.[6] For politicians, campaign contributions are both a door opener and a very tangible "thank you." Parker gets his calls returned—and gets an audience for his pet projects.

Tim Scott, who also has a shaved head and is frequently pictured with a broad grin, didn't have Booker's national reputation or his Ivy League resume, and he had not been in Sean Parker's orbit. But his political alignment and great personal story made him an obvious target for the EIG boys. Scott's grandfather was an illiterate farm worker who pretended to read the newspaper every morning so Scott and his brother would do the same. His mother was a nurse's assistant who raised two boys on her own after a divorce, often working double shifts to make ends meet. Scott's high school ambition was to play in the National Football League, but that dream died when, after driving his mother to an early morning shift, he fell asleep at the wheel, flipped the car, and broke his ankle.

Academics were not his strength, but Scott embraces that quality in speeches and in his 2020 autobiography (a standard tool for political up-and-comers, in which the author describes the adversities he has overcome). "I failed English and Spanish, and you fail both English and Spanish, no one calls you bilingual. They call you bi-ignorant because you can't speak any language!" he says.[7]

At an event, he joked: "When you fail civics and you end up as a US Senator, you know God has a sense of humor. That's for sure. You also realize after being there for a little while that I might not be the only person who failed civics in the United States Senate."[8]

Scott's parents split up when he was seven and he struggled for half a dozen years afterward, but he must have been an appealing teenager. He drew the attention of a couple of mentors, including the owner of a local Chick-fil-A who introduced him to the motivational teachings of Zig Ziglar and planted the seeds of a conservative ideology that Scott now embraces. Scott went to Presbyterian College in Clinton, South Carolina, for a year—where he found his Christian faith—and then transferred to Baptist College (now Charleston Southern University). After college he prospered as an insurance salesman and agency owner. He began his political career at age twenty-four by running for the board of a credit union. In 1995, at age twenty-nine, he was elected to the Charleston County Council with 73 percent of the vote.

Scott drew immediate attention from national Republicans, who didn't have very many other Black politicians on their bench. In a noteworthy move for an African American, in 1996 Scott cochaired the eighth (and last) US Senate campaign of South Carolinian Strom Thurmond, who had been a notorious segregationist. "He was a complicated man," Scott told the *Wall Street Journal*, "but people change their minds. They embrace truth. In the end Thurmond received around 30% of the black vote."[9]

Scott spent twelve years on the county council, one term in the state legislature, and then ran for the House in 2010 from a Charleston district that is about three-quarters white. With 68 percent of the vote, he beat Thurmond's son in a runoff and took a seat once held by nineteenth-century enslaver John C. Calhoun. In the House, Scott aligned himself with the Tea Party, voting to repeal Obama's Affordable Care Act, promoting a constitutional amendment to require a balanced federal budget, championing tax cuts, and opposing abortion rights and same-sex marriage.

He forged relationships with fellow travelers from South Carolina's congressional delegation as well as the Republican leadership, who put him on the House Rules Committee, which controls what happens on the House floor. In November 2012, he won reelection with 62 percent of the vote. Six weeks later, Governor Nikki Haley appointed him to the Senate to fill a vacancy. In 2014 he ran to fill the remaining two years on the term, and in 2016 won a full six-year term, finally giving him the luxury that other US senators have—six years between campaigns.

For the EIG boys, Scott had another appealing attribute: only a few months after he arrived in the Senate, the Republican leadership put him on the pivotal Senate Finance Committee, which handles all tax bills.

Like Booker, Scott was predisposed to the Opportunity Zones concept. While he was running his first race for a seat on the county council, he met NFL-quarterback-turned-politician Jack Kemp at a Republican event at the Elks Club in Charleston. Kemp, who spent eighteen years in Congress and four as George H. W. Bush's housing secretary, was the chief promoter of a precursor to OZs called Enterprise Zones. "I was starstruck," Scott says.[10]

Even before EIG connected with him, Scott was promoting what he called his Opportunity Agenda, which includes a proposal to give vouchers to poor children, children of military families, and children with disabilities to go to private schools and another revamping federal workforce training programs.[11] Scott and Booker, though ideologically at odds, had jointly sponsored a bill to give employers a tax credit for hiring apprentices. Bill introductions are so plentiful that the *Washington Post* rarely mentions them, but the novelty of the two African American Senators, who were "poles apart politically," working together was such a good hook that the newspaper wrote seven hundred words about the bill.[12] As a harbinger of what was to come, Booker and Scott said they might work together on other issues, including tax reform.

"You know we'll be really successful when you start noticing more and more senators shaving their heads," Booker joked to the *Post*. "It'll be an homage to our friendship."

In addition to his political skills and conservative passion, Scott had one other feature that would later figure in advancing Opportunity Zones: he was one of the nation's most prominent Black Republicans. Scott didn't often make his race a reason to vote for him, but he couldn't escape being asked about racial issues. When he arrived in the House, Scott got some advice from Patrick McHenry, a white Republican congressman from North Carolina, who knew that TV networks would be eager to put a Black Republican on the air almost daily. Be selective, McHenry advised. Don't go too fast. You're in this for the long haul. And don't feel you need to speak every time someone thrusts a microphone in your face. Scott took the advice.

But after the fatal July 2016 police shootings of Alton Sterling in Baton Rouge, Louisiana, and Philando Castile in a suburb of Saint Paul, Minnesota, Scott was moved to speak about race in a forceful and personal manner on the floor of the US Senate:

Because I shuddered when I heard Eric Garner say, "I can't breathe." I wept when I watched Walter Scott turn and run away and get shot in the back and killed. And I broke when I heard the 4-year-old daughter of Philando Castile's girlfriend tell her mother, "It's OK, I'm right here with you." These are people. Lost forever. Fathers, brothers, sons. Some will say and maybe even scream: But they have criminal records.

They were criminals. They had spent time in jail. And while having a record should not sentence you to death, I say, OK, then, I will share with you some of my own experiences...

Scott recounted several instances in the past in which he had been driving and had been stopped by a white police officer, and how frightened he was. He continued:

Even here on Capitol Hill, where I have had the great privilege of serving the people of South Carolina as a U.S. Congress member and as a U.S. Senator for the last six years—for those who don't know, there are a few ways to identify a Member of Congress or Senate. Well, typically, when you have been here for a couple of years, the law enforcement officers get to know your face and they identify you by face, but if that doesn't happen, then you have an ID badge, a license you can show them, or this really cool pin. I oftentimes said the House pin was larger because our egos are bigger. So we have a smaller pin in the Senate. It is easy to identify a U.S. Senator by our pin.

I recall walking into an office building just last year after being here for five years in the Capitol, and the officer looked at me, full of attitude, and said, "The pin I know, and you I don't. Show me your ID." I was thinking to myself, either he thinks I am committing a crime, impersonating a Member of Congress or what? Well, I will tell you that later that evening I received a phone call from his supervisor apologizing for the behavior. That is at least the third phone call I have received from a supervisor or the Chief of Police since I have been in the Senate.

So while I thank God, I have not endured bodily harm, I have felt the pressure applied by the scales of justice when they are slanted. I have felt the anger, the frustration, the sadness, and the humiliation that comes with feeling like you are being targeted for nothing more than being just yourself.[13]

Since that speech, Scott has become something close to the racial conscience of the GOP. That would prove important to the success of Opportunity Zones.

In March 2015, John Lettieri tapped his network. He asked a mutual friend to introduce him to Scott's chief of staff, Jennifer De-Casper. The chief of staff is important in every Senate office: someone has to keep tabs on details while the senator is posturing at hearings, doing press interviews, cajoling donors, flying home and back, and schmoozing with other senators. Some chiefs of staff basically labor to keep their boss out of trouble or to manage the staff; others become one of their boss's best friends.

DeCasper's relationship with Scott is more in the "best friends" camp, but their relationship is as unusual as the path she took to the job. DeCasper worked as a scheduler for her home-state senator, Republican Wayne Allard of Colorado, after she graduated from Colorado Mesa University. She left that job in 2002 for the University of Michigan Law School and then took a job as a state prosecutor outside of Denver. In 2008, the single mom of a toddler, DeCasper quit her job and moved to Washington without a plan. It was not a good time to find work. She took a job wielding glow sticks to direct planes across the tarmac of Washington's Dulles International Airport.

When Scott was putting together a staff in 2010 for his House office, DeCasper interviewed, first with a couple of staffers. The next day, with only a couple of hours' notice, she was invited back to meet Scott. She left work and rushed to Target to buy the right outfit.

DeCasper recounted their conversation to the Charleston newspaper, the *Post and Courier*, in 2017:

"It was the worst interview I'd ever had in my life. I ended up crying in the interview because he just touched a heartstring. . . . I just stopped the interview completely. He said, 'Do you want to talk about why you're crying?' And I said, 'No, I just want to be done. Just want to be done with this interview.'"[14]

Scott hired her anyhow.

DeCasper tells me years later, "As a prosecutor, I had seen another side of America. I told myself I was going to work for a person who worked for opportunity."

DeCasper had no clue who John Lettieri was, and she'd never heard of EIG. When they met, they began talking about their kids, and then Lettieri sketched out the OZ concept. His mission was to persuade Scott to put OZs at the top of his priority list. He knew a lot of people would be trying to recruit the new senator to promote their proposals, and he knew that if OZs were fifth or sixth on Scott's list, they were doomed. To succeed, he needed DeCasper to fall in love with the proposal. She did. Not everyone on Scott's staff agreed: one staffer invoked "the Heritage Foundation critique," referring to the conservative think tank's view that offering tax breaks to some but not to others is not conservative. DeCasper won the argument.

Scott had been talking with his staff about tweaking and expanding existing tax breaks for poor neighborhoods that had been used in Charleston but hadn't delivered the desired results. "I oftentimes refer back to my local-level service because it is, in fact, the most impactful service I had in preparation for being a United States senator," Scott tells me. "And I was looking for good ideas, and spotting them at times, even when I need to be pushed over a cliff by my chief of staff."

DeCasper, who is sitting in on our interview, laughs, points to my notebook, and instructs me: "Make sure you put that in there."

Scott met Sean Parker for the first time at Scott's Capitol Hill office on June 9, 2015, early in the evolution of the OZ proposal. Lettieri calls it "a mutual kicking of the tires."

"I remember being in the conference room with him and thinking to myself, 'I hope we're on the same page. I'm not sure we're on the same page,'" Scott recalls. "His politics are very different. But my thought is, and we say it all the time, 'we'll work with anyone, at any time, from anywhere, if we're pulling in the same direction.' That sounds good when you're saying it in a speech..." He laughs. "Sitting down with folks who may not be ideologically fused together is a bit of a challenge. But I found that his motivation and my motivation were similar enough. Our experiences are drastically different enough, where if we're both on the same page, this is probably a good thing."

DOOR OPENERS

Over 2015, with its key players in place, EIG lined up other complements to a legislative push. It hired a PR firm, Hamilton Place Strategies, led by Tony Fratto, a veteran of the George W. Bush Treasury and White House. Fratto put Michael Steel, who had been an aide to House Speaker John Boehner, on the account to help with the public rollout of the OZ campaign. It engaged a law firm, Steptoe & Johnson LLP, for legal work and lobbying, including by partner John Shadegg, a former Republican congressman from Arizona. And it signed up a lobbying firm of former Republican staffers, including Greg Nickerson, who had been a tax counsel on the House Ways and Means Committee staff in the early 2000s.

With Parker's money, the EIG boys were buying advice and door opening—pretty standard Washington stuff. In all, EIG spent more than $275,000 in 2014 and more than $800,000 in 2015 on lobbyists and consultants.[15] But it had plenty of cash: Sean Parker chipped in about $5 million in 2015 on top of the $3.5 million he and his friends had contributed in the two previous years. EIG ended 2015 with nearly $4 million in the bank.

The key to the strategy Glickman and Lettieri crafted was to establish the image of EIG as a credible think tank, not as a promoter of a tax break, which, after all, was its original reason for existing.

Their initial press release—March 31, 2015—talked in lofty terms about "forging a more dynamic, entrepreneurial, and innovative US economy for the 21st century," and said EIG would "convene leading voices from the public and private sectors, develop original policy research, and work with policymakers to advance legislation designed to bring new jobs, investment, and economic growth to communities across the nation." It did, however, emphasize "the uneven economic recovery" that had "left many communities behind." Sean Parker was identified as just one of half a dozen Silicon Valley names backing EIG.[16]

A couple of months later, in June, Parker wrote a 2,500-word manifesto describing his philosophy of philanthropy for the front cover of the *Wall Street Journal*'s Saturday "Review" section. For conventional philanthropists and foundations, he wrote, "the primary currency of exchange is recognition and reputation, not effectiveness." The result is "a never-ending competition to name buildings." In contrast, he placed himself among the "hacker" strain of philanthropists, interested in "impact that can be measured and felt."

"This new generation of philanthropists wants to believe there is a clever 'hack' for every problem," he wrote, in a very succinct self-description. One essential ingredient of success, he argued, was a willingness to "get political"—even though doing so has "the potential to sully your reputation." He noted his $600 million gift to his foundation and his philanthropic focus on cancer research but mentioned neither EIG nor Opportunity Zones.[17]

As the EIG boys knew well, there is a daily plethora of press releases with big names and canned quotes in Washington. They knew they needed to demonstrate to policy wonks and think tanks that they had some substance. They had to show politicians and their advisers they had big-name and bipartisan backers and thus at least a chance of success. They had to find a way to link their campaign to individual communities in a way that would appeal to members of Congress, their constituent-focused staffers, and to local press. All the while keeping Sean Parker engaged and enthusiastic, of course.

It was almost showtime.

CHAPTER FOUR

Once Upon a Time on the Isle of Dogs

In June 1978, the British Conservative politician Geof-frey Howe stood in a pub in the decaying London docklands then known as the Isle of Dogs. He was there to propose a plan for urban renewal different from anything in modern British history. Enterprise Zones would be an experiment, carried out in four or five "inner-city ghost towns," in which the government would eliminate many of the regulations and laws that had created the modern city. There would be no detailed planning controls, no rent control, no government grants or subsidies, no capital gains taxes, and the government would auction off all state land to private bidders—and then see what happened. In Howe's mind, it was to be a demonstration that free-market capitalism could succeed where government had failed.[1]

Howe was not the first to suggest such a scheme. The UK in the late 1970s was an economic basket case. Inflation and unemployment were high. Large swaths of land in Britain's cities where Victorian factories, wharves, and warehouses had once prospered were abandoned wastelands. In Liverpool, 15 percent of the land was vacant. London lost 11 percent of its population in the 1970s.[2] In fact, things looked so desperate that Howe's suggestion of luring private money to certain areas had been introduced a year earlier by a democratic socialist urban planner named Peter Hall.

In 1977, Hall had suggested "an extremely drastic last-ditch solution to urban problems" to be tried "only on a very small scale."[3] Hall's approach was even more radical than Howe's. He proposed zones in which taxes and regulation would be cut "to the absolute minimum" and "the normal range of social benefits would not be provided." In short, Hall sought to create Hong Kong of the 1950s and 1960s inside cities like Liverpool and Glasgow. He called them "freeports."

New policy ideas often take a long time to move from their origin in universities, musings of public intellectuals, or grassroots movements to mainstream acceptance and codification as laws. This was not the case with Enterprise Zones, in part because of the dire state of Britain's inner cities, but also because Howe's pitch came at a moment of political sea change. In 1979, Margaret Thatcher became prime minister and set about remaking British society with the guiding principle that less government was a good idea. Howe became her chancellor of the exchequer and cajoled an initially reluctant Thatcher to back his idea.

Parliament created Enterprise Zones in 1980, just three years after Hall introduced the idea. In designated areas, the capital gains tax on land—then 60 percent—was waived; so were property taxes on commercial, industrial, and retail property. Depreciation allowances were sweetened to reduce corporate income taxes. Planning approvals were streamlined.

"The primary aim... is to encourage industrial and commercial redevelopment in derelict or cleared areas of cities," according to a 1981 account by Stuart Butler, an early advocate of Enterprise Zones and now a colleague of mine at Brookings. "It is not the purpose of the zones to bring about the mixed use of existing buildings or to stimulate the housing market within the zones. Nor for that matter does the aim seem to be to encourage small new enterprises."[4]

Unlike the approach that Opportunity Zones would follow in the United States decades later, local governments in the United Kingdom had to apply for Enterprise Zone designation, and the national government chose. Of the initial twenty-five applications for Enterprise Zones, eleven were approved, with another dozen added over the years that followed. Gentrification was not an issue; hardly anyone lived in any of these zones. They resembled today's Opportunity Zones primarily in one respect—the prize of a tax break for those who put money in the areas.

The final version of Enterprise Zones was not exactly what Howe had outlined; provisions requiring the government to sell any land in the zone, ban rent control, and eliminate government labor rules were dropped. But the realization of so much of his project in such a short period of time was remarkable.

The Isle of Dogs area where Howe first proclaimed his vision is an Enterprise Zone success story: it's now London's booming Canary Wharf. What was once acres of decaying and abandoned docks is now a cluster of skyscrapers, home to the offices of some of the world's biggest banks and to the three tallest residential towers in the United Kingdom. But Canary Wharf is an exception. Overall, the evidence on the effectiveness of the British zones is, as scholars seem to conclude in nearly every study about place-based policies, "mixed." Some jobs were created, but at a very high cost per job.[5]

ENTERPRISE ZONES GET A QUARTERBACK

The idea migrated across the Atlantic with Stuart Butler. After finishing a PhD in American economic history at Saint Andrews in 1978, Butler took a job at the Heritage Foundation, a conservative Washington think tank that was to have substantial influence over Ronald Reagan's domestic agenda. At Heritage, Butler became an evangelist for Enterprise Zones, American-style. In his version, Enterprise Zones would be a grand experiment in reviving places like the South Bronx for people who lived in them, as opposed to bulldozing and displacing populations. Zoning and other rules would be suspended, minimum wage laws waived, and, perhaps, property taxes abolished.

Butler's goal, in contrast to that of the UK version, with its emphasis on incentivizing big building projects on largely unused land, would be to nurture small entrepreneurial businesses and encourage the creation of diverse, mixed-use city streets—the sort advocated by urbanist Jane Jacobs, author of *The Death and Life of Great American Cities*, with whom Butler corresponded. (Jacobs called Butler's version of Enterprise Zones "a potentially important idea for city neighborhoods in dire trouble" in a blurb for a book he later wrote about them.)

In Butler's mind, Enterprise Zones could demonstrate new ways to solve the vexing problem of urban poverty. "The existence of small zones where new approaches would meet no obstacles would give a major stimulus to the development of new ideas to create prosperity in the older cities," he wrote in a 1979 Heritage Foundation brief.[6] (In an unusual twist in the transatlantic exchange of ideas, Geoffrey Howe used Butler's essay to talk Thatcher into backing the idea.)

As in the UK, the idea quickly drew attention from prominent politicians. In May 1980, the charismatic Republican congressman and former NFL quarterback from Buffalo, New York, Jack Kemp, and a liberal Democrat from the blighted Bronx, Robert Garcia, introduced a bill to create Enterprise Zones in the United States. In their original version, local governments could apply to Washington to designate areas with high unemployment and poverty, but the local governments had to agree to cut property taxes by at least 20 percent. Like OZs, once a zone was designated, investors would enjoy lower capital gains taxes. Unlike OZs, there also would be additional incentives to create jobs, such as a cut in employers' share of Social Security payroll tax. Zone companies also got a corporate income tax break if at least half of their employees worked in the zone and at least half of their employees lived within it.

Kemp's argument resembled the one that Sean Parker and the EIG boys would use a generation later: Distressed communities suffer from a lack of capital. Give folks with money a tax break and the money will flow into these communities. "Virtually every survey shows that the major problem for inner city entrepreneurs is the absence of seed capital," Kemp argued. Cutting capital gains taxes, he said with characteristic hyperbole, would "unlock" capital and "support a whole new generation of budding entrepreneurs in America's inner cities where economic opportunity is needed most." Banks shunned blighted neighborhoods through a practice known as "redlining." Kemp wanted to "greenline" them.[7]

The idea got high-profile backing from Ronald Reagan, George H. W. Bush, and such prominent House Democrats as Charlie Rangel of New York and Dan Rostenkowski of Chicago. However, the business lobby was unenthusiastic, and the idea didn't win over the AFL-CIO, newspaper editorial pages, or the bulk of Democrats.

"It is difficult for me—as it is for many tax, business, and urban experts—to believe that merely the lure of lower tax rates will set off an eruption of business development in depressed urban areas," said

Shirley Chisholm, a Democratic congresswoman from New York and later the first African American to run for the presidential nomination of a major party.[8] Critics of OZs would echo Chisholm's analysis decades later.

Even though Kemp's Enterprise Zones never became federal law, he was such a good salesman that a lot of people think he succeeded. Adding to the luster of the label, states began enacting business tax incentives of various sorts that they called Enterprise Zones; forty-three states now have some version of them.[9]

Importantly for the EIG boys, the idea didn't die. Many economists and hard-line free-market conservatives see problems with place-based policies, but politicians love them. Elected politicians are, after all, place based. They lust for ribbon-cutting photos and press releases for projects in their districts for which they can take credit with voters.

The 1990s also saw the ascendance of Third Way centrist Democrats such as Bill Clinton and Al Gore, who warmed to public-private partnerships and were eager for ideas they could label as "reinventing government." That gave an idea like Enterprise Zones a new life.

THE CLINTON VARIATIONS

In 1993, after listening to arguments between those who preferred spending more money on cities and those who favored tax incentives, newly elected President Bill Clinton decided to propose both. After the usual back and forth with the White House, Congress created Empowerment Zones (tax breaks) and Enterprise Communities (grants, but no tax breaks). Like today's OZs, the Clinton zones offered a capital gains tax break, although it was more modest. Unlike OZs, which have no incentive aimed directly at hiring,

Empowerment Zones were crafted to boost employment, offering tax credits of up to $3,000 a year for each worker hired who lived in a zone.

The Clinton zone designations also relied on competition among communities. In order to be designated by the federal government, areas had to demonstrate that business, government, residents, and community organizations were involved in developing revitalization plans.

In the first designation round, the Clinton administration picked eleven Empowerment Zones and ninety-four Enterprise Communities. By 2001, 122 cities had been anointed, and by 2011 the tally, including a later designation called Renewal Communities, was up to 380.[10] By design, this was far fewer than the 8,764 Opportunity Zones created in 2017. The "race-to-the-top" concept was to foster competition and allow Washington to pick only the most ambitious and likely to succeed communities. Further encouraging competition, Congress set an absolute cap on both spending and tax breaks. In today's OZs, by contrast, there is no such limit and no competition to steer money to uses most likely to benefit people in a zone; anyone, in any of the 8,764 zones, with an investment that complies with the rules can claim the tax break.

Clinton's zones were not a big success, though. After digesting dozens of government and academic evaluations, the Congressional Research Service (CRS) said they found "modest, if any, effects and call into question the cost-effectiveness of these programs." Businesses and investors clearly benefitted, CRS said, but there was no evidence the programs had improved the economic well-being of local residents.

In a survey of the voluminous academic research on state and federal zones—some favorable, some not—economist David Neumark of the University of California, Irvine, a longtime critic of place-based policies, concluded: "It is very hard to make the case that research establishes the effectiveness of enterprise zones in terms of job creation, poverty reduction, or welfare gains." (Challenged by some of my Brookings colleagues to offer a better alternative, Neumark has sketched out a proposal for place-based federal subsidies for employers who hire people from low-income families.)[11]

Clinton wasn't done, though. In 2000, Clinton's last year in office, his administration looked for ways to steer private money to domestic emerging markets—as Sean Parker later would—and launched a program that moved in the direction of Opportunity Zones: the New Markets Tax Credit. The NMTC was different from its predecessors. For one thing, it wasn't restricted to low-income housing or historic preservation, but could be used to finance everything from industrial equipment and sewer plants to schools and stores. The NMTC was designed to draw private investment to low-income neighborhoods by providing investors (including banks) with tax credits that reduce their federal income taxes over seven years. Investors put money into local intermediaries called Community Development Entities, which are certified by the Treasury to sell NMTC tax credits. These Community Development Entities compete to get NMTC allocations: the Treasury picks winners based on their track records and plans. The entities then use the money they get from selling the tax credits to make loans or, less frequently, to invest in businesses operating in eligible communities.

The initial NMTC plan circulated in the Clinton White House didn't limit the total number of tax credits, but Treasury tax experts objected. Without some limits and screening by the Treasury, they warned, the provision would inevitably produce egregious cases of abuse and violate one of White House economic adviser Gene Sperling's principles: "Don't do anything that's going to have you on *60 Minutes* five or ten years from now."

As a result, more than 40 percent of the nation's census tracts qualify for NMTC under the law, but competition limits the number of places that reap the program's rewards. The Treasury picks Community Development Entities it deems most likely to serve the worst-off communities, up to a limit set by Congress. In the 2018 round, for instance, there were four dollars in applications for credits for every dollar awarded.

Consulted by Sean Parker years later, Sperling tried to talk him and the EIG boys into putting some similar restrictions on OZs. They refused, insisting there be no cap on the amount of tax breaks OZ investors could claim. Consistent with their Silicon Valley roots, they wanted scale.

Evidence on NMTC's effectiveness, though somewhat better than the earlier place-based policies, was, again, a mixed bag. Between 2001 and 2019, about $61 billion worth of NMTC projects were approved.[12] Since credits cover 39 percent of a project's cost, paid out over seven years, the cumulative cost to the Treasury over nearly two decades is roughly $24 billion. A 2013 Urban Institute evaluation commissioned by the Treasury concluded that of every ten NMTC projects in the early years of the program, only four would not have happened without the tax credits. Three would have happened anyway, although perhaps in a different place or at a later date. It didn't have enough information to draw conclusions about the remainder.[13]

Comparing neighborhoods that qualified for NMTC to those that came close but didn't, Matthew Freedman of Cornell University found that NMTC-subsidized investments did reduce poverty and unemployment rates, but a lot of that reduction was driven by people moving into neighborhoods, the dreaded gentrification phenomenon in which the better-off displace the poor. His bottom line: there were benefits, but they were "modest."[14]

The other knock on NMTC is that many would-be developers and investors find the whole process frustratingly complicated, costly, and bureaucratic—which, of course, is one reason the tax credits don't go to subsidize upscale condos or luxury hotels. The Government Accountability Office diplomatically says the program "could be simplified."[15] Brad Ketch, who runs a community development organization outside Portland, Oregon, is blunter: "Brain surgery is more simple than the New Market Tax Credit."

RETHINKING PLACE-BASED POLICIES

So Sean Parker's idea of offering tax breaks to invest in struggling areas wasn't as novel as he suggested. His spin was to avoid the restrictions that had limited the impact of previous attempts—the hope was that less bureaucracy, fewer rules, no cap on tax breaks, and more focus on attracting wealthy private investors would make the concept go viral, as Facebook had. The role of economists Jared Bernstein and Kevin Hassett was to create policy-world respectability for that effort. At EIG's behest but without any compensation (though Bernstein did get a $50,000 grant from EIG a few years later), the two wrote a twenty-page white paper with a wonky title, "Unlocking Private Capital to Facilitate Economic Growth in Distressed Areas," and forty footnotes. Waging a battle of ideas was the first step in the EIG boys' rollout strategy.

To define the problem OZs were supposed to solve, they pointed out that the distressingly slow recovery from the Great Recession of 2007–2009 had been "profoundly uneven," leaving many places struggling and at risk of a downward spiral of poverty and despair. "Distressed communities can be thought of as caught in a bad equilibrium outcome, where some economic shift has left the city with declining private activity and a falling tax base...a drop off of public investment and infrastructure, making it even more difficult to attract private capital."[16]

Their solution: the government should do more to draw private investment to left-behind places—a new place-based policy.

Economists generally hate such policies. Or they used to. Edward Glaeser, a prominent scholar of urban economics at Harvard, summarizes the case against them this way: Subsidies for declining places keep people in dysfunctional economies instead of encouraging them to move to more promising places, as Americans did for generations. Subsidies are often a windfall to people who happen to own real estate in a chosen community. (Pity the renters in Bilbao, Spain, who don't like contemporary art and whose rents have risen because of the success of the Guggenheim Museum there, he says.) Sinking money into infrastructure in declining places is often a waste of funds. He cites Detroit's People Mover, an expensive monorail that glides over largely empty streets where buses move swiftly and more cheaply.

But a few years after EIG was launched, some big-name economists, Glaeser among them, began to change their minds. At a Brookings Papers on Economic Activity conference in March 2018, I heard Larry Summers, a former Treasury secretary, say: "If I had been asked for a view twenty years ago, it would have been what I think would have been a standard view at Brookings, which is: Help poor people, not poor places. If you help poor people, a disproportionate share of the assistance will naturally go to poor places, but there's no particular reason to target poor places in a substantial way with your policies."

"This," he added, "is a relatively rare event. I have changed my mind on a significant policy question in part as a consequence of looking at data."

The data to which Summers referred didn't show that place-based policies had been the right solution all along, but rather that the nature of inequality and poverty in the United States had changed.

First, for decades the fortunes of regions of the United States had converged. Poorer regions, like the South, caught up with richer ones, like the Northeast. In 1950, for example, eighteen states had per capita incomes double that of Mississippi, the poorest state in the union. Today, Mississippi is still the poorest state in the union, but there is no state with double its per capita income.[17] Importantly, though, most of that convergence had already occurred by 1980. Over the past forty years, regional incomes have stopped converging. The South has stopped catching up.

There's been a similar trend in local unemployment rates. In the early 1990s, influential economists Larry Katz at Harvard and Olivier Blanchard of MIT showed there was no correlation between places with high unemployment in 1975 and places with high unemployment in 1985.[18] In other words, communities weren't permanently mired in despair. New data show that's no longer the case: places where lots of people weren't working in 1980 were also places where lots of people weren't working in 2010. And disparities in the fraction of men between the ages of twenty-five and fifty-four (generally too old to be in school and too young to be retired) who were not working were large: in Alexandria, Virginia, it was 5 percent and in Flint, Michigan, 35 percent—and that was before COVID-19.[19]

Second, Americans have become more stuck in place. For more than four decades after World War II, over 6 percent of Americans moved from one county to another every year, often in pursuit of better jobs.[20] Between 1940 and 1970, four million African Americans moved from the South to the cities of the North and West.[21] Northerners moved to the Sunbelt. City dwellers moved to the suburbs and beyond. But lately, people in the United States have been less mobile. In recent years, only about half as many Americans— about 3.5 percent— moved each year from one county to another. And the people most likely to move from decaying communities are highly paid, highly skilled, and highly educated workers. Their departure leaves their hometowns with an even greater concentration of less skilled, low-wage workers and, thus, with less of what economists call human capital, which is key to a community's economic prosperity.

Finally, there is new evidence of what one might call place-based determinism. In some of the most influential economic research in decades, Harvard's Raj Chetty combined census and tax data on *tens of millions* of people to show how the neighborhoods in which children grow up influence their earnings as adults, a phenomenon dubbed "zip code destiny."[22] On average, for instance, a child from a poor family in San Jose or Salt Lake City has a much greater chance of reaching the top of the income ladder than a child from a similarly poor background who grows up in Baltimore or Charlotte. Place matters, Chetty argues convincingly.[23]

"It is absolutely unavoidable that we will have more discussions about place-making policies over the next three to four years," Glaeser said at a February 2021 academic conference on Opportunity Zones that I organized at the Brookings Institution.[24] "America's spatial inequalities have gone up. Our geographic sclerosis has made the case for place-based policies better. But it is still possible to screw it up enormously."

This grim data on mobility and chronic place-based lack of opportunity was great news for the EIG boys. They had caught a wave, like Geoffrey Howe riding on the Conservative takeover of Parliament to create Enterprise Zones. EIG was launching their initiative at just the right moment. Bernstein and Hassett no longer had to convince experts that place-based policies were worth considering. But they did have to frame the problem in a way that would later allow them to advance their capital gains tax break as a solution.

Clearing the way for their approach also meant critiquing previous efforts. Bernstein and Hassett pronounced Clinton's New

Markets Tax Credit "more streamlined" than its precursors though "perhaps overcomplicated." They also said it wasn't structured to encourage investments big enough to revitalize an entire community, such as a new factory. The NMTC was too tilted toward real estate and, they said, while it might push a few investors "who were on the fence about investing in an area" to do so, it didn't attract much brand-new investment. Ironically, those charges would later be levied against Opportunity Zones. Another major failing of earlier attempts, Bernstein and Hassett argued, was that they "have not harnessed the power of intermediaries such as private equity firms, banks, venture capitalists, mutual funds, and hedge funds."

Bernstein and Hassett's bottom line was a mouthful: "A federal subsidy for private activity can knock the community out of the bad equilibrium and help it back on its feet." The translation: a tax break would nudge wealthy folks to put money into poor neighborhoods and revive them.

Expressly leaving details to others, the two outlined what would become OZs: a tax break, with many fewer strings than earlier programs, to lure the "very large stock of savings in the form of unrealized capital gains…built up in recent years" into giant mutual funds "constrained to invest in distressed communities" that offered investors deferred or reduced taxes on their capital gains.

While Bernstein and Hassett discussed the legacy and shortcomings of previous programs, few in the community development business—the foundations, low-income housing advocacy groups, purveyors of New Market Tax Credits or Low-Income Housing Tax Credits (created in 1986 to offer investors, often banks, a credit against their taxes for financing affordable housing)—paid much attention to the embryonic EIG campaign. This was fine with the EIG boys, who courted a few of those groups but generally shunned their advice. After all, part of their diagnosis was that these folks, and all the rules and constraints on the programs they administered and used, were part of the problem. They were barriers to people like Sean Parker and his peers putting money into low-income communities.

LIFTOFF

With the white paper formatted and printed with the EIG logo, the EIG boys moved to another item on their to-do list. They hired Atlantic Media, a mini–media conglomerate, to produce their launch event.[25] The outfit, then owned by wealthy Washingtonian David Bradley, had both news products (*The Atlantic* magazine) and an events-for-hire business.

A launch event is a staple of Washington initiatives. Big-name speakers are used to draw a crowd to hear the pitch for a new idea. The EIG launch on the morning of April 15, 2015, was staged from the broadcast studio at the (now defunct) Newseum, a couple of blocks from the US Capitol. The ringmaster was Steve Clemons, who moved between think tanks and blogging and was then essentially a professional moderator and convener for Atlantic Media events.

Bernstein and Hassett, with Amy Liu of the Metropolitan Policy Program at Brookings seated between them, were the opening act. Behind the panelists was a blue backdrop decorated with EIG's name and logo (a copper diamond with "E I G" etched into it) repeatedly interspersed with *The Atlantic*'s logo.[26]

There were jokes about Clemons's loud striped socks—something of a fad among panelists in Washington. Clemons tried to suppress the academic jargon, but Hassett talked about "Nash equilibria," arguing that no one would invest in a bad neighborhood unless other people did, but since other people didn't, no one would.

"So we're gonna cooperate or everyone's screwed," Clemons translated.

Hassett fantasized that someday big mutual fund companies would offer OZ funds as an option alongside stock and bond funds, that investing in them would become "a social norm," and that Silicon Valley companies would tell their employees they were expected to put some of their income into such funds. (He didn't explain how *that* would work.) "And then when they make money, the thing will snowball and feed on itself because I think there is actually profit to be made by turning these places around," Hassett concluded.

After about forty-five minutes of such wonkery, Booker and Scott came on stage. Interviewed by Clemons, the senators talked in generalities—about their states, their respect for each other, and their apprenticeship bill. There were more jokes about loud socks, a Tim Scott trademark, and some banter about whether EIG was pronounced "eye-g" or "ee-g." (The founders say simply E-I-G.) Clemons tried to steer the conversation toward the Bernstein-Hassett idea without much success.

"There are a lot of options out there, a lot of models at work," Scott said.

Booker riffed on the urgent need to strengthen US schools to make the country more competitive with China. The senators didn't appear to be very well briefed about the point of the event. In the closing moments, Booker did talk about "public-private partnerships, which I think that EIG is really focused on," but quickly pivoted to praise "social impact bonds" and to talk about the importance of reducing recidivism.

The session got zero press coverage—there was no news—but that wasn't the point. This was a coming-out party aimed at Washington insiders. It was about branding EIG as a credibly bipartisan outfit with connections to two of the Capitol's rising stars. A photo of the two senators in front of the logo-covered wall and the hashtag #RethinkRenewal has a permanent home on the "About" page of EIG's website.

Parker wasn't at the event and went unmentioned, but he was making occasional trips to Washington to schmooze with members of Congress and stay in touch with his team over long dinners like the one at Blue Duck Tavern.

FROM WHOLESALE TO RETAIL: THE DISTRESSED COMMUNITIES INDEX

The Atlantic launch event was wholesale; the next step was retail. There's a cliché in Washington that "all politics is local," but clichés sometimes persist because they are true. From his time as a Senate aide, Lettieri knew that congressional staff lust for easy-to-grasp visualizations and super-local data. That led to the creation of a popular tool, EIG's Distressed Communities Index, which amalgamated data on schooling, housing vacancies, employment, median income, poverty, and changes in the number of businesses to identify "the most economically depressed" zip codes in each state.[27] Nevada, Georgia, Mississippi, and Tim Scott's South Carolina had a quarter or more of their populations living in economic distress, according to the index.

The idea was to create an analysis and a simple visual tool that captured the huge and growing gaps between places that were doing well and those that weren't. It would help EIG make the point to individual senators and representatives that the country's worrisome economic inequality wasn't only between rich and poor people but also between prosperous places and left-behind places. The project was an enormous undertaking—eight hundred thousand pieces of data in all. EIG hired Matt Lockwood from Google's map unit, whom Glickman knew from his Georgetown days, to oversee the data viz. Hamilton Place Strategies, the PR firm, was also recruited to assist, as was Peter Merrill's number-crunching shop at PricewaterhouseCoopers.

The index didn't get much attention when EIG quietly unveiled an early version in July 2015, but the big launch, including the website, came in February 2016. EIG gave the *New York Times* a jump on the story and got a headline on the front of the business section with a lead paragraph that was exactly what the EIG boys had hoped for: "The gap between the richest and poorest communities has widened since the Great Recession ended, and distressed areas are faring worse just as the recovery is gaining traction across much of the country."[28]

The media blitz wasn't limited to the *Times*. Visitors driven to EIG's website loved the multicolor maps that allowed them to zero in on their own zip codes. Traffic was so strong after the *Times* piece that the website went down. The site also provided local media across the country with all the data they needed to cover economic distress in their own areas. "We realized journalists want to write their own stories," Lockwood says. "We gave them the tools."

EIG made a deal with the Associated Press to provide access to the data.[29] Scores of headlines followed: "The 10 Most Distressed Cities in America"..."San Antonio Still Leading in Inequality"..."Glen Lyon Residents Upset by 'Distressed' Status Report"..."The Recovery Passed Over Much of Milwaukee"..."Far from Flourishing: Rural Communities Join Urban Centers as Poorest Zip Codes in the Lehigh Valley"..."WV Has the Third Most Distressed Communities"..."Toledo's Economic Distress: No End in Sight Soon."

EIG's research also created a hook for Robert Siegel, the host of NPR's *All Things Considered*. Prompting Lettieri during an on-air interview, Siegel said: "There is only one core city that ranks as a prosperous area in the United States of America. Just wait for five seconds to tell us so people can guess. They won't."

Lettieri waited a few beats, and then replied: "It's Bismarck, North Dakota."[30] (Bismarck would later get three Opportunity Zones, though.)

Through this initial launch period, one thing went unmentioned: the specifics of an Opportunity Zone tax break. The omission was deliberate. EIG was defining the problem in way that would make it easier to sell Opportunity Zones as the solution.

CHAPTER FIVE

A Bill Is Born

C ENSUS RECORDS SHOW THAT IN 1910 WALTER LAIDLAW, A Presbyterian minister, lived on Hamilton Terrace in Manhattan with his wife, Jennie, his son and stepson, his mother-in-law, and two Irish immigrant servants.[1] Similar demographic information about Laidlaw's neighbors in Manhattan Ward 12 and how the neighborhood changed over time is easily accessible today—in part because of the work of Laidlaw himself.

The US Constitution mandates a national census every ten years to allot seats in the House of Representatives. Laidlaw made the idea more granular; he created the concept of organizing basic census data by smaller, uniformly drawn geographic areas. His original goal was to put the charitable work of New York churches on a scientific basis, but the idea caught on. In 1910, seven other big cities (Baltimore, Boston, Chicago, Cleveland, Philadelphia, Pittsburgh, and Saint Louis) also used this "census tract" approach, although none analyzed and published the data in as much detail as New York.[2] Over the twentieth century, the concept expanded to cover more and more of the country, though it wasn't until the year 2000 that every square inch of the United States was in a numbered census tract—65,443 of them that year.

As Laidlaw intended, the boundaries of census tracts are relatively stable over time, allowing for meaningful comparisons from one decade to the next. Today they range in size from 1,200 to 8,000 people each, averaging about 4,000 residents.[3] As the nation's population grows, tracts in growing communities are sometimes subdivided. So the total number of tracts steadily rises over time, offset by merging of tracts in places with shrinking populations.

After EIG's launch, Glickman and Lettieri needed to advance Opportunity Zones as the specific solution to the problem Bernstein and Hassett had outlined. Part of this was technical—crafting the details of the tax code provision that would create OZs. To define the "places" in the place-based effort, they would build on Laidlaw's census tracts.

Census tracts had major benefits: they were predefined areas with lots of readily available demographic data on poverty and income, and they were already used by the government to identify places eligible for the New Markets Tax Credit. They had some significant shortcomings, though. While the boundaries of a census tract often coincide with a city, county, or state border, they aren't necessarily drawn to reflect what residents or real estate developers consider neighborhoods. As a result, they can be somewhat arbitrary measurements of poverty and lack of opportunity. Prosperous, high-priced areas may be mashed together with struggling, poor ones, potentially creating a misleading snapshot of a community based on the "average" person in the tract.

Early in the process of crafting the tax provision's details, someone on the EIG team—it's not clear who—wondered aloud about the arbitrariness of census tract boundaries. What if one side of a street was inside an eligible tract and the other was outside? EIG's solution was to outsource the designation decision: allow governors to give OZ status to a census tract that didn't qualify as a low-income community, provided it was contiguous to a tract chosen as an OZ and its median family income was no more than 125 percent of that adjacent tract.

This detail got next to no attention as the bill took shape. Although only some governors used the flexibility to select "contiguous" tracts that didn't seem all that deserving, the provision would end up tarnishing OZ's public image. In fact, the bad press resulting from exploitation of loopholes or general lack of accountability would become somewhat of a theme in the first few years after Opportunity Zones were created. A few bad examples can taint even a well-intended program.

With census tracts defining places, EIG needed a process for selecting which tracts deserved OZ designation. The stated intent was to aim the incentives at neighborhoods that truly needed them, as opposed to neighborhoods that didn't. At the Plaza Hotel meeting in March 2014, Peter Merrill of PwC had explained how the New Markets Tax Credits law determined which tracts were deemed "distressed communities." For that program, "low-income communities" were basically defined as areas with a poverty rate above 20 percent or median income below 80 percent of the metro area median. Parker and the EIG boys thought it would be simpler, and politically expedient, to piggyback on the NMTC definitions as opposed to creating their own—but that presented a different problem. Using the New Market Tax Credit definition would make more than 40 percent of all the nation's census tracts into OZs. The EIG boys knew they would never be able to sell OZs as targeting "distressed communities" if that much of the country qualified.

The NMTC had a built-in mechanism for limiting the number of "distressed communities" that got aid: Congress put a cap on the program and the US Treasury chose among competing applicants. But giving Washington that much control was antithetical to what the EIG boys were trying to do. That approach, they argued, would interfere with the flood of unrealized capital gains they imagined they would be unlocking and directing to needy neighborhoods. The OZ architects wanted to get rid of the bureaucratic red tape.

Once again, the EIG boys' solution was to outsource decision making to the states. Governors would be allowed to designate up to a quarter of their states' eligible tracts as OZs, a feature EIG turned into a marketing point: we are moving decision-making outside of Washington and closer to the people. Booker and Scott liked the idea—they were eager for local officials to have some say.

"You want to give the governors some skin in the game," Parker said. "Letting governors make decisions with the input from their mayors and communities is important. It allows them to focus on the places where they have engaged leadership at the community level."[4] Governors would know best which 25 percent of zones were the best fit, he figured.

While the solution sounded good to those suspicious of Washington, it gave an enormous amount of discretion to governors to identify the places that qualified for the place-based tax break. Allowing contiguous tracts to be blessed as OZs meant governors could choose from a universe of 56 percent of all census tracts in the United States, some of which really didn't need another government subsidy.[5]

The law also required governors to make their designations within just a few months after the bill became law. State governments aren't equipped to digest and implement an entirely new federal law that quickly. Every state made rushed decisions. The inevitable result was more than a few permissible but questionable OZs, which splattered mud on the whole enterprise before the first dollar was invested and underscored the weakness of a lobbying and legislative effort that evaded significant vetting of the details.

SCORING CAPITAL GAINS

Arguing over the tax rate on capital gains has become a staple of political campaigns, with Republicans favoring lower rates—some of them arguing for zero—and Democrats generally favoring higher rates, though occasionally supporting lower rates for favored purposes, such as small businesses. In the 2020 presidential campaign, for example, Donald Trump said he wanted to cut the top capital gains tax rate from 20 percent to 15 percent. Joe Biden said he wanted to double it to 39.6 percent to match his proposed top marginal tax rate on other income.

Amid all the persistent political combat, the capital gains rate has trended downward since the early 1970s and, with the exception of a few years after the 1986 Tax Reform Act, has been lower than the rates on other income, often substantially so. The debate usually goes like this: Politicians and economists on the left argue that a lower rate for capital gains is simply a tax break for the rich that doesn't do much good for the economy. Politicians and economists on the right argue that lower capital gains taxes encourage saving and investment and risk-taking, spurring business formation, entrepreneurship, and innovation, with accompanying benefits to economic growth.

Most Americans don't care about the capital gains tax rate because they make most of their money in wages, not by selling stocks or real estate or businesses or art. Cutting capital gains tax rates directly helps the wealthy, almost exclusively. More than two-thirds of all long-term capital gains reported on tax returns are reported by people in the top 1 percent; only 10 percent by those in the bottom 90 percent.[6] Moreover, most of the income reported by people at the very top is from capital gains, not wages and salaries. So rich people—and the politicians to whom they contribute—care a lot about capital gains tax rates.

The capital gains tax has one unusual characteristic. Unlike most other taxes, when you pay is largely in your control. Under current law, people don't pay the tax when their shares of stock or property go up in value, only when they decide to sell them. As a result, the levy is sometimes seen as an unwelcome excuse for investors to hold onto assets until they die and pass them to heirs, capital gains tax-free. This is sometimes called the "lock-in" effect; some argue that it stops money from moving to its most productive uses.

What is certain is that people like Sean Parker and his friends were sitting on enormous sums of unrealized (i.e., as yet untaxed) capital gains. Parker and his peers in the top 1 percent hold about half of all unrealized gains, and 40 percent of the wealth of the top 1 percent is unrealized gains.[7] At the time of Facebook's initial public offering, Parker's shares were worth about $2 billion, almost all of which represented taxable capital gains.

EIG drew a lot of attention for its estimates—which look reasonable—that there was $6 trillion in unrealized capital gains in 2017 that OZs could potentially unlock.[8] It said that about two-thirds of that amount was in family portfolios of stocks and bonds and the remaining third on corporations' books. Of course, this money isn't buried in the backyard, waiting for someone to dig it up. It's invested in stocks, bonds, real estate, businesses, and art. Every sale has a buyer, so "unlocking" these capital gains doesn't magically increase the amount of money available to invest; that only happens when people save more and consume less. But unlocking does move money around. Indeed, that was part of the rationale for OZs.

Convinced the existing programs to direct capital to down-trodden communities were flops, Parker and the EIG boys wanted something different. They believed that tax incentives aimed directly at businesses in OZs wouldn't work because many businesses have other ways to reduce their taxes, and because most small businesses don't make big decisions based on tax breaks. Alternatively, they thought, big up-front incentives to investors generally require so many strings to be sure the money goes for the intended purpose that there are too few takers.

As Glickman puts it, the OZ concept was to give just enough of an up-front lure to draw investors, but to offer a big reward only for investments (in businesses or in real estate) that prove profitable after ten years. "If you don't create any value, there's no appreciation, and you don't get anything," he says. (Never mind that back in the Clinton years, looking for ways to encourage investment in new and small companies, Congress had already cut capital gains tax rates for investments in certain small firms—those with assets of $50 million or less—though not hotels, restaurants, financial institutions, real estate companies, or mining companies. During the Obama years, the capital gains tax on these investments was eliminated altogether—up to $10 million or ten times the original investment, whichever is greater. Inevitably, at least one diligent accounting firm boasts it has devised ways for clients to combine the benefits of that tax break with the OZ tax break.)[9]

As the OZ tax break took form, Parker and the EIG boys bounced options off various people to be sure the cuts were sufficiently generous to get investors to actually move their money into OZ neighborhoods. Early versions were deemed not generous enough.

An early "discussion draft" of the legislation, never made public, said that an investor who sold an asset had to put *all the proceeds*—not just the profits, but the original investment as well—into an OZ to qualify for the tax break. That wasn't considered sufficiently attractive. Before the bill was finalized, the wording was changed to say an investor has to put only the profits—not the gross proceeds—from the sale of an asset into an OZ. The original investment can be used for whatever purpose the investor desires. This gave OZs an edge over other real estate tax breaks.

But every step to sweeten the OZ tax break for investors risked putting OZs in political peril. Increasing the cost to the Treasury and the impact on the federal debt would give opponents on the left an easy talking point and deficit-phobes in the center and on the right a reason to resist. The key was to craft the bill, with help from Peter Merrill of PricewaterhouseCoopers, so that the official Joint Committee on Taxation (JCT) estimate of forgone tax revenues over ten years (the period that Congress uses) was small—no matter what the true long-run cost was.

The challenge was to provide investors with a good reason to put money into an OZ without generating a price tag that would be an impediment to the bill's passage. One early version of Opportunity Zones would have allowed investors to defer paying capital gains tax on the initial gain they rolled into an OZ until the OZ investment itself was sold. But that was too expensive within the ten-year window. The clever solution: the final version requires OZ investors to pay the initial capital gains tax in 2026 so JCT number crunchers show a substantial inflow of revenues to the Treasury in that year, reducing the ten-year tab (though not the much larger long-run cost to the Treasury in forgone tax revenues).

The twist: when 2026 gets closer and OZ investors start fretting that they're going to owe taxes, Congress can amend the law to extend the tax due date by a year or two. As long as the new due date is within the rolling ten-year window, the price tag on such a change in the law will be, officially, zero. This maneuver can be repeated year after year. Indeed, a bipartisan pair in the House introduced legislation in February 2021 to push the due date from 2026 to 2028.[10]

This is how Washington works: a billionaire-financed organization with a focused legislative agenda hires a former congressional staffer to advise on crafting a tax proposal that not only looks much

less costly than it truly is, but also includes a feature that will make
it easy for Congress to push off investors' tax due date.

AN IDEA BECOMES A BILL

In its waning moments, the 113th Congress of 2013 and 2014
managed to avoid the ignominy of being named the "least productive" in modern history. That title remained with the 112th. But
the reprieve was hardly earned by impressive effort. The last-minute
legislation included a lot of fluff like naming federal buildings and
post offices. And it didn't do anything to change the perception and
the reality that the bitterly partisan Congress was gridlocked.

Throughout EIG's early years, Glickman and Lettieri knew this
dysfunction meant they faced an uphill battle getting Opportunity
Zones into law. The 114th Congress of 2015 and 2016 wasn't much
better than its recent predecessors. Even with their carefully culti-
vated bipartisan strategy, the EIG boys braced for failure. Getting
anything significant passed into law seemed, at best, difficult.

Glickman, Lettieri, and their congressional allies spent the early
part of 2016 fine-tuning the details of the OZ proposal, based on
Parker's consultations in Silicon Valley and their conversations in
Washington. For instance, EIG and Cory Booker's staff asked community development experts at the Urban Institute—including
Brett Theodos, a public policy PhD who had evaluated earlier tax incentives and spending programs aimed at distressed communities—
for advice. But when Theodos and his colleagues said the design
was too broad—too many geographies, too many sorts of projects,
too much potential for real estate speculation—and that vetting of
some sort from Washington was essential, their advice was rejected.
Glickman and Lettieri, then and now, insist that OZs are not and
should not be viewed as a program or a conventional tax credit, but

as something bolder and grander. But ultimately OZs should be and will be evaluated like other tax incentives, weighing the cost of forgone tax revenues against the benefits the tax break actually produces for the communities and people it is supposed to help.

On April 27, 2016, three years after EIG was chartered, Opportunity Zones made their debut on Capitol Hill. Cory Booker and Tim Scott introduced the "Investing in Opportunity Act" in the Senate. Ron Kind, a Wisconsin Democrat, and Pat Tiberi, a Ohio Republican, did the same in the House. An early suggestion that the bill be labeled something like "domestic emerging markets" was dropped when Booker dumped on it—and pushed for "opportunity" in the title.

By year-end 2016, Booker and Scott had nine cosponsors in the Senate. In the House, there were sixty-one—twenty-two Democrats and thirty-nine Republicans—including nineteen members of the Ways and Means Committee, though notably not the chairman, Kevin Brady.[11] This modest success—attracting 15 percent of the members of the House as cosponsors—was made easier by the fact that no one, not even the EIG boys, thought this bill was going anywhere soon. What's more, sponsoring doesn't obligate a member of Congress to vote for a bill if it does ever come to the floor, particularly if it is embedded in a bigger piece of legislation. It's more like signing on to a statement of principles than scrutinizing a change to the tax code. Who could be against promoting economic opportunity in poor neighborhoods?

In the 2015–2016 session of Congress, 9,664 bills were introduced; only 329 became law. The Investing in Opportunity Act was not among them. That wasn't a surprise to Glickman and Lettieri. They knew how DC works. The EIG boys were playing a long game.

Bill introductions are an occasion for press releases. In a joint statement, senators Scott and Booker and representatives Tiberi and Kind lauded EIG for championing policies "to connect communities with the capital they desperately need." They boasted that the proposal was "designed to be very low cost to the taxpayer, with no tax credits or public sector financing involved." Of course, the notion that there wasn't any public financing involved obscured the reality that, from the point of view of the federal deficit, there's no difference between reducing someone's taxes and giving them a tax credit; at the end of the day, there is less money in the Treasury's coffers.

The legislators also set a standard useful for measuring whether Opportunity Zones are delivering on their promise today: OZs, they said, would connect "struggling communities with the private investment they need" and "dramatically expand access to the capital and expertise needed to start and grow businesses, hire workers, and restore economic opportunity in struggling communities."[12]

OZ's congressional debut drew little press attention. *USA Today* noted it.[13] Scott's and Tiberi's hometown papers wrote stories. EIG distributed testimonials from recognizable names across the political spectrum. Andrew Yang, not yet as prominent as he would later become as a Democratic candidate for president, wrote in *Forbes*: "Basically, there's a lot of money out there that's being held for investment and tax purposes that is not being conveyed to entrepreneurs in struggling parts of the country. If we create a system of financial incentives to make it more appealing to invest in early-stage businesses, it can only help move the needle."[14] The *Daily Beast* website celebrated the proposal as a "bipartisan plan to wage a smart war on poverty."[15]

Given the bill's low profile and low odds of passage, most skeptics of targeted tax breaks or trickle-down economics didn't bother raising their voices. One of the few discordant notes came from Angela Rachidi, a former deputy commissioner in New York City's Department of Social Services, who was tracking anti-poverty efforts at the conservative American Enterprise Institute. Echoing criticism of the old Enterprise Zone proposal, she said it would take a lot more than directing investment dollars to poor neighborhoods to meaningfully reduce poverty. "Improving the health of low-income Americans so that they can work, addressing home and family responsibilities that limit work, and taking a hard look at how government benefits might contribute to non-work are equally essential," she wrote.[16]

Sean Parker weighed in, too. If OZs become law, he said in an EIG press release, they will provide "a vital new pathway for investors and entrepreneurs to kickstart economic growth in distressed areas across America."[17]

The press was, in general, skeptical of Parker's political acumen—to the extent it took note. An August 2016 piece in the *Los Angeles Times* read like a political obituary:

> The 36-year-old Silicon Valley oligarch once vowed to rattle the established order of Washington. But several years into a multiplatform, multimillion-dollar effort that seeks to transform politics through technology, campaign cash and a few big ideas, the renowned rule-breaker is finding that the rules of politics are not easily broken.
>
> Parker is a curiosity in Washington: a billionaire eager to engage in politics, but without a signature cause. His agenda is murky and can even be contradictory. He might emerge as the anchor donor in a big campaign to rid money from politics during one election, and then take a lead in funding efforts to protect some of the most entrenched incumbents in another. His ideology defies definition.[18]

Parker did, in fact, have a vision—just not the typical DC one. He was approaching politics like a venture capitalist, throwing money at things that looked promising with the knowledge that some—perhaps, most—would fail. And not all his efforts failed. In 2016, Parker put $8.8 million behind a referendum to legalize recreational marijuana use in California; it passed.

PLAYING THE FIELD

With the bill finally unveiled, EIG moved into its next phase: the attention-getting PR campaign. It looked for ways to create data that would get attention in the media and help build the case that something like OZs was needed to revitalize the American economy. It commissioned a poll of 1,200 millennials that found them less inclined to be entrepreneurs than older generations.[19] It published an "Index of State Dynamism" that combined seven metrics to create a gauge of states' economic vitality going back to 1972.[20] "Americans are less likely to start a business, move to another region of the country, or switch jobs now than at any time in recent memory," EIG said. The rankings were like catnip to local newspapers, as EIG's communications team knew they would be.

EIG then leveraged the political opportunities created by this media attention. In June 2016, for example, Lettieri told the Senate Small Business Committee that one of the best ways for the government to broaden access to capital and spur entrepreneurship was to create Opportunity Zones, which he described as "a targeted incentive that corrects a market failure to generate prosperity in US communities." Scott pressed the case with his fellow Republican senators, arguing that they could not afford to let the public think that only Democrats cared about poor people.

EIG tapped its network to spread the word. Jack Kemp, the Republican congressman and early advocate for Enterprise Zones, had died in 2009. Lettieri asked a Republican lobbyist working for EIG to connect him to Jack's son, Jimmy. Lettieri explained to Kemp that OZs were based on his dad's Enterprise Zones.

Jimmy Kemp had, in fact, already approached Representative Paul Ryan, at that point chair of the Ways and Means Committee, with the idea of picking up where his dad—a prominent supply-sider advocate of lower taxes—had left off. Ryan was a Jack Kemp protégé and talked with substantial passion about the need to reduce poverty. But, according to Kemp, Ryan was reluctant to pursue anything as ambitious as far-reaching tax reform. "I know what I can get done and what I can accomplish," Kemp says Ryan told him.

"I left disappointed," said Kemp.

Kemp gave EIG his blessing, and Jack Kemp's files, and joined an EIG advisory council early in 2016, but he was sure OZs were a lost cause—especially as far as Ryan was concerned—and he told Lettieri as much. Ryan, who became Speaker of the House after John Boehner abruptly resigned, never did push to put OZs into legislation.

Kemp was, though, impressed with Sean Parker's commitment. The two men bonded over food allergies—like Parker, two of Kemp's sons have them. "Sean didn't like to hear from his accountants that he couldn't take capital gains and put them in distressed communities," Kemp told me, "so he said, 'OK, I'm going to change the tax code.'"

Kemp also deployed his family's Jack Kemp Foundation (from which he draws a $150,000 annual salary) to give visibility to Tim Scott, who preached at foundation forums that "conservative principles are truly the way to eliminate and eradicate poverty."[21] Those principles generally boiled down to declaring the War on Poverty a failure and advocating less government spending, fewer federal restrictions on states, more school choice, bigger tax breaks to encourage work and investment, and an emphasis on personal responsibility.

BETTING ON CLINTON, READY FOR TRUMP

All in all, 2016 was a good year for the EIG boys. They'd built a small think tank, crafted a tax break that would be ready to grab a ride on the next big tax-bill train, and recruited a bipartisan group of supporters.

EIG was also a runner-up to much bigger outfits as the best US think tank in economics and finance in a ranking by Britain's *Prospect* magazine. "With roots in Silicon Valley, it is entirely fitting that this tank focuses on the problems caused by the over-concentration of economic dynamism within the US, in work that one judge called 'grim and well-argued,'" the magazine said.[22]

Like most political junkies in Washington, Glickman and Lettieri expected Hillary Clinton to win the presidency. With a Democrat in the White House, they figured Cory Booker would be their best advocate, and a shield against left-leaning Democrats who were skeptical about any capital gains tax cut for the rich.

In the early innings of the 2016 presidential race, Parker was courted by a few of the Republican contenders—Marco Rubio, Rand Paul, Jeb Bush. "He was sending a clear signal," the *Los Angeles Times* wrote. "Innovators like him would not be taken for granted [by Democrats] again."[23] But when Republicans turned to Donald Trump, Parker lined up behind Clinton, hosting a fundraiser for her in his backyard; some five hundred donors attended and together pitched in over $1 million for her campaign.

Of course, Clinton didn't win. Trump did. But EIG's diversified political portfolio—particularly the support of Tim Scott—had positioned it well for a Republican Congress and a Trump presidency.

Trump himself hadn't been involved in any of EIG's maneuvers, but a March 2016 exchange between Trump and the *Washington Post*'s editorial page editor caught the EIG boys' attention:

"What would you do for Baltimore, let's say?" the editor asked.

Trump replied, "Well, number one, I'd create economic zones. I'd create incentives for companies to move in."[24]

When the time came, real estate developer and tax-break enthusiast Donald Trump could be recruited.

CHAPTER SIX

An Archipelago of Tax Havens

ON JANUARY 20, 2017, DONALD TRUMP WAS SWORN IN AS
president with a brash and harsh agenda. He promised to
build a border wall that Mexico would pay for, temporarily ban
Muslims from entering the country, impose tariffs on goods made in
China and Mexico, repeal Obamacare, and—most importantly for
the EIG boys—cut taxes.[1] At a retreat a few days later in Philadelphia, Republican members of Congress (the GOP controlled both
houses) trimmed their list to two items: health care and tax reform.[2]

While the first few days of the Trump administration set the partisan tone of the next four years—anti-Trump protests in Washington, DC, led to more than 2,000 arrests while the White House
press secretary sparked a public row over the size of the crowd at
Trump's inauguration—congressional Republicans kept their focus
on the top policy issues. The staff on the House and Senate tax-
writing committees got to work on alternatives early in the year.

Despite EIG's successes in 2016, Opportunity Zones were not
part of the discussion. Cutting corporate taxes was at the top of the
congressional to-do list. Big companies had convinced politicians,

including many Democrats, that the corporate tax rate was too high, putting the United States at a competitive disadvantage. Top Trump economic policy officials also wanted to cut the corporate tax rate, although the president himself vacillated between whether repeal of the Affordable Care Act (ACA, also known as Obamacare) or tax reform was his top priority. In April, the White House issued a vague, one-page, bullet-point wish list of tax cuts.[3] Capital gains rates weren't mentioned, let alone Opportunity Zones. (Ironically, one bullet point was to "eliminate targeted tax breaks that mainly benefit the wealthiest taxpayers.") Gary Cohn, the former Goldman Sachs executive who became chair of the White House National Economic Council and a key player in tax reform, and Treasury Secretary Steven Mnuchin showed little if any interest in OZs.

The EIG boys were undaunted, and Lettieri's Republican connections suddenly became crucial to the mission. The insider network he and Glickman had spent four years building produced a juicy dividend. Kevin Hassett, who'd coauthored the OZ white paper for EIG, became chair of Trump's Council of Economic Advisers, the three-member panel of economists who advise the president. His collaborator, Jared Bernstein, greeted the news with an enthusiastic tweet: "Great choice! He's a conservative economist who cares a lot about people (tho way too into corporate tax cuts.)"[4]

There was one other voice keeping OZs alive in the White House: Ja'Ron Smith. A Howard University alumnus with an undergrad degree in business and a master's in divinity, Smith had worked on then representative Mike Pence's staff in the House before moving to the Senate office of early EIG supporter Tim Scott. Smith left Scott's office in 2015 for an outfit funded by the conservative Koch brothers; his connections with then vice president Mike Pence got him a job working on urban affairs in the White House in 2017.

Smith, who stood out in the Trump White House with his shaved head and bushy black beard, had been and continued to be a strong proponent of OZs. In his compact office in the Eisenhower Executive Office Building, a large color photo of Trump speaking at a rally decorating the wall, Smith told me he came up with the name "Opportunity Zone" while working on Scott's staff. (Others don't recall that.)

Smith's first few minutes of fame came in August 2018 when Trump counselor Kellyanne Conway was asked on ABC's *This Week* for the name of the highest ranking African American on the White House staff. After filibustering for a few minutes by talking about Ben Carson, the Housing and Urban Development (HUD) secretary, she remembered "Ja'Ron, who has been with us since the beginning."[5] (Smith left the White House a few days after Election Day 2020. "In four years, President Trump has delivered for Black America," he wrote in a farewell tweet, citing, among other accomplishments, Opportunity Zones. He is now executive director of another nonprofit backed by the Koch brothers.)[6]

TAX REFORM OR BUST

In the spring and summer of 2017, Republican leaders had difficulty maintaining momentum on tax reform. House Republicans proposed a "border adjustment tax" that would have taxed imports and exempted exports. That blew up and was ditched. A group called the "Big Six"—Treasury Secretary Mnuchin and economic adviser Cohn from the administration, Ryan and Brady from the House, Majority Leader Mitch McConnell and Senate Finance Chair Orrin Hatch from the Senate—labored to hammer out a Republican consensus on tax cuts.

As the clock ticked with little visible progress, the press, largely unaware of what was going on behind the scenes, was relentlessly skeptical about the chances of a big tax bill. "Now that Mr. Trump has revealed his hand," the *New York Times* wrote after Trump released his April 2017 wish list, "the obstacles he faces for getting tax overhaul done this year are even more apparent."[7]

The odds looked even worse by July, after the GOP failed to repeal the Affordable Care Act. The vote fell short in the Senate on the "no" votes of three Republicans—John McCain, Susan Collins, and Lisa Murkowski. That defeat led some Washington pundits to conclude that, given Democrats' united opposition, the Republican leadership couldn't muscle *anything* through the Senate.

In fact, the embarrassing inability to deliver on the promise to repeal the ACA galvanized Republicans in the Senate. They needed to get *something* done before the year was out. What's more, the Republicans' business constituency, particularly multinational corporations, was pushing hard. Two distinct groups in the Senate—Republicans who wanted tax cuts at any cost and Republicans who worried about the budget deficit—finally reached a compromise, clearing one obstacle to a big tax reform bill.

This was the moment EIG had been waiting for. With tax reform looking viable, they activated their network to get OZs included in whatever bill emerged. Pat Tiberi talked up OZs with every member of the Ways and Means Committee. His enthusiasm for OZs and the personal connections he'd formed over sixteen years in Congress brought many House members around, although he still faced strong opposition from both flanks. Left-leaning Democrats were skeptical about making rich people richer to help the poor. On the right, OZs were condemned as crony capitalism, and some Republicans objected to any provision that had the government so explicitly picking winners and losers. But the biggest obstacles in the House came from the leadership, Speaker Paul Ryan and Kevin Brady, chair of the Ways and Means Committee. (Ryan had picked Brady over Tiberi for that prime post in 2015.)

"Paul was fascinating because of his Kemp background, but he didn't like the tax credits and he didn't like anything that added to complexity. He said, 'you need to talk to Kevin,'" Tiberi told me.

Tiberi didn't get much more out of Kevin Brady. "Kevin was really focused on simplification. He was never opposed, but he was never for it. He never said no. He knew a majority of Republicans were for it, but every Republican had something else that was more important."

So OZs were left out of the House version of tax reform. In fact, hostility to targeted tax breaks was so strong that, had it become law, the House bill would have also killed existing tax credits for historic preservation and Clinton's New Market Tax Credit. Community groups, banks, and developers who used the tax credits watched anxiously; some worried that Opportunity Zones might end up as a substitute for the NMTC.

Ryan has since become an OZs enthusiast, celebrating them as "a component of our poverty-fighting agenda to boost economic growth and job creation." In an interview, he insists he didn't oppose the provision but simply wanted to see the Joint Committee on Taxation cost estimate—the all-important score Peter Merrill had helped the EIG boys structure—to be sure it wouldn't show a big widening of the deficit over a ten-year horizon.

"I just have a long history with the idea and believed in it, and as soon as Kevin [Brady] got a good score, I just was in a good place to say, 'Put it in and keep it in,'" said Ryan, adding, "But Tim Scott got it there."

On that last point, there is no debate. Individual senators often exaggerate their roles in passing a piece of legislation. Not in this case. Tim Scott takes, receives, and deserves credit for getting OZs into the tax bill.

THE CORE FOUR

That Scott played such a major role in the creation of OZs was a combination of his hard work and political skills—and a little luck.

With enormous pressure to get a tax bill done by the end of 2017, fierce Democratic opposition, and a slim majority in the Senate, the leadership needed to fashion a tax bill that nearly all Republican senators would vote for.

Advancing a successful bill demanded strong leadership, but Orrin Hatch, the eighty-three-year-old chairman of the Senate Finance Committee, was near the end of his career. Moreover, as the failure to repeal Obamacare demonstrated, the Senate had changed. Every senator needed to be courted, not just those on the relevant committee. So, rather than acting as the unquestioned commander of the effort, Hatch picked four senators to work on both the substance and the schmoozing needed to get a viable bill.

They were called the "core four." Rob Portman of Ohio, a former US Trade Representative, handled the international business tax piece. Pat Toomey of Pennsylvania, a reliable conservative (and a skeptic of targeted tax breaks like OZs), handled the other business provisions, including the contentious issue of how to handle partnerships, sole proprietorships, and other businesses whose profits are taxed as income to their owners, the so-called pass-throughs. Tim Scott, who was younger and close to other senators from the Southeast, took charge of explaining changes to the tax code for individuals. A later addition, John Thune of South Dakota, a member of the GOP leadership team, rallied the large Republican contingent from the Midwest.

Scott made clear to the Senate Finance Committee staff that, whatever else ended up in the bill, he expected OZs to be there. Hatch was sympathetic. For one thing, he needed Scott's help to pass the tax bill. But EIG's networking played a role in firming up Hatch's support.

In October 2016, Lettieri and Glickman hitched a ride on a bus tour organized by AOL founder Steve Case. Known as the "Rise of the Rest," the tour was designed to encourage venture capitalists to invest outside the East and West Coasts. At a stop in Salt Lake City, the EIG boys met Jeremy Keele, an adviser to Jim Sorenson—heir to one business fortune, builder of another, and one of Utah's richest men.

"We hit it off," Keele says. "They said, 'Hey, there's this idea we've been working on.' We got pretty excited about it because we had for a long time been looking for policies that could drive capital into low-income communities."

Keele introduced the EIG boys to Sorenson. Big on impact investing—investing both for profit and social good—Sorenson embraced the concept almost instantly. (In January 2021, Sorenson was named to EIG's small board of directors.)

Locking up Sorenson's support paid off a year later. A big contributor to Republican campaigns, Sorenson promoted OZs in his meetings with House Speaker Ryan and, substantially more successfully, with his home-state senator, Orrin Hatch.

Keele recalls one meeting in Hatch's office amid the flurry of activity around tax reform in which Sorenson made the case for OZs. According to Keele, Hatch summoned committee staffers who were working on the bill and said, "Is there any reason we can't put in this Opportunity Zone stuff?"

With Tim Scott in the core four and Hatch advocating for OZs, EIG's chances of success were rising. The White House, though, remained uninterested. They had way too many bigger priorities for the tax bill, like how deep a cut in the corporate tax rate they could get.

Then came Charlottesville.

"VERY FINE PEOPLE"

In August 2017, a rally organized by neo-Nazis and other white nationalists to protest the removal of a statue of Robert E. Lee from a public park, turned violent. A counterprotester was killed after a white supremacist rammed his car into a crowd; nineteen others were injured.

Asked about the events during a briefing on August 15, 2017, Trump famously said, "You . . . had people that were very fine people on both sides."[8]

That was too much for Tim Scott. He responded on Twitter that same day: "There is absolutely NO gray area when it comes to condemning groups who breed on racism, hate and division." He didn't mention Trump by name but said, "Let us not repeat history with ambiguity when it matters the most. From my house to the White House, let's be clear."[9]

A couple of days later, Scott told a VICE News video interviewer, "I'm not going to defend the indefensible. . . . What we want to see from our president is clarity and moral authority. And that moral authority is compromised."[10]

The White House noticed. Sarah Sanders, the White House press secretary, called Scott's office and asked if the senator was interested in talking to the president face to face. Scott's office told her they'd get back to her. There was some debate among the Scott staff: Would anything he said change Trump's position? Would people say Scott was crazy for trying?

In the end, Scott decided one doesn't turn down an invitation from the president.

During the tense ride to the White House, Scott told Jennifer DeCasper, his chief of staff, that they needed to pray for "clarity and guidance in this unusual and possibly contentious meeting." She agreed and, fearing a confrontation between her boss and the president of the United States, said, "Can you also ask that when this is over, I am still fully employable. I have a kid, you know."[11]

As Scott and DeCasper made their way through the layers of security, Scott says he wondered: "Were the Black faces looking back at me applauding me? Hoping I would stand up for their invisible pain? Wondering if I would succeed? Did the white faces understand why I had to be there? Did they understand why this was important not only to me but to all people of color, as well as to the spirit of our country?"[12]

It was almost a month after the Charlottesville protests, early in the afternoon of September 13, 2017, when Scott and DeCasper walked into the Oval Office. Like other Washington insiders, they knew what they would see: the heavy, nineteenth century Resolute desk, the gold drapes, the array of battle flags, the Rose Garden through the windowpanes. Seeing Vice President Mike Pence there was a surprise, though. Also in attendance were press secretary Sarah Sanders and Mary Elizabeth Taylor, an African American woman in her mid-twenties who was then working in the White House legislative affairs shop. (Taylor made headlines in June 2020 when she quit her job as the State Department's assistant secretary for legislative affairs, saying that Trump's handling of racial tensions "cut sharply against my core values and convictions.")[13]

Trump underscored the significance of Scott's visit by inviting him to sit in one of the two armchairs in front of the fireplace. The armchairs are a place of honor where the president usually positions visiting heads of state. On many other occasions, Trump sat behind the massive desk, and his supplicants sat facing him. The press wasn't invited. The White House photographer was, and the White House released a photo of the two men.[14] Scott was wearing bright magenta socks with big blue polka dots ("in the great tradition of George H. W. Bush," he says). The initial caption, unfortunately, identified the senator as "Tom Scott."[15]

Scott told me he had braced for a confrontation with Trump: "a more aggressive conversation with me defending my position and he defending his." That didn't happen. Trump mostly listened. "I told him how his comments that there were good people on both sides in the Charlottesville tragedy hurt my heart" and that growing up in South Carolina "meant daily encounters that left me with an absolute sense of dejection, the sense of not being complete because of the color of my skin."[16]

Trump said little. As the forty-minute meeting neared its end, Scott recalls the president said, "Tell me what I can do to be helpful to the people I've offended."

Scott was prepared. His answer: help me get Opportunity Zones into the tax bill. Trump hadn't heard of Opportunity Zones, but as a real estate guy it didn't take him long to grasp the concept. He promised to do what he could. It was a well-timed pitch. Trump was very focused on getting a tax cut through Congress.

Later that afternoon, the phone rang in Ja'Ron Smith's office. It was Marc Short, then the chief White House lobbyist. "Tell me about Opportunity Zones," he said. "The president likes it. The president wants to see if we can get this into tax reform."

Smith's reaction? "Excitement. It was kind of the missing link," he says. He immediately called Shahira Knight, who was coordinating tax reform for the White House National Economic Council, to be sure this was really happening. It was, she assured him.

The next day aboard Air Force One, returning to Washington after inspecting hurricane damage in Florida, Trump was asked by a reporter about his meeting with Scott. His reply: "He...has legislation, which I actually like very much—the concept of which, I support—to get people going into certain areas and building and constructing and putting people to work. And I told him yesterday, that's a concept I could support very easily."[17]

Thanks to Tim Scott, Opportunity Zones had momentum in the Senate. Without any serious deliberation or careful analysis from administration economists or Treasury tax experts, Opportunity Zones were now on the White House priority list, too.

By a remarkable coincidence, on the same day Scott was at the White House, Sean Parker was on Capitol Hill, making the case for OZs to be included in the emerging tax reform bill. In an impressive display of lobbying prowess, Lettieri arranged for him to see Paul Ryan, Kevin Brady, and Majority Leader Kevin McCarthy in the House, and Orrin Hatch in the Senate.

The basic pitch: "How are you going to do a once-in-a-generation tax reform and not do something for the left-behind parts of the country?" Parker and Lettieri reminded the House leaders that their proposal was popular: they now had eighty-one House cosponsors (forty-five Republicans and thirty-six Democrats, including well over half the members of Brady's Ways and Means Committee). Ryan talked about his affection for Jack Kemp, whom he considered a mentor, and made the connection with Kemp's Enterprise Zones, but talked about his determination to pass a "clean" bill in the House, to simplify the tax code rather than complicate it. Brady made similar points. Parker and Lettieri got no commitments. A few weeks later, in October, word leaked that lead OZ sponsor Pat Tiberi was going to leave Congress at year-end, which didn't help the EIG boys' bargaining position in the House.

The meeting with Hatch was strikingly different. For one thing, Hatch was a songwriter. (His tune "The Answer's Not in Washington" was recorded by Mormon singer Janice Kapp Perry.) He had been very engaged in the early 2000s debates over Napster and the use of the internet to share and distribute music. He not only knew who Sean Parker was, he admired him. Equally if not more important, Parker assured Hatch that they had Tim Scott's backing. Hatch voiced support for the goal of offering left-behind places an assist, but added emphatically: "If you've got Tim Scott, you're good."

THE FINAL SCORE

In November, two months after Scott's visit to the White House, Hatch presented the Senate Finance Committee with an initial "chairman's mark"—or draft—of the tax bill. Opportunity Zones weren't in it. But when the chairman offered his second version, it included the language Scott's staff and the EIG boys had written.

During the following days of markup, Opportunity Zones were never mentioned once. No member of Congress questioned whether they were a good idea or heard anyone critique the details. That isn't a model of good government or careful program design. "When you legislate that way, and you don't discuss it at the markup, you don't involve the other party, and you drop it at the last minute, it is an invitation to trouble," complains Senator Ron Wyden, who was the senior Democrat on the Senate Finance Committee at the time. "When we made the point that process was an invitation to trouble, we were just cut out."

The lack of scrutiny was just fine with Tim Scott and the EIG boys, though. Getting the provision into the bill was like singing with a large choir—it was best if no one noticed you.

The EIG boys had spent years trying to get the right people to notice OZs, but calling attention to them now had only downsides. First, it would alert critics of such tax breaks to push back. Second, highlighting the inclusion of Scott's pet project could lead more senators to press for their own. If those requests turned into arguments or conflict, they would endanger the few requests already included.

Now that the OZ provision was in a larger tax bill that had a serious chance of passage, it got closer examination by congressional technicians. The lawyers in the Senate's Legislative Counsel began fine-tuning the bill's language to avoid any ambiguity. The Joint Committee on Taxation's staff, a nonpartisan group of tax lawyers, economists, and accountants, went to work estimating OZs' cost. EIG had spent months working out the details of the OZ bill, but these examinations would be more intense than anything the bill had faced before, potentially exposing flaws in the design or—more seriously—pushing up the cost estimate. From Scott's office, Shay Hawkins kept in close touch with the JCT staff. "They saw lots of holes. We had to close them up," he says.

In determining OZs' overall score, one key feature was immutable. Investors who deferred taxes on a capital gain by investing in an OZ would face a capital gains tax bill on that initial gain in 2026. If taxes were triggered in that year, congressional scorekeepers could project a surge of revenue to the Treasury within the all-important ten-year window, reducing the price tag on OZs. The JCT estimated the provision would lose around $1.5 billion a year in tax revenues for several years, then bring in $10.8 billion in fiscal years 2026 and 2027, for a net ten-year tab of just $1.6 billion—essentially breakeven. (In hindsight, that ten-year estimate was probably on the low side.) Outside the ten-year window, things were less rosy; the Treasury stood to lose billions, because any profits made on OZ investments held for more than ten years escape capital gains taxes completely.

The JCT staff sought to limit the possibility that OZs would be exploited as a tax shelter well beyond the proponents' intent. The original bill, for instance, said that a taxpayer could invest directly in an OZ property, business, or partnership, *or* through a Qualified Opportunity Fund, much as one can buy shares of stock in a company or shares in a mutual fund. The final version required that all OZ investments go through a fund, and that funds must hold at least 90 percent of their assets in OZs. The aim was to make it easier for the IRS to monitor and audit OZs.

With so many provisions of the tax bill in play, and so much time pressure, the JCT and the Legislative Counsel didn't catch everything; the wording of the OZ statute has several glitches. In a detailed summary of the Tax Cuts and Jobs Act published a year after it was signed into law, JCT footnotes highlight a couple of places where "a technical correction may be necessary to reflect this intent." This is a polite way of saying the drafting of the statute was so convoluted that the law didn't say precisely what those who voted for it intended, a not infrequent occurrence with big tax bills rushed through Congress. (A couple of tax lawyers at Ballard Spahr were blunter, writing that the Treasury would have to draft rules "to interpret an ambiguous statute that cannot properly function as written.")[18] In the old days, Congress would have quietly passed a technical corrections bill a few months after a major tax bill was enacted. Brady drafted such a bill, but partisan gridlock interfered with even this normally uncontroversial measure.

Although the OZ provision moved along with no unwanted attention or controversy, the overall tax bill became mired in partisan warfare. Excluded from the bill's drafting, Democrats were united in their opposition, arguing it would cut corporate taxes too deeply, benefit upper-income taxpayers more than others, and widen the budget deficit. McConnell needed at least fifty of the fifty-two Republican senators on board. Just past midnight on December 2, McConnell muscled the Senate version of the tax bill through by a vote of fifty-one to forty-nine. He kept all his party in line except Senator Bob Corker of Tennessee. Corker voted against that version of the bill because he worried about the size of the budget deficit the big tax cuts would produce.

On the other side of the Capitol, the House passed its version with no provision for Opportunity Zones. Because the House and Senate bills were different, a conference committee was convened to sort things out. The committee held an open session—with no mention of OZs—but the real work was done in private. This was where Tim Scott and EIG's network would manage to keep OZs in the final bill.

As before, the single biggest issue was preventing Republican defections in the Senate, but now the stakes had been raised. Senator John McCain of Arizona, stricken with cancer, was in the last months of his life and couldn't be counted on to show up for the final vote. And Republicans knew they would lose another vote at the end of the year—an Alabama senator who had lost a special election to a Democrat. By January, Republicans would have only a one-vote majority.

There are a number of time-honored tactics for squeezing votes out of reluctant senators and representatives. One of the most common is to include a member's pet provision in a bill. The Tax Cuts and Jobs Act has a few of those; Scott's OZs was one. Friends of the liquor industry got another. Deb Fischer of Nebraska got a new tax credit for employers who offer paid family leave. Marco Rubio of Florida threatened to hold up the bill unless the child tax credit was expanded; he won.

Fortunately for supporters of Opportunity Zones, there was not much late resistance to OZs from House Republicans. In fact, they saw the Senate's OZ provision as a solution for a totally different political problem: what to do for hurricane-ravaged Puerto Rico? Some Republicans suggested exempting companies in Puerto Rico from parts of the new corporate tax code, but that would have turned the island into a gigantic tax haven. The OZ language allowed the governor of Puerto Rico, like the governors of the fifty states, to designate up to a quarter of low-income census tracts as OZs. But, since nearly all of Puerto Rico is low income, Ryan's staff suggested making nearly all of the island an Opportunity Zone.

BYRD DROPPINGS

Though Opportunity Zones—and the larger tax bill—looked likely to pass, there was one last hurdle: the Senate's Byrd Rule, named for the longest serving senator ever, Robert Byrd, who represented West Virginia for over fifty years. Adopted by the Senate in 1985 and written into law in 1990, the Byrd Rule applies to bills, like the Tax Cuts and Jobs Act, that are considered under a parliamentary process known as reconciliation, which allows them to be passed with a simple majority (instead of the more common sixty votes). The Byrd Rule says reconciliation bills cannot include "extraneous" provisions, defined as those that don't affect federal spending or revenues. (The rule was intended to prevent senators from sticking unrelated items onto a budget bill that couldn't be filibustered.) If a senator objects to a bill provision based on the Byrd Rule—and the Senate parliamentarian (the official interpreter of Senate rules) agrees—the provision can remain in the bill only if sixty senators agree to keep it.

Republicans knew they wouldn't get the eight Democrats needed to have sixty votes for anything. Democrats knew that they couldn't block final passage of the bill. To make passage as painful as possible, they scoured the text for potential Byrd Rule problems. As a result, Republicans couldn't leave anything in the bill that could prompt an objection. Byrd Rule disputes are usually handled behind closed doors with the parliamentarian. The two sides give the parliamentarian memos and sometimes appear in person; if the parliamentarian decides something is extraneous, the proponents generally cut it to avoid a fight on the Senate floor that they cannot win.

Provisions erased from a bill to avoid a Byrd Rule objection are known—I'm not making this up—as "Byrd droppings." The Puerto Rico provision the House proposed became a Byrd dropping, though it became law later, making 98 percent of the island's land an Opportunity Zone.

Two sections of the Opportunity Zone provision became Byrd droppings, because they didn't affect revenues or spending directly. Though the core of the OZ program was left intact, the elimination of those two elements would later prove troublesome to OZ defenders.

One gave governors some guidance in designating OZs from among the eligible census tracts. It didn't bind them to anything but said they should "strive" for "contiguous clusters of census tracts" and should favor tracts that were already the focus of efforts to attract investment, had successfully used the New Market Tax Credit or other incentives, or had "recently experienced significant layoffs due to business closures or relocations." The guidance was vague and nonbinding but, without it, governors were essentially on their own when it came to choosing OZs.

The other would have required the Treasury to report annually to Congress on the number of OZs, the amount of assets they hold, the composition of those assets (real estate versus businesses), the fraction of OZ tracts that actually got investments, and "an assessment of the impacts and outcomes of the investments in those areas on economic indicators, including job creation, poverty reduction, and new business starts." Without that provision, the Treasury was not required to demand or publish information on OZs, an issue that OZ critics later raised repeatedly.

The Treasury did eventually require Opportunity Funds to list their investments on IRS Form 8996 and investors to list their OZ investments on Form 8997. It is not yet clear what of this content will be available or when it will be released to the public or researchers. Several members of Congress have introduced bills to require more reporting and, in some cases, public disclosure. Despite bipartisan support, none of them had passed by spring 2021.

With the Byrd Rule problems cleared, and the potential defectors Rubio and Corker falling into line, the final version of the Tax Cuts and Jobs Act passed the Senate on a party line vote, fifty-one to forty-eight, on December 20 at 12:30 a.m. (Along with other Democrats, Cory Booker voted no.) McCain didn't make it to Washington for the vote, but it turned out McConnell didn't need him.

That afternoon, Trump invited all the congressional Republicans to the White House for an outdoor celebration, complete with a band playing "Hail to the Chief." Scott stood just behind Trump's left shoulder. Trump called him to the podium, introducing him as "a very, very special man.... He helped us solve some problems." Trump didn't mention OZs, but Scott did: "The Investing in Opportunity Act has been included, which will bring trillions of dollars into poor communities, because of your willingness to listen."[19]

Scott's prominent role at the White House provoked, as it had before, harsh attacks on social media. "What a shocker," tweeted Andy Ostroy, who described himself as a "proud Democrat" and "filmmaker/producer." "There's ONE black person there and sure enough they have him standing next to the mic like a manipulated prop. Way to go @SenatorTimScott."

Scott's quick reply: "Uh, probably because I helped write the bill for the past year... and have worked on tax reform my entire time in Congress. But if you'd rather just see my skin color, pls feel free."[20]

Ostroy deleted the tweet.

(Scott has mastered the sharp retort on Twitter. When someone once called him a "house nigga," he replied with a single word: "Senate.")

A QUIET WIN

Parker felt vindicated: "I told everyone, 'You know I think this is going to pass.' And everybody was like, 'Yeah right.' The crusty, curmudgeonly tax policy experts, who had spent their whole ca-reer[s] trying to advocate for some minor change in the tax code, laughed our idea off. They'd say, 'You're going to pass the most ambi-tious development economics program since the Great Depression, and you're going do it without an advocacy campaign, just because it's a great idea? Yeah. Uh-huh. That's going to happen.' And well, it did."[21] (Chalk up that hyperbole about "the most ambitious devel-opment economics program" to Parker's exuberance at his success.)

Parker emerged from his victory with a view of Congress that, while short of utopian, was far more positive than the one public opinion polls suggest the general public holds. "As soon as you step outside of politically charged hot-button issues—at one point, they would have been called wedge issues, but now are even more toxic, radioactive political issues that are used to sow division—you find that members of the Congress are idealistic enough. They're idealis-tic in that they got elected because they wanted to actually change things."

He came away with a clear notion about why he succeeded while so many others have failed—and insists it wasn't because members of Congress knew he was willing to write big checks to their cam-paigns. "If you come to the table with something that's inherently designed to appeal, to be bipartisan, and you're really serious, and with the analysis and the data and the people necessary to get it done, and really see it through to completion so that you're not just showing up as a kind of fly-by-night character with an idea and then disappearing,... then they seem very happy to work with you," he told me.

In other words, getting something done in Washington means following the EIG playbook, a good formula for those who can af-ford it.

As it turned out, hardly anyone else noticed Parker's victory. Press accounts of the tax bill overlooked OZs, with one exception. The editorial page editor of the *Denver Post*, Megan Schrader, looked through the JCT spreadsheet that listed every provision of the tax bill and spotted OZs. "Sounds a bit like the US Treasury will get to create onshore tax havens for friends," she tweeted.[22]

When she pressed the offices of Colorado's senators, Republican Cory Gardner and Democrat Michael Bennet, both of whom had endorsed the OZ bill, they defended it as "bipartisan," just as the EIG boys had hoped. The goal is worthy, she wrote in her opinion column, but the provision is likely to "open up yet another loophole in the U.S. tax code ripe for abuse by tax avoiders and evaders who have no intent to comply with the spirit of the law" and be marketed to wealthy clients looking for "a safe place to park their money tax-deferred."[23]

A month after the Tax Cuts and Jobs Act passed, on January 29, 2018, the *New York Times'* Jim Tankersley—who had been following EIG and OZs but was preoccupied with more newsworthy parts of the tax bill—wrote a largely favorable piece about what he called "a little-noted section" of the new law.[24] "It's very exciting," Michael Tubbs, the mayor of Stockton, California, ranked by EIG as the eighth most distressed large city in America, told him. "It makes communities like Stockton more attractive for investment." It was about the last nice thing the *New York Times* would ever write about OZs.

A few months later, I heard a longtime veteran of Washington tax battles derisively tell a closed-door meeting of corporate tax executives that Congress had created "an archipelago of tax havens across the country."

That was not the spin that Sean Parker and the EIG boys had been hoping for.

CHAPTER SEVEN

Choosing the Zones

S O WHERE ARE THOSE 8,764 OZs, THAT ARCHIPELAGO OF TAX shelters?[1] A glance at a map shows them—by design—scattered across the country: small patches of land in the densely populated East, bigger ones in the sparsely populated West. Each began as one entry on a list of tens of thousands of eligible census tracts prepared by the Treasury and sent to the nation's governors, who were empowered by Congress to winnow the list. The law provided few clear legal standards or criteria for picking OZs from the eligible tracts. The wording of the statute didn't require the Treasury to vet the governors' choices—and it chose not to do so.

The zone-choosing saga demonstrates both the shortcomings of the OZ design (few rules or mandates, lots of discretion, little required accountability) and the approach the Mnuchin Treasury took in implementing the law (as few restrictions on governors and investors as possible and the lightest oversight it could get away with). Not surprisingly, this approach led to some questionable choices, and some egregious choices, that got OZs off to a bad start, PR-wise.

Some governors picked wisely; some did not. Some tracts were down and out; some were already rising. Prosperous downtown Portland, Oregon, is an Opportunity Zone. So is downtown Berkeley, the Little Tokyo neighborhood of Los Angeles (half a mile from the city's financial center), and already gentrifying tracts in West Oakland, California. The area surrounding the Mall of America in Bloomington, Minnesota, which the local newspaper describes as "booming," is an OZ; even before the designation, it was the site of five new hotels, with four others on the way.[2] The city government of Austin, Texas, one of the fastest growing metro areas in the country, asked for four Opportunity Zones; the governor allotted it twenty-one.[3]

The governor of South Carolina picked a tract in the popular ocean-side resort town of Myrtle Beach, the second-fastest growing metro area, percentage-wise, in the United States during the 2010s. In Indiana, the state chose a downtown Indianapolis tract that includes the Eli Lilly corporate headquarters and the historic Fletcher Place district, and in which a quarter of the households made $100,000 or more a year.[4] Fifty-two OZs are home to a stadium or arena where a professional baseball, basketball, football, hockey, or soccer team plays. Some are in gritty neighborhoods; some not.

An Opportunity Zone in Transylvania County, North Carolina, a couple of hours drive west of Charlotte, includes mile-high peaks and forest slopes dotted with waterfalls.[5] It's beautiful, but an unusual choice for OZ designation. In February 2020, a Republican state legislator asked his congressman for help making an after-the-fact change in the boundaries of the OZ, the only one in the county. "Sixty-five percent of the land area composition of the Opportunity Zone resides inside of the Pisgah National Forest, and development on national forest property is prohibited," Chuck Edwards complained. At the time, Edwards said he was optimistic Congress would pass a bill allowing the lines to be redrawn to include the site of an abandoned mill. He is still waiting.

Not all the Opportunity Zones chosen by governors were dubious or confusing choices. A lot fit both the letter and the spirit of the law—they designated poor and struggling communities desperately in need of private capital—but so many other OZs are more attractive to investors that money may never flow to these poorer zones, even with the lure of the tax break.

So how did the selection that produced such disparate results work? It was a three-part process. The law set the parameters. The Treasury filled in some details. And the governors made the choices.

THE BUREAUCRATS GO TO WORK

After the Tax Cuts and Jobs Act passed at the end of 2017, there were plenty of questions about exactly how OZs would work. This is typical. Congress always leaves details for the executive branch to handle. The architects of OZs had outsourced many of the stickier decisions to governors, but the Treasury made several important calls before turning the process over to the states.

The first question was organizational: which office at the Treasury would handle OZ implementation? The law gave the secretary of the treasury sole discretion.

The logical choice to oversee OZs was the Community Development Financial Institutions (CDFI) Fund, an office within the Treasury that already administered place-based programs like the New Markets Tax Credit and provided grants and technical assistance to Community Development Financial Institutions, bank-like entities in downtrodden neighborhoods. The staff at the CDFI Fund had been in touch with the EIG boys early on—well before the OZ provision was even attached to the Tax Cuts and Jobs Act. Months later, when Opportunity Zones surprisingly became reality, the CDFI Fund staff expected to be the primary overseer of OZs, partnering with the IRS, which is involved in anything touching the tax code. And some in Congress expected the same. Although the statute itself wasn't specific, the accompanying conference committee report—one way Congress documents legislative intent—said that Congress intended "that the certification process for a Qualified Opportunity Fund will be done in a manner similar to the process for allocating the New Markets Tax Credit" and added that the law "provides the Secretary authority to carry out the process."[6]

But the CDFI Fund didn't end up with the job. First, OZ proponents were eager to distinguish Opportunity Zones from the more complicated New Market Tax Credit process the CDFI Fund manages. Second, Kipp Kranbuhl, the Trump appointee who had come to the Treasury from the private-equity business and oversaw the CDFI Fund, didn't grab what might ordinarily have been his turf. Among Trump appointees at the Treasury, the line was that the OZ tax break was not a "program," and thus it shouldn't be administered by the CDFI Fund shop. (That would become a mantra for the whole administration. A later White House report on OZs opened with this sentence: "The Opportunity Zones initiative is not a government program." So what is it? "It is a once-in-a-generation initiative to lift Americans out of poverty and bring economic and community revitalization to the areas that need it most."[7] Lofty words for a capital gains tax break.) In contrast, the nonpolitically appointed staff at the CDFI Fund viewed OZs as, well, a program that needed to be administered.

Since Kranbuhl didn't take the assignment, and no other political appointee at the Treasury thought OZs would be a big deal, Dan Kowalski, a twenty-year veteran of Capitol Hill, put up his hand. Kowalski has the dry, precise presence expected of someone who put in many years on the staffs of House and Senate budget committees. In 2016, he had moved to the Trump campaign as a

$13,500-a-month staffer, working on a campaign economic policy task force and serving as deputy to the campaign's policy director, Stephen Miller, who later became a controversial White House aide.

At the Treasury, Kowalski formally became a "counselor" to the secretary—a title used to avoid the hassle of the Senate confirmation required to give someone an official post such as "assistant secretary." Among Treasury staff, he was seen as the White House's agent in the building, keeping an eye on the secretary and his top lieutenants, who weren't viewed as Trump loyalists. Kowalski didn't have all that much to do at first. He was assigned a large corner office with a big window overlooking Pennsylvania Avenue, but it was farther from the secretary's suite than any other on the third floor of the nineteenth-century building, a fact about which he frequently complained. Kowalski was enthusiastic about being the point man on Opportunity Zones. Not only did it give him something substantial to work on, but he also saw the provision as a tangible way to deliver on Trump's campaign promises to do something for economically struggling communities.

Kowalski is neither a lawyer nor a tax expert, but, after Mnuchin gave him the job, he became the program's key decision maker in the federal government. Kowalski signed off on all the big OZ policy calls, including those addressing questions left unclear by the law's language. One such decision, which would later have on-the-ground implications, defined "contiguous" tracts. Did the tracts have to share a substantial border with an OZ, or would a mere touching corner suffice? The latter, he decided.

Though he was in charge of OZs' rollout, Kowalski lacked the staff needed to quickly come up with a list of eligible census tracts. He turned data-driven tasks like the list making over to the experts at the CDFI Fund. So, by default, the CDFI Fund staff, who had initially lost out on the OZ oversight job, ended up with substantial input.

For example, determining which tracts were eligible for Opportunity Zone designation wasn't just a matter of pulling a list from a database. The CDFI Fund needed first to decide which years to pull data from. The official data on poverty and income levels come from the Census Bureau's annual American Community Survey. Because any one year's surveys aren't large enough to provide statistically reliable data for every census tract, the data are averaged over five years. By early 2018, the most recent available data covered 2012–2016, but the CDFI Fund decided not to use it. The data hadn't been thoroughly vetted yet and the CDFI Fund had a tight deadline to meet. They had to get lists to the states ASAP so governors could then submit their choices to the Treasury by the end of March 2018. As a result, the CDFI Fund team decided to use the older 2011–2015 numbers. (The Treasury did later allow states to use the 2012–2016 data in certain circumstances.)

A lot can change over any five-year period, but for much of the country, 2011 and 2015 were quite different, economically speaking. In that interval, the unemployment rate, for instance, had fallen from 9.1 percent in the wake of the Great Recession to 5 percent. What's more, the differences between the economic conditions (the readings used to determine an area's poverty and income levels) of 2011–2015 and 2018 and beyond (when investment decisions were made) were profound in some communities. By 2018, some places that qualified as "low income" using 2011–2015 data were already gentrifying and drawing plenty of investment without extra incentives.

A few examples of up-and-coming areas eligible for OZ designation sit just a few miles from the Treasury building in downtown DC.[8] One includes the blocks around Audi Field, DC United's new soccer stadium at Buzzard Point. Even before OZs existed, investors already had planned to invest hundreds of millions of dollars there. Another encompasses the NoMa neighborhood, just north of Union

Station, where office buildings and pricey apartments were already sprouting before developers even heard about OZs. Illustrating just how broad the criteria were, the city's tony Georgetown neighborhood was eligible, largely because the students in Georgetown University dorms pulled down the median income. (The mayor of DC designated Buzzard Point as an OZ, but neither NoMa nor Georgetown.)

The Treasury compiled the list of tracts eligible for OZ designation in early February 2018, light speed for a government agency. They sent governors spreadsheets with more than 41,000 eligible tracts, over half of all census tracts in the United States. The list included 31,680 tracts that met the legal definition of "low income." The other 9,453 tracts didn't qualify as low income, but were eligible because they were "contiguous" to a low-income zone and their median income was no higher than 125 percent of the adjacent OZ.

Governors were told to pick up to a quarter of the eligible tracts in their states for OZ tax breaks. Smaller states (and DC and US territories) with fewer than one hundred low-income tracts were permitted to choose a total of twenty-five zones. All the selections were consequential and long term. Once chosen, an Opportunity Zone would keep the designation for ten years, and there was no provision in the law to change a zone's status—no matter how much the zone changed.

From that list of eligible tracts, governors were free to make their decisions however they liked. Some states—California, Michigan, Nevada, and Vermont among them—posted proposal choices for public comment before submission to the Treasury. In Indiana, an advisory panel of citizens was convened. Kansas solicited "letters of interest" from local governments, and the governor picked at least one zone from every community that responded. Colorado asked local authorities to make their case for designation and decided to allocate most of the state's OZs to rural communities, instead of more prosperous urban centers. Florida decided each of its sixty-seven counties should get at least one OZ.

The wide latitude given governors combined with the large number of eligible tracts—including some that already were magnets for private investment—meant more than a few selections drew skeptical press attention. Nevertheless, the designations were clearly allowed under the wording of the law and the Treasury's decision not to use its authority to limit or scrutinize governors' choices. Indeed, much of the OZ story is about what the law allowed, not how people bent it.

Some of the criticized OZ designations appear to reflect the difficult choices facing states, rather than corruption. In Michigan, for example, the state designated much of downtown Detroit. This included tracts (one of which was eligible only because it was contiguous to a low-income OZ) where Dan Gilbert—cofounder of Quicken Loans, owner of the Cleveland Cavaliers basketball franchise, and an early EIG supporter—already had invested nearly $2 billion to reinvigorate the central business district.[9] The investigative website ProPublica called attention to the designation in October 2019, suggesting that Gilbert's relationship with Donald Trump improperly influenced the state's choices;[10] Gilbert angrily denied that.[11]

Detroit's official response illuminated a quandary that had little to do with political favoritism, even if it benefited developers like Gilbert. "The City recommended the eligible areas where it believed developers were more likely to find profitable investments," a city spokesperson told ProPublica. "To do anything else would have been pointless."

This was a fundamental question confronted by thoughtful governors: should a state designate the worst-off neighborhoods, even though they had little chance of drawing private investment, or should it pick less challenging areas that private investors were likely to find most attractive?

THE POLITICS OF OZ

There was, however, politics behind plenty of the designations. After all, we're talking about state capitols.

In New Hampshire, Governor Chris Sununu, a Republican, drew attention from the local press and criticism from Democrats for picking a three-hundred-square-mile tract that, among other things, included his family's Waterville Valley ski resort, even though other tracts in the state had higher poverty rates or lower median incomes. (His family said in 2018 that it didn't have any plans to take advantage of the tax break "at this time.")[12]

In Florida, ProPublica reported, developer Wayne Huizenga Jr., son of the billionaire founder of Waste Management and AutoNation, lobbied Florida's governor to add three tracts to those initially proposed by the city of West Palm Beach. The tracts encompassed a marina for three-hundred-foot-long superyachts and, as he observed in his letter to the governor, a site where he was planning a $120 million luxury apartment complex. Governor Rick Scott granted Huizenga's wish. Photos of the yachts on the ProPublica site and in the *Miami Herald* made the selection look outrageous.[13] EIG's critique of the story pointed out that northern parts of the tract were distinctly down-and-out and the target of redevelopment efforts by a local nonprofit.[14] ProPublica fired back that two other census tracts to the south were not selected as OZs, despite being considerably poorer and less white than the one that included the marina.[15] EIG didn't challenge ProPublica's reporting that Scott also picked a zone in Tampa at the request of a firm controlled by another billionaire donor, Tampa Bay Lightning owner Jeff Vinik.

Governor Scott told local reporters the allegation of favoritism was "ridiculous," and asserted, inaccurately, "the ultimate decider was Steve Mnuchin's shop."[16] The governor's office said Scott's focus "was on supporting job creation in low-income areas in the state, based on federal requirements and what would offer the best return on taxpayer dollars. That's what guided every decision he made."[17]

But all those stories—tarnishing the image of OZs and undermining the EIG boys' efforts to paint them as data driven—ran long after the Treasury had certified the governors' choices.

GILMAN'S TRIC

Perhaps the most extensively documented case of alleged political favoritism came from Nevada, one of the last states to finalize its choices. Under the Treasury's rules, governors were to rely on the list of eligible tracts compiled using 2011–2015 census data to determine if a tract was low income. The same data would also be used to determine if a tract contiguous with a low-income tract could get OZ designation. The Treasury later amended those rules so that if a tract qualified as low income using 2012–2016 census data, the state could pick that one, too. The amended rules did not, however, allow using the newer data to decide if a *contiguous* zone was eligible. That proved to be a problem for a tract in Storey County, a sparsely populated expanse of scrubby desert and low, rolling mountains.

The Storey County tract encompassed a 165-square-mile industrial park known as Tahoe Reno Industrial Center (TRIC) already home to, among other things, Tesla's Gigafactory, which makes batteries and motors in what Tesla claims will be the world's largest building.[18] The tract didn't have enough poor people to count as a low-income community, wasn't initially eligible for designation, and thus didn't make the list of OZs Nevada sent to Washington. But it ended up on the final list after an aggressive lobbying effort and a little rule bending at the Treasury.

Central to the saga is Lance Gilman, a real estate developer with a stake in TRIC who was also a Storey County commissioner and owner of the county's first licensed brothels. In January 2018, Blockchain LLC, a California start-up in the cryptocurrency business, bought the last large parcel available in TRIC—and hired Gilman to coordinate marketing and government relations.[19] At an April 17 meeting of county commissioners, Gilman said the county was using a lobbying firm headed by former Nevada congressman Jon Porter to help get the TRIC tract designated as an OZ. He said he was "cautiously optimistic" that then governor Brian Sandoval would pick the TRIC tract.[20]

Sandoval didn't. Before sending its choices to Washington, the state asked the Treasury whether a tract like TRIC, which was not a low-income tract but contiguous to one under the 2012–2016 data, would qualify. It was told by the CDFI Fund staff that it wouldn't. Indeed, they had rejected a similar request from Vermont. On April 13, Dean Heller, Nevada's Republican US senator, called Secretary Mnuchin to press the issue. On April 20, Sandoval sent the Treasury a list of sixty-one tracts in the state it proposed to make OZs. Tract 32029970200, in which TRIC was located, didn't make the list. An uproar ensued. Storey County politicians eventually persuaded their counterparts in Dayton, in neighboring Lyon County, to offer to drop one of Lyon's three OZs so Storey County could get one.

On May 8, Sandoval talked to Mnuchin on the phone to argue Storey County's case. The Treasury says Mnuchin made no promises but told the governor his staff would review the request. That same day, Sandoval made the request in writing, proposing to withdraw the nomination of a census tract in Lyon County and add the TRIC tract in its place.[21] Storey County commissioners flew to Washington on May 9 to meet with the state's congressional delegation and press the issue. Mnuchin's calendar shows he met for an hour with acting IRS commissioner David Kautter on May 9; the subject of that meeting hasn't been disclosed.[22]

Sandoval's request alarmed staff at the IRS and elsewhere in the Treasury. "Several states have asked for a deviation, akin to the request made by Nevada, and the answer has been consistently that such a deviation is not permissible," Mireille Khoury of the IRS counsel's office wrote in a May 16 email to colleagues.[23] She warned that granting Nevada's request would invite unwelcome scrutiny of the IRS implementation of the Tax Cuts and Jobs Act and open the door to accusations that the process for picking OZs "was influenced by political considerations or bias." The then head of the CDFI Fund office, Annie Donovan, expressed similar concerns.

Overriding those warnings, Kowalski granted the Nevada request. "We issued a policy memo internal to IRS saying that we made a mistake here. The nominating instruction should be modified in the future to reflect that a non-LIC [low-income community] contiguous tract could be nominated on the newer data, and that, in fact, Nevada's petition was correct and that they should be designated," Kowalski says. He says he offered Vermont the same deal, but that state stuck with its original choices.

The official word to Nevada from the Treasury came in a June 15 letter from the IRS commissioner to Governor Sandoval. Four days later, Gilman recounted the successful lobbying campaign with glee at the Storey County commissioners meeting:

"So, unfortunately, in the first approvals, Storey County was overlooked. And Lyon County got a significant share. . . . So a team of folks—and you know I'll leave out some—but I'll tell you a team of folks got very, very busy working with the county governments and at the federal level with the Treasury, and it was an outstanding effort on behalf of everyone."

Gilman singled out the Storey and Lyon county managers, lobbyist Jon Porter, Senator Heller, and Governor Sandoval. "We actually traded a very small Opportunity Zone in Dayton....And that allowed much of Storey County to come in as an Opportunity Zone. So, tremendous opportunity. We'll see the fruit of our actions here in the next four or five years. But truly an incredible event to attract a lot of capital here in our economic development."[24]

It took only a week after the Treasury's formal decision for Khoury's fears about bad publicity to come true. The headline on well-sourced *Washington Post* reporter Damian Paletta's story on June 22 read, "After Nevada GOP push, Treasury changed lucrative policy benefitting one county."[25] He gave the credit to Heller and Sandoval, and noted that at the end of April 2018, Gilman contributed $5,000 to Heller's reelection campaign, the largest single contribution he'd ever made to a federal candidate.

The story didn't end there. In October 2019, the *New York Times* said billionaire Michael Milken, who pled guilty to securities fraud in 1990, had interests in a company that owned land in the Storey County tract. Milken had been publicly and privately very enthusiastic about OZs, even telling some acquaintances he was buying land to take advantage of the tax break. "Symbol of '80s Greed Stands to Profit from Trump Tax Break for Poor Areas," the *Times* headline said.[26]

Mnuchin, the *Times* noted accurately, participated in a closed-door session on Opportunity Zones with Milken, Sean Parker, and others at the annual Milken Institute Global Conference on April 30, 2018. The *Times* knew the two men had talked but had no proof Milken had asked Mnuchin for help in designating Storey County. Both Mnuchin and Milken vehemently deny that Milken had done so. Lower-level Treasury officials who objected to the Storey County designation tell me they never heard Milken mentioned. Milken's lawyers hired a former Milken aide to write a twenty-four-page rebuttal to the *Times* story; it essentially pointed the finger at Gilman, Heller, and Sandoval.[27] In a *Wall Street Journal* op-ed, Milken blasted what he called the *New York Times*' "journalistic mendacity."[28]

Lost in all the noise: even before the OZ tax break was enacted, TRIC had drawn millions of dollars in private investment, not only from Tesla but also from Alcoa, Golden Gate Petroleum, Home Depot, Kaiser Aluminum, Mars, PetSmart, and Walmart, and housed Google and Switch data centers.[29] In other words, it didn't need the extra boost from the OZ tax break Gilman and his political allies managed to get; the big winners will be the existing landowners and the wealthy investors who put their money there.

DOWN AND OUT IN PALO ALTO

In a couple of big states, Democratic governors, who were somewhere between disinterested and hostile when it came to OZs, made particularly jarring choices.

In New York, Governor Andrew Cuomo, famously critical of Trump and, so, skeptical of a tax break branded with his name, initially considered not picking zones at all. In the end, he made some eyebrow-raising calls, all of which were legal under the wording of the OZ provision in the tax bill and the absence of any Treasury rules or guidance. For example, fully one quarter of New York State's Opportunity Zones are in trendy Brooklyn (which has 13 percent of the state's population). They include a neighborhood near the Williamsburg Bridge where the median value of owner-occupied homes is around $1 million. An OZ in Queens' Long Island City (median household income $130,000) was already so attractive it almost became home to Amazon's HQ2 with all sorts of state subsidies, though (at least according to Amazon) no plans to tap the OZ tax break.[30] The project ran into community and union opposition, and Amazon backed away. But the headlines offered evidence for the narrative that money was flowing to tracts that didn't need the extra incentives of a capital gains tax break.

On the West Side of Manhattan between 50th and 59th Streets, a few blocks from Central Park and not far from some of the city's most expensive properties, Hell's Kitchen is in an OZ. Well before OZs, in November 2016, the neighborhood already was appealing enough for billionaire investor Bill Ackman to sign a deal to move the headquarters of his hedge fund to a rehabbed office tower there; the ground floor hosts a Jaguar Land Rover dealership.[31] Impoverished Far Rockaway, Queens, this was not.

Years later—after Biden beat Trump and the political terrain shifted in Washington—Lettieri complained to me the Trump Treasury didn't do enough to prevent governors from making bad choices. "Where a Treasury Department has wanted to find a lot of authority, they find it, and where they've wanted to be extremely hands-off, they found that rationale as well. That's true of every administration," he said. Lettieri figures that areas where governors made bad choices—he singles out Cuomo as an example—drew 99 percent of the criticism and "100 percent of the justified criticism of Opportunity Zones."

Along with tracts already profiting from gentrification or pre-OZ investment, several areas around college campuses ended up as Opportunity Zones. They were full of students who report little income and, due to the way the Census Bureau does its counting, that pushed college towns' poverty rates above the 20 percent threshold, making them OZ eligible. Governors didn't have to anoint them, but several did. Areas around Liberty University in Lynchburg, Virginia; University of Illinois in Urbana-Champaign; Purdue University in West Lafayette, Indiana; and the University of Louisville in Kentucky are all OZs.

California governor Jerry Brown was a high-profile offender, at least initially. After some public criticism of the governor's list, which included Stanford University's campus as an OZ, EIG sent an open letter to the governor, its *only* such public complaint. It wrote:

> California's data-only approach fell short in several particularly egregious places. For example, three of the state's recommended tracts— 5130 in Santa Clara County (covering Stanford University's campus in Palo Alto), 28.01 in San Diego County (covering San Diego State University's campus in College Heights), and 4237 in Berkeley, Alameda County—all have high poverty rates thanks to large student populations but are nevertheless parts of communities that clearly do not align with Congressional intent for Opportunity Zones. Similarly, San Francisco County's tract 178.01 (in the South of Market Area) combines a high poverty rate with some of the highest incomes in the state thanks to a recent influx of wealthy residents and business owners. Meanwhile, a recommended tract in Westwood (7011) is nearly entirely comprised of a Veterans Administration medical campus and thus may contain no real opportunity for private investment in the first place.[32]

The public comment period worked to some extent. The state dropped those tracts before submitting its final choices to the Treasury. However, Brown's final selections did include downtown Berkeley (adjacent to the University of California campus), already gentrifying tracts in West Oakland, and neighborhoods in San Francisco that had high poverty rates because of public housing complexes but already were changing and drawing plenty of private money. EIG could wince at the designations—many of which did draw negative headlines—but the law they had conceived and championed made them perfectly legal.

MOVING OUT

One of the biggest fears community groups and OZ skeptics had was that the program would accelerate gentrification in already gentrifying neighborhoods. To be sure, not everyone considers gentrification evil—and there's evidence the process isn't as economically harmful to folks who live in those neighborhoods as some argue—but the stated purpose of OZs was to improve the lives of OZ residents, not displace them.

Measuring gentrification by looking at how neighborhoods had changed between 2000 and 2016, the Urban Institute found that relatively few tracts eligible for OZ designation were experiencing "socioeconomic change" (its euphemism for gentrification), but the ones chosen as OZs were more likely to be gentrifying than those passed over. In some states—New York, in particular—the chosen zones had seen substantial gentrification since 2000; Delaware, Connecticut, and Maryland were close behind. Among cities, zones chosen in New York City, Oakland, Seattle, and Washington, DC, ranked particularly high on the already gentrifying scorecard.[33]

Yet, as EIG pointed out in a seventeen-page rebuttal, some tracts that showed up as gentrification hot spots on the Urban Institute's list seemed reasonable OZ choices. "One such example is tract 13121011800 in the English Avenue neighborhood in Atlanta, where more than one-third of homes remain vacant, life expectancy is nine years shorter than the national average, and past revitalization efforts have consistently come up short. A relatively new student apartment block in the northernmost corner of the tract may help push the poverty rate above 50 percent (and may well be the driver behind the socioeconomic change captured in Urban's analysis), but the number of boarded up homes and empty parcels woven throughout the neighborhood confirm that the tract—literally on the wrong side of the railroad tracks from Georgia Tech University—continues to struggle."[34]

My Brookings colleague Adam Looney used a different gentrification measure: house price appreciation from 2012 to 2016. He found most states selected tracts in which house prices had appreciated faster than in eligible communities that weren't chosen (although some were in states with pretty low house prices). EIG pooh-poohed his measure, too, arguing that a lot of the places on the list were rural towns that didn't fit the popular notion of gentrification, even if home prices had risen.

Looney concluded that the law gave states too much flexibility and didn't provide incentives for states to choose places like the communities Tim Scott described when he talked about OZs.[35]

EIG disagreed. "The challenge," it said, "was for governors to identify places with clear needs, but also clear capacity to attract and absorb new investment—places where an incentive for private capital could catalyze a broader economic turnaround if combined with the right local strategies. The results show that governors embraced the task, adapting the selection process to their own unique circumstances in order to strike a delicate balance between need and opportunity at the local level."[36]

THE GOOD NEWS

Were questionable OZ choices the tip of the iceberg or exceptions? Looking across the country, on average, states picked tracts that—at least on the surface—looked needier than those that were eligible but not picked. Of the 8,764 tracts designated as OZs, only 198 qualified because they were contiguous to low-income tracts. (The law allowed up to 5 percent of OZs to be in that latter category; in the end, only 2.2 percent were.)[37] About 35 million people live in OZs, a little over 10 percent of the US population.

Said Adam Looney, no fan of OZs: "Across a range of indicators like child poverty and educational attainment, states' selections are, on average, more disadvantaged than the low-income tracts they did not select, and selections had larger minority populations." Yet Looney also reported that "some states selected zones that were, on average, better off on many dimensions than low-income areas they skipped over." Georgia and Hawaii stood out for allocating the largest share of their picks to the most distressed neighborhoods. At the other end of the spectrum, West Virginia, Mississippi, New Mexico, Alabama, Arkansas, Kentucky, and Louisiana picked places that were much less distressed than the alternatives.

Of course, the averages obscure the reality that designating a census tract as an Opportunity Zone didn't mean anyone would sink any money into it. Nothing in the design of OZs directed money to those zones most in need of investment as opposed to those that already looked very attractive to developers.

Indeed, the Urban Institute found a lot—not the majority, but nearly a third—of tracts designated as OZs already were magnets for private investment. In some places, that reflected a deliberate decision by governors' offices, who understood that, given the design of the incentive, zones in their state would be competing with zones in other states for money. They picked accordingly; anointing the worst-off tracts might mean attracting very little money.

Although the OZ law doesn't permit the subsequent designation of any census tract that didn't make the initial cut, property owners and local officials in a handful of places successfully lobbied the Commerce Department and Census Bureau to widen the boundaries of OZ-blessed census tracts to include their property. For instance, according to a February 2021 Bloomberg report, an OZ investor encouraged the local government in Saint Croix, US Virgin Islands, to successfully press Washington to more than triple the size of one census tract, hoping to expand an Opportunity Zone so it includes an airport, an oil refinery, and an industrial park. And the owners of the Pittsburgh Penguins, along with city officials and union leaders, succeeded in their quest to expand a downtown OZ-designated census tract to include a development site once occupied by the hockey team's arena. The team's owners told Bloomberg they didn't plan to exploit the OZ tax break, but its developer-partners said they intended to.[38] But in May 2021, the IRS slapped them down, saying that the boundaries of OZs were fixed in 2019 and wouldn't change even if the boundaries of an OZ-designated census tract were altered.

TAXPAYER FRIENDLY

During this process, the states were flying blind—in one sense. They had to select their OZs well before the Treasury laid out regulations that would answer lots of lingering questions about exactly how the zones would work. States submitted their choices for OZs by March 2018 (although some got one-month extensions). The Treasury issued the first set of regulations in October 2018. Three hundred comment letters later, the final set were finally issued in a 544-page document in December 2019, fast by Treasury standards but a lag that frustrated the EIG boys and Tim Scott—and a lot of tax lawyers, wealth advisers, developers, and investors.[39]

In fairness, filling in details that a law doesn't spell out is always a contentious process. For OZs, it was further complicated by the wording of the statute—vague in some places—and by intense interest from the White House, including from Ja'Ron Smith and the Council of Economic Advisers. Additionally, there were so many other parts of the 2017 tax law to parse that the Treasury's Office of Tax Policy, which works with the IRS on such chores, couldn't give its full attention to OZs.

To implement Trump's signature legislative achievement as soon as possible, Steve Mnuchin began convening a "daily tax implementation meeting." Sometimes OZs got left in the dust. One senior staffer in the Tax Policy shop told me he looked at the OZ provision of the statute, thought it'd be unworkable, and moved on. One of the office's career lawyers kept pressing to push OZ regulation writing higher on the priority list without success. Mnuchin's calendar shows he met for half an hour with Sean Parker on March 13, 2018. The two had crossed paths during Mnuchin's time in the movie business in California. Parker says both he and the Treasury secretary saw OZs as a way to move venture capital to impoverished neighborhoods. Still, nothing much happened on the rule writing until Mnuchin came back to Washington from the Milken Institute conference at end of April 2018 and started asking questions about OZs.[40]

The pace of the rollout of OZ rules made at least one person very impatient. Steve Wynn is a casino owner who sold $2.1 billion worth of shares in Wynn Resorts in March 2018 after he was forced from the company after former employees accused him of sexual misconduct. The sale would stick him with a huge capital gains tax bill—unless he could put the money into an OZ fund. The law gave him 180 days to invest any capital gains; that is, until September. For Wynn, an OZ investment was a great opportunity to save money on his big payday, but without the rules it was hard to know precisely what was kosher.

On June 4, 2018, with about three months left on his OZ time clock, Wynn and his tax lawyer came to Washington to meet with Kowalski to press for faster work on the regulations. Mnuchin dropped by the meeting, his calendar shows. As a six-figure donor to Republicans and, until the employee complaints surfaced, the finance chair of the Republican National Committee, Wynn had substantial political clout. Despite Wynn's efforts to speed up the process, though, the first regulations weren't issued until October, a month after his 180-day window for investing in OZs closed. (Wynn didn't respond to my inquiries about whether he did, in the end, make OZ investments.)

When the rules finally did emerge, many of them dealt with arcane issues very important to a very few, very interested people. Overall, though, there was one refrain throughout the Opportunity Zone conferences I attended and the conversations I had. As Steve Glickman put it at a January 2020 webinar, the regulations got "consistently more *taxpayer friendly*." Indeed, nearly every time the Treasury had to make a choice, it chose a more *taxpayer-friendly* option; in other words, it gave rich investors more leeway in avoiding taxes. A Google search turns up 29,100 hits that refer to OZ regulations as "taxpayer friendly."

The law, for instance, said that Qualified Opportunity Funds had to hold 90 percent of their assets in OZ property—either real estate or an OZ business. If the asset was a business, then "substantially all" of the business's tangible property had to be in an OZ. The Treasury's regulations defined "substantially all" as 70 percent. That means, structured carefully, an OZ fund could have 63 percent of its tangible assets in an OZ (70 percent of 90 percent) and 37 percent elsewhere.

The tangled wording of the statute effectively limited the tax break to property *acquired* by an OZ fund after December 31, 2017. That led people who had property in an OZ purchased before that date to conclude that if they wanted to cash in, they would have to sell their land or building. But the Treasury, with some justification, stretched the definition of *acquired* to include *leased*. That decision, coupled with other rules, allows property owners to start their own OZ fund and lease their own property to themselves—and get all the OZ tax breaks.

Another taxpayer-friendly tilt revolved around the provision that if an OZ fund bought a property with an existing building, the investment could qualify for the tax break only if the owner spent at least as much as the original purchase price in improvements. The Treasury decided the value of the land (as opposed to the building) didn't count in that calculation. So if an OZ fund bought a property for $800,000, of which $480,000 was for the land and $320,000 was for the building, as long as it spent at least $320,000 in improvements the whole $800,000 qualified for the OZ tax treatment. After some prodding from outsiders who worried people would use the OZ break to speculate on empty land,[41] the IRS said generic anti-abuse provisions would thwart someone who bought an empty lot, put a shed on it for a parking lot attendant, and then tried to claim it was an OZ-eligible investment.[42]

In a move particularly welcomed by investors and money managers, the Treasury and IRS also expanded the tight investment time window. To jump-start the program and reduce the risk that OZs would do little more than shelter investors' profits from taxes, the statute originally gave OZ funds only six months to put at least 90 percent of investors' cash into buildings or businesses in an OZ. Developers, entrepreneurs, and their lawyers and accountants complained loudly that this was impossible; it often takes years to get permits for a new building, for example. The Treasury and IRS opined—despite there being nothing specific in the law that allowed them to—that funds had thirty-one months (with certain loose restrictions) to put the money to work; that was later extended to sixty-two months (that's five years).

All that came before the COVID-19 pandemic led the IRS to ease all sorts of restrictions. In June 2020, for instance, it told investors they had until year-end 2020 to invest any capital gains in an OZ fund even if that took them beyond the statutory 180-day deadline. In the very last days of the Trump presidency, it pushed that deadline to March 31, 2021. It also gave OZ funds more time to put their cash to work.[43]

To the frustration of the EIG boys and some investors, the initial rounds of Treasury regulations focused on defining the rules for real estate investments, leaving lots of questions about investing in start-ups and other businesses hanging until final rules were issued in December 2019. Writing rules for investments in businesses was far trickier than for real estate because, unlike buildings, businesses can have operations outside the zone and can move. The delay undercut OZ proponents' argument that this place-based incentive, unlike its predecessors, would spark investment in job-creating businesses in down-and-out neighborhoods. At one point, Lettieri tells me, one Treasury political appointee (he won't say whom) said favoring real estate was intentional because some at the Treasury didn't think directing money toward risky start-up businesses was wise. Treasury insiders say the bigger issue was that the place-based nature of the OZ statute wasn't as well suited for investments in businesses as Parker and the EIG boys' rhetoric suggests.

Requests for the Treasury to limit investors' ability to exploit OZ tax breaks in ways that didn't fit the program's intended purpose did not get a warm welcome. One group of affordable housing ad-vocates asked the Treasury to require detailed reporting, including the number of jobs created by an OZ investment, the number of rental housing units available before and after an investment, and how many of those housing units remained affordable for folks with incomes well below the median.[44] Others wanted OZ funds to at least identify the intended benefits to the community, or even be re-quired to certify that investments would create jobs for low-income individuals, develop affordable housing, or provide other value to the neighborhood.

The IRS and the Treasury refused, arguing that such rules would reduce the flow of OZ money. The agencies were, they said, seek-ing "a balance between providing taxpayers with a flexible and effi-cient process for organizing QOFs [Qualified Opportunity Funds], while ensuring that investments in such vehicles will be properly directed toward the economic development of low-income communities. The suggested recommendations, while potentially helpful for directing such investment and limiting abuse, likely would present numerous obstacles for potential QOF investors and ultimately reduce, rather than increase, the total amount of investment in low-income communities."[45] At a public meeting on OZs at the Federal Reserve Bank of New York in July 2018, Tim Scott's aide Shay Hawkins said, "My boss is for reporting, but not if it reduces OZ financing by a single dollar," according to someone who was there.

As a result, OZ funds have limited paperwork and reporting to do. No one needs the IRS's blessing to create an OZ fund, as you would, for instance, to create a 501(c)(3) nonprofit. One "self-certifies," as the jargon of the industry puts it. The IRS requires OZ funds to fill out Form 8996 so the agency can check that they are following the rules. The initial two-page version of the form, published in 2018, required only basic dollars and cents totals. After criticism, the IRS revised the form in January 2020. Now four pages, it requires the census tract location (though not the address) of OZ fund real estate holdings and the federally issued Employer Identification Number of any OZ business. Investors in OZ funds who are taking advantage of the capital gains break file the separate, two-page Form 8997 with their annual tax return.

Before he left office at the end of the Trump administration, Kowalski said the government planned to use census data along with the IRS filings to evaluate OZs. It's not clear how much, if any, of this information will be made public or provided, anonymized, to independent researchers. Data from 2018 wasn't collected in an easy-to-crunch digital format, so any serious analysis is years away. Later information was collected digitally, but it takes a long time for the IRS to process. Even basic data for 2019—how much money went to which OZs—wasn't expected to be available until mid-2021. This lack of data makes it much harder to judge the success of OZs, and harder for anyone (inside or outside of government) to spot the ways clever lawyers and accountants are exploiting the law's loopholes and interstices.

CHAPTER EIGHT

Don't Blame the Players, Blame the Game

Anthony Scaramucci wasn't the first to jump into the OZ pool, but he did it with a bigger splash than almost anyone else.

Scaramucci—or The Mooch, as he has been known since grade school—was a media-hungry financier with a mixed bag of political convictions when he started a stint as Trump's White House communications director in July 2017. Two days into his new role, Scaramucci publicly vowed to find and fire "un-American" leakers within the White House.[1] He himself was fired nine days later, after his profanity-splattered criticisms of other top Trump aides—some of whom he believed to be leaking to the media—were quoted in the *New Yorker*.[2]

After leaving the White House, Scaramucci wrote one of the long series of insider tell-all books about (his eleven days in) the Trump administration. He also returned to his life as a high-profile money manager at the hedge fund he'd founded in 2005, SkyBridge Capital. When the Tax Cuts and Jobs Act passed later in 2017, he began plotting his entry into the OZ business, launching an OZ fund in 2018. It would, he said confidently, raise an eye-popping $3 billion and be "a game-changing product" for his company. Even before it was cleared to begin soliciting money, Scaramucci asserted the fund already had drawn "tons of investor interest."[3]

Like many other OZ funds, this one was open only to what the Securities and Exchange Commission calls "accredited investors," those with a net worth of at least $1 million (not including their home), or income of at least $200,000, or total assets of at least $5 million. The minimum investment was $100,000.[4] OZ funds are not for the typical American.

On a conference call with potential investors in December 2018, Scaramucci said one of his fund's first projects would be a Moxy Hotel on the site of a gas station in Oakland. "For those of you who have yet to go to Oakland, California, or that part of the Bay Area, I can tell you that it's fully gentrifying. Oakland is effectively becoming the Brooklyn Heights of San Francisco," he said. "We think we're going to be building a swank, boutique hotel there that's going to create excessive economic rents."[5]

As Scaramucci honed his OZ pitch in public, he took care to talk up the attractiveness of the tax break to investors while emphasizing the social benefits of OZs to anyone else who might be listening.

"A lot of capital in the United States is trapped," he said on Fox Business in January 2019. "You bought Amazon at a dollar and it's trading at $120, and you don't want sell, you don't want to realize that gain, but you want some diversity for your family. This is an opportunity where you can chip off some of that . . . and you can move it into one of the nation's Opportunity Zones."[6]

As is his style, Scaramucci talked big. "Let's say we can deploy a trillion dollars," he said on Fox. "This is a real opportunity to go into areas of the country that need the help where you can supply capital and start that fertilizing." A trillion dollars? No one else was talking numbers that big.

In that January 2019 interview, Scaramucci also said his fund already had more than $2 billion in real estate deals in its pipeline, including the Oakland hotel and a port project in Tim Scott's state of South Carolina.

Whatever the accuracy of his forecasts, Scaramucci has an impressively extensive personal network. It extends to Richard Branson, the British billionaire entrepreneur, who has spoken at Scaramucci's conferences and hosted Scaramucci and his wife at his Virgin Islands retreat, Necker Island. So, when one of Scaramucci's partners told him Branson's firm had unveiled plans for a Virgin Hotel in an OZ in New Orleans, Scaramucci called his friend, connected with his North American operation, and agreed to invest about $35 million in the $80 million project—the first investment of his OZ fund. This wasn't a project spurred by OZs: plans for the hotel were unveiled in January 2017, nearly a year before OZs were written into law.[7] Groundbreaking was in May 2019, and the opening was set for mid-2021.

The 225-room "experiential lifestyle hotel with a premium room product," according to the fund's prospectus, is in New Orleans's Warehouse District, in an artsy, gentrifying area on the edge of an OZ that doesn't resemble the down-and-out zones Tim Scott and the EIG boys talk about. Virgin, accurately, describes the neighborhood as "an up-and-coming area...directly next to the central business district and home to a growing number of new restaurants, galleries and shops."[8]

The tract is a textbook example of how data from 2011–2015 can green-light OZs in areas that aren't really struggling today. Although more than a quarter of the residents were below the poverty line in the 2010–2015 census data—hence the OZ designation—the median income was above $65,000 and the median house price nearly $450,000. Scaramucci argues the project fits the goals of the OZ law because it'll create 220 hotel jobs.

Did Scaramucci's plan to build a swank hotel in a gentrifying area align with the declared intent of Opportunity Zones? Not really. Was it totally legit under the OZ law? Absolutely.

I began to sense a theme developing:

Don't blame the players. Blame the game.

SALTING OZs

For years, Scaramucci has thrown lavish annual events called SALT (for SkyBridge Alternatives) in Las Vegas. Like everything else he did, the SALT conferences—once known as "Davos in the Desert"—married pizzazz and entertainment with traditional panels of experts. In 2010, Bill Clinton spoke. The 2012 edition featured Al Gore, Sarah Palin, and a party with Maroon 5.

Scaramucci's four-day SALT conference in May 2019 at the Bellagio in Las Vegas is a pep rally for Opportunity Zones. One panel, "Investing in the Land of Opportunity," has some familiar names: EIG's John Lettieri joins Dan Kowalski from the Treasury and executives from Scaramucci's OZ fund.

Another features Chris Loeffler, whose Caliber real estate fund is building an OZ operation in the Southwest, in dialogue with his lawyer, Marc Schultz of Snell & Wilmer, a Phoenix-based law firm. "Tax programs like the Qualified Opportunity Zone program are a once in a lifetime, maybe twice in a lifetime opportunity," Loeffler says.[9]

Caliber's first OZ project is a new DoubleTree by Hilton Hotel adjacent to the Tucson Convention Center, a long-contemplated project that had trouble getting off the ground until Caliber raised OZ money for it. On top of the OZ tax incentives, the hotel got a property tax abatement from the city and a sales tax break from the state.

"There haven't been a lot of tax programs where you can layer all these things on like we can with this, so it's been a great thing for us and we're looking at every possible tax benefit we can gain with these investments," Loeffler says.

Schultz chimes in: "Well, a lot of the incentives in the tax code don't allow you to double dip with municipal bonds. And this particular incentive has no prohibitions with using this with any other incentive, and so it obviously would be malpractice for a developer not to consider other incentives."

Don't blame the players. Blame the game.

Later on, HUD secretary Ben Carson, the pediatric neurosurgeon who was one of the several unsuccessful Republican challengers to Donald Trump in 2016, makes an appearance. He uses the occasion to unveil new HUD incentives for developers building multifamily housing in OZs, part of a concerted effort by the Trump administration to do whatever it could to concentrate federal spending in OZs. Carson alternates between reading his prepared remarks and ad-libbing, as is his custom, not always making sense: "Every street in every city, every stretch along every country road has the power to be a zone where opportunity is found," he says.[10]

Carson is followed by a panel—"Opportunity Zones: A Bipartisan Solution to Address the Uneven Recovery"—that includes Jim Sorenson, the billionaire Republican OZ fan from Utah; Steve Case, the founder of AOL and an early EIG backer; and Stephen Benjamin, a Democrat, the first African American mayor of Columbia, South Carolina, (then) president of the US Conference of Mayors, and an OZ evangelist. (Eight census tracts north of Columbia's downtown are Opportunity Zones. As of January 2021, Columbia had yet to land its first OZ dollar, though local officials said there were a few glimmers on the horizon.)

That panel is moderated by Steve Glickman, who had left EIG in 2018 to start an OZ advisory firm. Onstage he describes OZs as the first new attempt in twenty years to undo the harsh reality that "your destiny, your chance to achieve the American dream [is] defined by your zip code." The OZ concept, he says with exaggeration, "started" with "a group of bipartisan economists" led by Jared Bernstein and Kevin Hassett. He is echoing the bipartisan branding he and Lettieri had worked so hard to create for Opportunity Zones— no reason to let up now.[11]

Scaramucci's SALT conference is glitzier than other OZ conferences—it has bigger names on stage and a more select audience—but it is hardly unique. The gold rush is on.

THROUGH THE GRAPEVINE

In spring of 2018, after governors had finalized their choices for OZs, word about the OZ tax break began to spread. Real estate developers and real estate investment funds saw OZs as a way to raise money. Tax lawyers, financial planners, and accountants saw a way to make money by saving their clients money on taxes. Third-party administrators who manage paperwork and compliance for money managers saw a new market for their services. Virtually unnoticed when the Tax Cuts and Jobs Act was signed into law, OZs were beginning to show signs of frenzied anticipation.

An early mover in the nascent OZ industry was Novogradac, a national accounting firm with a Washington policy shop that already had substantial expertise in advising people who tap the New Markets Tax Credit and other targeted tax breaks. The firm publishes the *Novogradac Journal of Tax Credits*, a full-color, eighty-page monthly filled with updates on tax breaks for renewable energy, historic preservation, low-income housing, and community development. A typical article is headlined: "New Mexico State Solar Tax Credit Offers a Promising Addition to the Growing Industry."

Novogradac is one of those behind-the-scenes players that leverages expertise to influence legislation and arcane IRS regulatory decisions. Its founder, Mike Novogradac, says the firm's goal is to "try to bridge the gap between what policy makers want to do and what we think will actually happen." He is a regular donor to Republican Senate campaigns; he gave them $84,000 in the 2019–2020 cycle.[12]

Representative Pat Tiberi, one of the original congressional sponsors of OZs, says he connected Novogradac and EIG as the legislation was being drafted. Mike Novogradac advised making the provision more generous to investors than in the original outline.

With the early, inside word on Opportunity Zones, it made sense for Novogradac to form an OZ Working Group in late 2017, while the big tax bill was still moving through Congress. The group brings together investors, syndicators, lenders, for-profit and nonprofit developers, consultants, law firms, and others "to suggest consensus solutions to technical Opportunity Zones incentive issues" and to make recommendations to government rule-writers.[13] Its marketing brochure promises members get "direct access to the legislation sponsors, Treasury and the IRS."[14]

Since OZs became law, Novogradac has become a combination online bulletin board, cheerleader (with posts like: "What State and Local Governments Can Do to Support Federal Opportunity Zone Investments"), and quasi-official scorekeeper. Novogradac's list of OZ funds and its running tally of the sums they say they've raised, though incomplete, is one of very few public sources of quantitative information on OZs.

Because Novogradac had been working with the EIG boys, the firm was primed when the Tax Cuts and Jobs Act passed. At the end of January 2018, before many of its competitors had heard of

Opportunity Zones, Novogradac featured an hour-long panel on OZs at its New Markets Tax Credit Conference in San Diego with three lawyers, a venture capitalist, and a Novogradac accountant.

One attendee, Olivia Byrne, a real estate lawyer at K&L Gates in Washington, DC, says the conference is where she first heard about OZs—and recognized their potential. She and one of the firm's lobbyists wrote a very short blog post in March 2018 with the headline: "Opportunity Zones—A Golden Opportunity?"[15]

"I've never had so many calls on an article," she says. "Two or three a day! Everyone pulled it up."

At Bisnow, a commercial real estate news and events company, chief executive Will Friend says he didn't hear about OZs until the firm's annual Miami gathering of real estate industry CEOs in April 2018. "People were just starting to talk about it and one CEO suggested it was the biggest thing coming down the pike since the EB-5 program," Friend says. (EB-5 is the visa offered to foreigners who make investments in the United States.)

"I was on the phone with our team within minutes and asked that they become as much of an expert as they could on the subject in the next two days," Friend recalls. "I wanted to know everything there was to know about the program and how we could bring people together around the subject."

Bisnow organized its first OZ conference in Los Angeles in the summer of 2018 and did three others that year. The firm began 2019 with conferences on OZs in Baltimore and Chicago in January. By the year-end, they had sponsored fourteen more—from Boston to Sacramento. Bisnow reporters counted forty-five OZ conferences sponsored by other firms on the calendar in 2019.

Bisnow, OZ Expo, and other conferences had a simple business model: recruit tax lawyers, accountants, real estate developers, fund managers, OZ enthusiasts, and a politician or Trump administration official to talk from the podium. Sell sponsorships to outfits that provide administrative services to OZ funds, such as real estate information services, accounting firms, and the like. Offer continuing education credits for lawyers and accountants who need them. And sell tickets at around $500 a pop to folks looking to invest in OZs or folks trying to raise money from OZ investors.

THE TRUMP EMBRACE

The conferences gave Trump administration officials a platform for building OZ enthusiasm. Opportunity Zones were not born in the Trump White House. But after Tim Scott maneuvered them into the Tax Cuts and Jobs Act, the White House embraced them as its own.

Steve Mnuchin, for example, was late to the OZ party, but once he arrived, the Treasury secretary's public enthusiasm was nearly unbounded. In a September 2018 interview with *The Hill*, he said, "I think there's going to be over $100 billion in private capital that will be invested in opportunity zones."[16]

The estimate startled Treasury number crunchers. None of them had a calculation anywhere near $100 billion. Nevertheless, the Treasury PR shop put the number in press releases, and other administration officials attributed it to Mnuchin as authoritative.[17] Scaramucci told me his initial $3 billion target for his OZ fund reflected that estimate. "I said, okay, we could easily be 3 percent of that market, given the joint venture partners that I had and the distribution mechanisms." Trump converted Mnuchin's assertion from a prediction to an after-the-fact accounting. "Countless jobs and $100 billion of new investment, not government investment, have poured into 9,000 of our most distressed neighborhoods," he said.

Asked about this claim by a pesky reporter from FactCheck.org, Lettieri said, "I'm pretty sure nobody knows where that number [$100 billion] comes from."[18]

Mnuchin had a lot of other things on his plate, especially after COVID-19 tanked the economy, but Ben Carson, the HUD secretary, did not. By executive order, Trump created a White House Opportunity and Revitalization Council to "amplify the impact of this tax incentive," and named Carson to chair it.[19]

Carson became an evangelist for OZs, telling audiences that, as a neurosurgeon, his mission was to return an organ to its full, healthy function, and as HUD secretary he was doing the same with Opportunity Zones, which he described as "areas that, like an afflicted organ, are no longer achieving their full function due to decades of neglect."[20]

At an OZ Expo I attend at a Brooklyn hotel in the summer of 2019, Carson takes the stage in front of ten-foot-by-twenty-foot photo of himself and spells out the basics to a crowd that already knows them: "Unlike previous community investment programs in earlier decades, anyone can invest in Opportunity Zones, whether they are a large institutional entity or an ordinary individual. And in some cases, the capital gains tax for investors can be reduced all the way down to zero." Never mind that few "ordinary individuals" have the capital gains needed to invest in an OZ fund.

Then Carson looks up from his prepared text and adds, "Some people have complained this is just a mechanism for rich people to get richer. News flash: rich people are going to get richer anyhow—so why not give them an incentive to invest that money in a place that has been neglected."

The folks at the table at which I am sitting look at each other with raised eyebrows and bemusement. *The rich are going to get richer anyhow* was not one of those carefully crafted EIG talking points, even if it did match the worldview of many OZ proponents.

Carson gets a standing ovation, but he can't rouse a crowd like Scott Turner, who follows him to the stage. A speech communica-

tions major who ran track and played football at the University of
Illinois, Turner played in the NFL for a decade, worked as an aide to
a Republican congressman, made an unsuccessful run for Congress
from California, won a seat in the Texas legislature, launched a quix-
otic Tea Party–backed challenge to the incumbent speaker of the
Texas House (losing 127–19), worked as "chief inspiration officer"
at a Dallas-based software company, started a custom clothing line
with his wife, and performed as a motivational speaker or, as he puts
it, led a "speaking ministry." In April 2019, Trump named him to
be the full-time, $180,000-a-year executive director of the council
Carson chairs.

At the Brooklyn OZ Expo, Turner opens with a long story about
how he made it to the NFL even though, to his deep disappointment, he didn't get invited to the annual NFL Scouting Combine
where teams scout draft prospects.

"I know I'm going to the Combine," says Turner. "I'm the fastest
person on the field. So I start looking in the mailbox. For my invitation." He pantomimes peering into a mailbox. "All my boys that
were getting their invitations so I would go home and go to class and
come home and look in the mailbox. Boom! Nothing. Maybe it's a
typo, maybe they don't have my address right, something. I know
I'm getting invited. Every day. Nothing."

The accountants, tax lawyers, real estate developers, and small-
time, tax-phobic investors stop looking at their cell phones or
whispering to each other or paging through the program. They are
mesmerized as Scott goes on. His teammates go to the Combine in
Indianapolis, he says. He does not.

"I jumped in my 1987 Maxima with no windshield wipers,"
Turner continues. "And I drove over to Memorial Stadium. That's
the stadium there in Champaign, Illinois. Memorial Stadium was
three tiers, sat about 88,000 people.... It's February. It's cold in

Illinois and I went over to that stadium all by myself. No one there encouraging me, no one there saying, 'Hey, you can do it.' Matter of fact everybody says, 'You crazy. You're not going to the NFL Combine in Indianapolis.' I didn't want to hear all that chatter. I shut it out. And I stood at the bottom of that stadium and I looked up to the top. And I said, 'I'm going to get from here to there as fast as I can.' I took off…Whoomp! One step at a time, two by two, three by three. Over and over from the bottom to the top. Over and over again."

Then his agent called and said twenty-two NFL teams were coming to Champaign-Urbana to take a second look at some players, and said Turner could work out for them, too. Turner did, running the forty-yard dash in 4.3 seconds (the NFL record is 4.22 seconds), and ending up as a seventh-round pick of Washington's NFL team.

So what does this have to do with Opportunity Zones. Well, nothing and everything.

"How long are you willing to hold onto your dream?" Turner asks the crowd. "To your vision? I wasn't willing to throw in the towel. I was not willing to take no for answer."

Then he segues to OZs. "America is experiencing great prosperity but not every American is experiencing that prosperity." Opportunity Zones are the answer. "This is not another government program. This is a mission," he says, with emphasis on the last word.

"Y'all feelin' me?" he asks. The audience—mostly middle-aged, mostly white, mostly male—nods and grunts in agreement as if they are parishioners in Turner's church. "Is everyone with me? Raise your hands if OZs make you uncomfortable?"

Few do.

"It's a different paradigm. This is an opportunity to have a generational impact. People are literally leaving their careers and investing their lives in OZs.…This could revolutionize our country.…What will you do? Why are you here?"

Scott gets a very long standing ovation. The crowd is genuinely enthusiastic. When he leaves the podium, he is surrounded by people who want to ask a question or take a selfie with him. And then the conference turns quickly to a panel on technicalities of the latest IRS guidance on OZs.

President Trump himself became one of the loudest promoters of Opportunity Zones. His personal celebration of them hit a zenith in his 2020 State of the Union address to Congress. "This is the first time that these deserving communities have seen anything like this. It's working," he told assembled lawmakers and other guests.[21]

Then he pointed to one of his props in the gallery: Tony Rankins from Cincinnati, who was seated next to Ivanka, the president's daughter. "After struggling with drug addiction, Tony lost his job, his house, and his family. He was homeless. But then Tony found a construction company that invests in Opportunity Zones. He is now a top tradesman, drug-free, reunited with his family."

Rankins "made an incredible comeback thanks to Opportunity Zone investments!" the White House tweeted. The official GOP Twitter account added that "an opportunity zone in Cincinnati has given him a second chance."

A few days after the State of the Union, Trump called Rankins to a stage in Charlotte, North Carolina, at an Opportunity Now Summit. Rankins told the crowd that without the OZ bill "I wouldn't be standing here before you right now."

The story had little resemblance to the truth. Travis Steffens of R Investments—who had connected the White House to Rankins through an acquaintance at the Small Business Administration—had hired Rankins off the streets, as he had other homeless people, but he'd done that before OZs existed.[22] Steffens had been doing real estate projects in low-income neighborhoods for years, neighborhoods that were now in OZs. He had raised OZ money for an ambitious project to turn a Cincinnati warehouse into R Academy, where homeless people would learn construction skills while building tiny homes for other homeless folks. And he did have some other OZ projects in the works. But Rankins wasn't actually working in an OZ-financed construction project at the time; his was across the street from an OZ border.

Rankins did get an unanticipated benefit from the publicity: several dentists offered to fix his teeth. He later showed up in a video ad for Trump's reelection campaign.[23]

Ivanka Trump is another OZ cheerleader. In November 2018, the Jack Kemp Foundation decided to bestow its annual award on Sean Parker for, as Jimmy Kemp put it, his "visionary role in fulfilling the promise of my dad's Enterprise Zones."[24] When Kemp asked the Trump administration to send a representative to the event, Ivanka volunteered. She didn't say much—talking points about "creating the incentive for private-sector capital" to be invested in places that had been overlooked for generations—but she did help ticket sales.

A photo of the one-time bad boy of the internet with the daughter of and adviser to the president of the United States and Senator Tim Scott memorialized the event—and crystalized the long, strange journey of Opportunity Zones from the kernel of an idea that had popped into Sean Parker's head to legislation celebrated by President Trump as the centerpiece—pretty much the only piece—of his strategy to help poor communities and, particularly, Black Americans.

For Trump, Opportunity Zones became his go-to argument whenever he wanted to claim he was doing great things for African Americans. "My Admin has done more for the Black Community than any President since Abraham Lincoln. Passed Opportunity Zones with @SenatorTimScott," he tweeted in June 2020.[25] At a Labor Day 2020 press conference, he said OZs "really turned out to be a tremendous thing, especially for African Americans."[26] And the Trump administration aggressively deployed some of its very few

Black appointees to publicly promote Opportunity Zones, including Ben Carson, Scott Turner, and Ja'Ron Smith.

THE FAMILY BUSINESS

For the EIG boys, the association with the Trump administration was a mixed blessing. It gave OZs lots of publicity. At the White House's insistence, agencies across the government scrambled to tailor existing programs to target OZ communities. Trump even issued an executive order that OZs (and "other distressed areas") be given preference as locations for federal offices.[27] And Trump's Treasury issued regulations that generally made OZs more appealing to investors. But the president's embrace branded OZs with Trump's name, largely destroying the bipartisan sheen the EIG boys so treasured. They didn't initially anticipate how much the polarization and partisanship in Washington and antipathy to Donald Trump among Democrats, and, importantly, among the press would threaten Opportunity Zones. To headline writers, OZs became simply a "Trump tax break." Trump-suspicious reporters went looking for (and often found) Trump real estate cronies who were cashing in.

This is because OZs were initially—and to a large extent still are—exploited as a real estate tax break. Trump, many of his friends, and his son-in-law, Jared Kushner, are in the real estate business. It was easy for the press to find examples of how they were benefitting from the tax break the White House was so aggressively promoting.

In late 2018, for instance, Bloomberg reported that the company owned by Jared Kushner's family (in which he has a big stake but claims he didn't have any role in managing while working in the White House) spent more than $13 million to buy a twenty-four-room hotel and two single-family houses along the waterfront in Pier Village, a summer tourist spot in Long Branch, New Jersey, near a luxury apartment building and hotel the firm began building before the tract was designated an OZ.[28]

About the same time, a digital real estate investment platform called Cadre—founded in 2014 by Kushner, his younger brother, and a friend—started an OZ fund, drawing attention from investigative reporters at the Associated Press. The headline: "Ivanka, Kushner could profit from tax break they pushed."[29] Ivanka, the AP said, had talked frequently with Tim Scott during the Tax Cuts and Jobs Act deliberations—though most of those calls, Scott says, were about the child tax credit. The AP cited a transcript of an Oval Office event on Opportunity Zones in which the president said Ivanka had been "pushing this very hard." Perhaps, but her role in getting OZs into the tax bill was insignificant.

In any event, Kushner reported in a February 2020 ethics filing that he was selling his stake in Cadre, then valued at between $25 million and $50 million, in part because the firm was seeking foreign investors.[30] In May, after the onset of the COVID-19 pandemic, the company laid off 25 percent of its workforce.[31] In July, Kushner put off the sale and the company agreed not to seek foreign investors as long as he was an owner.[32]

The stories by Bloomberg, ProPublica, and the *New York Times*—about the zones governors chose, about luxury hotels and condos going up with OZ money, about people in the president's orbit dabbling in OZs—created a narrative about OZs that stuck: Opportunity Zones were another tax break for the very rich cloaked in rhetoric about helping poor neighborhoods. There is a lot to that narrative, though it is incomplete. There *are* OZ projects that live up to the stated objectives of the EIG boys and their congressional allies, but it's hard to make the case that they represent the bulk of the projects financed by OZ investors.

As OZs drew attention from national media, they even figured in an episode of *Billions*, the Showtime TV series that the *New York*

Times's Andrew Ross Sorkin helped create.[33] In the show, hedge fund titan Bobby Axelrod (Damian Lewis) competes with a rival for rights to develop an OZ in Axelrod's hometown of Yonkers, New York. About all the show got right is that there are Opportunity Zones in Yonkers—three of them. Lions Gate Entertainment Corporation, the studio behind *Orange Is the New Black*, and Great Point Capital are using $10 million in OZ equity to build a $100 million production studio there.[34]

OZ fund managers confide privately that some family offices (who invest money for wealthy families) backed off of OZs, saying their clients didn't want to find themselves, or a deal in which they invested, on the front page of the *New York Times*.

After the bad publicity, some Democrats who had been OZ enthusiasts from the start backed away. Representative Ro Khanna, who had been in on conception, tweeted after one *Times* story: "The problem with opportunity zones is Trump's failure to target communities that are truly left behind. No affluent community should be part of an opportunity zone."[35]

Never mind that the bill he backed failed to instruct the Treasury to overrule governors' choices.

While he agreed to cosponsor the original bill—which put few restrictions on the tax break and demanded little of the Treasury in that regard—Khanna told me subsequently the backers "assured me they were in talks with the administration to have regulations to make sure it would be targeted. That was botched."

Representative Ron Kind, the lead Democratic sponsor in the House, was unhappy with the choices made by the Republican governor in his state of Wisconsin. The college town of Madison got ten zones. Kind says his district had 40 percent of the eligible communities but only 15 percent of the chosen zones. "We were working under the assumption that the states would know best, and I think we may have been fooled," he says.

OZs did draw support from some unlikely places. Charlamagne tha God, a radio show host and actor, came to DC in spring 2019 to talk up OZs with the Congressional Black Caucus. He shared photos of himself and Tim Scott with his 3.6 million Instagram followers and lauded Scott for "leading the charge" on OZs.[36]

ABOUT THAT $3 BILLION

As for Scaramucci, in April 2019 he said investors were holding back until the Treasury issued OZ regulations; his fund, he said, had raised "just over $10 million." By autumn 2019 he had pared his $3 billion goal to $300 million. "A lot of people misplaced and outsized the demand for what we thought we could achieve," he told a commercial real estate conference in October, less than a year after launching his fund with bravado. "I still think it's a success for us, but it's nowhere near as successful as we thought it would be."[37]

As of year-end 2020, Scaramucci's fund had drawn just $40.6 million, a bit more than 1 percent of his original target. The hotel project in Oakland went ahead with OZ investors, but without Sky-Bridge. In fact, the fund's only project is the Virgin New Orleans hotel, though Scaramucci told me in mid-August 2020 that he was eyeing a second project—a commercial storage facility near a port in the southwestern United States. The fund had $5 million in cash as of December 31 and told shareholders that it "could potentially commit to one or more additional development deals...but this will be dependent upon a variety of factors," including the willingness of investors to put money into the fund.[38]

Scaramucci has no time for those who challenge the OZ concept. "If a person doesn't like the rich," he says, "well, too bad. They're always going to be among us. And they are going to want incentives to move and dislodge their capital."

I ask him why OZs didn't take off as he had anticipated.

The tax break, as juicy as it seems, isn't generous enough to get investors to take the risk of investing in these distressed communities, he says. His solution? Even bigger tax breaks for investments, perhaps a sliding scale that offers deeper tax cuts for investment in the worst-off zones.

CHAPTER NINE

So What Happened on
the Ground?

I NOW UNDERSTOOD HOW AN IDEA PUSHED BY A SILICON VALLEY billionaire ended up as a stowaway (as Glickman puts it) on Donald Trump's big tax-cut bill. I was hearing OZs hailed as the most important anti-poverty tool since the War on Poverty itself, and I was hearing them attacked as a giant giveaway to the rich, especially to Trump's real estate buddies. I wondered what OZ investments were doing on the ground. Were they improving the lives of people in left-behind communities? Or primarily showering tax breaks on wealthy people for making not particularly risky investments, with limited benefits to poor neighborhoods and the people who live in them?

I knew the truth lay somewhere beyond the partisan, Trumpphobic headlines and overblown boosterism. With 8,764 OZs, one can find half a dozen examples that prove almost any point. I also knew that, unfortunately, few answers would be found in any kind of official accounting. Neither Congress nor the Treasury, at least initially, required any public reporting, so it's nearly impossible to get even basic data. There is, so far, no authoritative way to tell how many of the OZs actually got any OZ money.

It's even challenging to come up with a solid total of how much has been invested in OZ funds to date. Novogradac, the accounting firm, posts a tally of funds that volunteer data: it counted 1,002 funds, of which 708 had raised money—a total of $16.3 billion as of April 13, 2021.[1]

A form called Schedule D, filed at the Securities and Exchange Commission (SEC), gives a glimpse of how much a firm intends to raise in private placements, which are exempt from most SEC disclosure rules. Although filers don't have to reveal if they are OZ funds, the names sometimes give clues. A name like "Alpha Opportunity Zone Fund I" is a giveaway, "Dukes Business Consulting" less so, although both are listed on a directory of OZ funds.[2] And Schedule D filings don't always reveal how much money a fund has actually raised.

Moreover, there are lots of missing data. Wealthy family offices that create their own funds generally don't talk about what they're doing. Neither do big corporations using OZs to shelter their own capital gains—telecom companies putting cell phone towers on top of buildings in Opportunity Zones, for instance. Enterprising Bloomberg reporters searched Delaware's corporate records and found 1,800 entities with telltale words or initials—such as QOZB—in their names. Among the corporations was AT&T, which changed the names of two entities after the reporters called.[3]

Until the IRS releases official data, even government estimates are informed guesswork. Extrapolating from Novogradac and SEC filings, Trump's Council of Economic Advisers estimated that about $75 billion in private capital had flowed into OZ funds by the end of 2019, representing the first two years of OZs, though it acknowledged it could be off by tens of billions of dollars.[4] (By comparison, about $275 billion went into venture capital investments in the

United States during 2018 and 2019.)[5] Some in the industry think that $75 billion estimate may be on the high side: only a handful of funds have raised hundreds of millions of dollars, so there would have to be a lot of smaller funds to get the total up to $75 billion by year-end 2019.

How much of that estimated $75 billion will go to projects that would have happened without OZ tax breaks? Relying on previous economic research showing how investors responded to changes on tax rates in the past, not on any OZ-specific data, the White House economists figured that nearly two-thirds of its estimated $75 billion will go to projects that would have happened anyway (roughly half for projects that would have happened in the OZs without the tax break and half for projects that would have happened elsewhere). Thus, a little more than a third (36 percent) would be entirely new investment that wouldn't have occurred without OZs, the stated purpose of the program. A June 2020 Urban Institute "early assessment" of OZs, based on seventy in-depth interviews, found that "most project sponsors report that OZs were not critical for filling a financing gap or increasing the social impact goals of their venture."[6]

Other than calling attention to a community, the OZ designation has zero direct effect if no money flows to that place. It would hardly be surprising if most of the big bucks went to tracts that were attracting private money before the tax break arrived. After all, OZs offer investors the same-sized tax break for investing in the most appealing Opportunity Zones or in the most distressed. There is no extra bonus for taking the risk of investing in the poorest, neediest, and most desperate tracts.

In the first analysis of its kind, JCT economist Patrick Kennedy and Berkeley grad student Harrison Wheeler got access to about three-quarters of the 2019 tax returns filed by OZ funds. In an April 2021 paper, they reported that 7,402 of the 8,764 OZs—84 percent—got no OZ investment at all. Nearly all the $18.9 billion in OZ investments reported on those returns went to just 450 zones, and they are much better off economically than zones that didn't get any money. Half the money went to just 1 percent of the zones. New York, Los Angeles, Salt Lake City, and Phoenix drew the most OZ money. Kennedy and Wheeler also found that the average household income of investors in OZ funds was a whopping $1,083,766, around fifteen times the income of the typical American household.[7]

For all the attention that "impact investors" seek and get, most investors are more interested in their financial bottom line than the social bottom line. So the question is whether the OZ incentive is lucrative enough and focused enough to induce the typical profit-seeking, tax-reducing investor to put big bucks into a poor neighborhood for a project that wouldn't have got financing otherwise.

I do see two clear trends. First, most OZ money through early 2021 was going to real estate—with multifamily housing particularly attractive after COVID-19 cast a shadow on hotels, retail, and office projects. Relatively little money was going to operating businesses, in part because the regulations on OZ businesses came later, in part because so many people have so much practice reducing their taxes by investing in real estate, and in part because the design of the tax break wasn't as well suited to businesses as it was to real estate (which is permanently located at a specific place.) At an October 2019 House committee hearing, Jennifer Vasiloff from Opportunity Finance Network, a trade association of community development financial institutions, said OZs weren't drawing money to existing small businesses because "most investors are expecting double digit returns, prefer real estate to small business investments and largely shun the more challenging geographies that need an infusion of capital the most."[7] And the EIG boys' talk of getting lots of big institutional money managers to create and successfully mass-market OZ funds to lots of investors didn't materialize.

Second, OZ fundraising did not live up to the hype of the early conferences and press releases. Anecdotes can be misleading. Both friends and foes of OZs describe every real estate project in a zone as an OZ investment whether or not the investors are actually using the tax break. Folks in the industry say money did begin to trickle into OZs in 2018, particularly into real estate deals already in the works. Some investors waited for the Treasury to finish writing the rules in December 2019 before locking up their money for ten years, though the extra capital gains kick the law offered for investments made before year-end 2019 prompted some investors to pounce. Then, not surprisingly, the onset of the COVID-19 pandemic in March 2020 led to an abrupt slowdown, amplified by the IRS decision to delay deadlines for putting capital gains into OZ funds because of the pandemic. Money began flowing again during the fall of 2020, helped by a rising stock market that left many wealthy investors with substantial capital gains. But on the very last day of the Trump presidency, the Treasury again delayed a deadline for putting capital gains into an OZ fund, giving investors three more months, until March 31, 2021, to equivocate. It's possible that finalized rules, a stable post-COVID-19 economy, calls to harness the OZ incentive to speed the recovery from the pandemic, and perhaps Biden's call for higher capital gains tax rates, which would make the incentive even more attractive, could lead to more investment in the future, but it's unlikely OZs will ever match the exuberant projections of 2018.

Years from now, we may know how much money went into what kind of investments in how many Opportunity Zones. Today, the only way to tell is to scour the internet and ask around. I cast a wide net. I talked to scores of people across the country, from Portland, Oregon, to Baltimore, Maryland, to find out where the money went and where it didn't. My reporting found a kaleidoscope of results—some expected, some surprising, and some bizarre.

CHAPTER TEN

Portland: Tax Breaklandia

I STARTED MY QUEST IN PORTLAND, OREGON, FOR SEVERAL REA-
sons. In some other states, reporters found suggestions of political
favoritism or corruption in the zone picking. There is no sign of that
in Oregon. Economically, Oregon isn't as poor as states in the Deep
South nor as rich as states in the Northeast. It has an urban corridor
along I-5 with large rural areas to the east. It has poor parts and
rich ones. On average, the census tracts Oregon chose as OZs were
neither the most nor the least economically distressed among those
eligible; they were about average.[1] So, while Oregon is politically left
of center and whiter than most states, it seemed a good laboratory to
test what Opportunity Zones are doing.

Shortly after the Tax Cuts and Jobs Act passed in December 2017,
Chris Harder, director of Business Oregon, the state's not-so-subtly
named economic development agency, began seeing references to
OZs on Twitter and elsewhere. He asked his government affairs dep-
uty, Nick Batz, to look into them. "It creates domestic tax havens,"
Batz replied in an email that captured the essence, if not the details.
"If I'm an investor, I park my capital gains in the safest company

I can find in one of these zones and wait ten years to withdraw... tax free."[2]

After New Year's, the email traffic around OZs grew heavier. The office of Governor Kate Brown, a Democrat, inquired: What is this program? Is this something we should be caring about? The White House was sending emails to governors' offices promoting OZs, but Harder and others wondered: Is this just a talking point for the administration or is this a program?

Over the next few months, however, Harder, Batz, and the governor's office determined that OZs were a real program—and one that demanded extraordinarily quick decisions. The US Treasury told Oregon that 366 of the state's 834 census tracts were eligible to be OZs. Brown had until March 21 to tell the Treasury which 86 tracts the state wanted to designate.

The state would have to make these determinations without really understanding what the brand-new program was. On February 2, Nick Batz sent the governor's chief economic adviser, Jason Lewis-Berry, a five-page memo outlining the basics. "Nothing really like this has been tried before," he wrote in an email. "It remains to be seen how quickly and effectively capital can be mobilized....At present, there are uncertainties about specific mechanics that may not be resolved for at least several months."[3]

Illustrating just how baffling OZs were to governors' offices, Batz (correctly) said the law offered tax breaks for investments in businesses as well as in "tangible property," but (incorrectly) predicted the tax incentives "may not be amenable to common models of strictly real estate re/development."

Early afternoon the next day, a Saturday, the governor's chief of staff, Nik Blosser, emailed Lewis-Berry: "The biggest question I have is how much investment this is likely to incite—I'm assuming Business Oregon is doing this analysis."[4] (They weren't. Even a year later, the agency's spokesman, Nathan Buehler, told the *Oregonian*: "The answer is we don't know.")[5]

There was one more wrinkle. In the name of simplicity, the definition of taxable income in Oregon, as in many other states, mirrors federal rules. So, a cut in federal capital gains taxes would also be a cut in the state's 9.9 percent capital gains tax (the same rate as its tax on ordinary income), reducing Oregon's revenues. So the state would have to pick its eighty-six opportunity zones without answers to two big questions: How much would OZs' capital gains tax break reduce state revenue, and what would their eventual economic payoff be?

Business Oregon, working with the governor's office, took charge of the process using information they did have. They did number crunching—poverty rates, unemployment rates, housing prices. They made spreadsheets. They wrestled with the perennial tension between Oregon's rural communities and its urban centers. They checked with the leaders of the state's nine Native American tribes. They reached out to the organizations of Oregon's city and county officials. They enlisted their own regional offices. On February 26, Business Oregon announced a website "to solicit input from the general public." It set a deadline of 5:00 p.m., March 14, for responses. Government often moves slowly, but the OZ law forced states to move with unusual speed, which left little time for deliberation.

Harder saw the selection process in terms of a national competition for capital. If the state picked the worst-off tracts, Oregon risked not drawing any money at all—particularly if neighboring states took the other option. But if it picked tracts already ripe for investment, it risked offering tax breaks for projects that would have happened anyway—plus the likelihood of bad headlines. (The negative headlines did, in fact, materialize.)

Communities across the state lobbied to get their tracts designated, although one neighborhood with three eligible census tracts asked the governor *not* to pick theirs: Cully, a residential section of Northeast Portland that long had organized to resist gentrification. Leaders of four community groups and a parish priest sent the governor a letter: Our neighborhood is "already threatened by outside investment that works against the interests of lower-income residents and people of color," they wrote. They feared that locating an Opportunity Zone there would make gentrification even more profitable. Keep us off the list, they pleaded. They got their wish.

Ultimately, the state decided on two sets of zones: One scored high on prospects for growth and demonstrated ability to attract out-of-state business investment. The other comprised poorer communities long starved for investment. The decision to designate some choice tracts led to a controversial call. Nearly all of Portland's central business district was designated as Opportunity Zone territory.

BEST DRAW IN THE COUNTRY

Despite highly publicized and sometimes violent 2020 street protests and the COVID-19 recession, Portland still has the feel of a boomtown. Nike, growing ad agency Wieden+Kennedy, Adidas, Intel, Columbia Sportswear, spillover from Seattle-based Amazon and Silicon Valley–based Google, and proliferating design and software firms all prosper alongside a still-lively manufacturing sector tied to the agriculture, food processing, timber, and transportation industries long the economic bedrock of the Pacific Northwest.

The city's population—655,000 at last count—has grown by about 25 percent since 2000, much faster than the country's as a whole. Prosperity and coolness make the city a people magnet: 60 percent of today's Portlanders were born outside of Oregon.[6] *U.S. News & World Report* ranks the city among the top ten US metro areas in which to live, a notch above San Francisco.[7] Portland is better educated than many other big US cities: half the city's adults have a bachelor's degree or better. Given the number of designer coffee shops and craft breweries, Portlanders apparently drink lots of coffee and lots of beer. The Census Bureau says Portland has more bicycle commuters per capita than any other US city.[8]

Land use in Portland reflects its geography—the city is bisected by the Willamette River—and its affection for urban planning. The downtown, with its shiny office towers and several OZ designations, is on the west side of the river. To the north of the central business district is the Pearl District: once rail yards, warehouses, and factories, now dotted with boutiques, restaurants, condos, and the nationally famous Powell's bookstore. All this is Opportunity Zone territory. Further west are the rich folks in their big houses.

Bordering the east side of the river is a half-mile-wide strip of small factories and construction crew garages, preserved by city planners hoping to keep jobs there. Some of those jobs are gone, some remain. The Eastside, as it's known, is still gritty in parts, still home to small machine shops and produce wholesalers, still crisscrossed by railroad tracks and overpasses. But it is pulsing with renovation and home to a growing number of twenty-first-century jobs in software, PR, marijuana, and distilleries. (As we stand outside an Eastside coffee shop, a passing freight train loudly sounds its whistle. "That's our anti-gentrification plan," jokes Ethan Seltzer, a retired urban planning professor at Portland State. "It works.") Much of the Eastside is Opportunity Zone territory, too.

Further east are residential neighborhoods, some filled with two-story Craftsmans, others with small bungalows. If you keep going east, roughly 160 blocks from the river, you get to neighborhoods like Rockwood, where many poor, and often African American or Hispanic, folks have moved after being pushed out of closer-in neighborhoods on the city's north side.

One of Portland's distinguishing features is important for understanding the local Opportunity Zone dynamics. The city preserved a significant amount of low-income housing downtown and in the Pearl District as those areas were redeveloped into mid-century modern furniture shops and Peruvian tapas restaurants. That means several downtown census tracts look poor enough to qualify as OZs even though they are hardly starved for investment, particularly since the Treasury used census data averaged over 2011–2015; a lot had changed in downtown Portland since the beginning of that period. (The city was hit hard by the early 2000s tech bust and the 2007–2009 Great Recession but began bouncing back around 2014.)

"Every single census tract in that Opportunity Zone in downtown Portland is prime property," says Jonathan McGuire, a local accountant who has been advising clients on OZ deals. "West of the Rocky Mountains, there is no other metro area where the entire center of town is an Opportunity Zone, and especially on the West Coast, no other downtown can sport the zone quality in both location and price of entry."

McGuire's sentiment is widely shared. An online real estate platform put Portland's OZs among the top ten OZs in the nation in terms of "most promising near-term growth potential."[9] In marketing material for his OZ fund, one local developer boasts "Portland may well have gotten the best draw in the country for urban opportunity zones."[10] Only seven of Oregon's eighty-six OZs are in Portland, the state's most urban and wealthiest region, but they appear to have lured the most out-of-state money—and rank among the OZs most attractive to investors nationally. So much for Steve Glickman's talk of Opportunity Zones as "a Marshall Plan for the heartland."

In a play on the city's nickname, Portlandia, *Bloomberg Businessweek* boiled it down to a two-word headline: "Tax Breaklandia."[11]

Portland offered a good case study: Did OZs spur new investment or give tax breaks to projects that would have happened anyhow? And who got the bulk of the benefits?

THE LOOPHOLE AT 250 SW TAYLOR STREET

The stated purpose of OZs in Portland and elsewhere is to spur investment in neighborhoods that need it, or at the very least to encourage new investment in zones just beginning to turn up. But, as with any legislation, there are loopholes that get exploited.

Here's a doozy: a new building, conceived, financed, and started before the Tax Cuts and Job Act was passed, can qualify as "new"— and thus eligible for the OZ capital gains tax break—provided an OZ fund buys the building just before it gets an official certificate of occupancy. Folks in Portland didn't invent this maneuver: I heard a Hollywood hotel developer describe it at that Las Vegas expo, although he was just speaking hypothetically. The developers of 250 SW Taylor in downtown Portland took full advantage of it.

Between 1892 and 2017, 250 SW Taylor was the site of a brick and stone six-story Romanesque building that was initially the Ancient Order of United Workmen Temple—home to a fraternal organization that offered services including insurance to its members. Over the course of a century, a variety of tenants shared the building while many neighboring buildings were torn down and replaced with modern towers.

By 2016, 250 SW Taylor was valued by preservationists (it had been designed by a noted local architect) but hadn't any tenants. A couple of local developers and a San Francisco real estate firm sought and received city approval for a new building—nine stories of offices on top of ground floor retail—in October of that year, fourteen months before the Tax Cuts and Jobs Act became law. Demolition began in August 2017.[12]

In October 2017, before passage of the OZ law, NW Natural, the local gas utility, chose the new building over thirty-three other contenders and signed a lease to make the building its new headquarters.[13] The structure features the large glass panels popular in office towers these days but is distinguished by vertical reddish-orange stripes of terracotta cladding. In a nod to the tenant's business, the lobby has a huge gas fireplace.

The building sits a few blocks from the parks and bike trails along the Willamette River. Across the street is a three-building complex of office and convention space known as World Trade Center Portland; a Starbucks occupies the first floor. There's a Marriott AC Hotel nearby. This is not the sort of neighborhood Tim Scott talks about when he preaches the virtues of Opportunity Zones. And yet, 250 SW Taylor—a building that was already green-lighted, under construction, and leased to a major tenant by October 2017—would qualify for the OZ tax break. Legally.

On September 25, 2019, an outfit called AB PR QOZB I Property LLC was registered by Prospect Ridge, a New York City real estate investment firm.[14] QOZB is short for Qualified Opportunity Zone Business. A week later, on October 1, the new outfit bought the nearly completed building at 250 SW Taylor for $141.25 million, taking a $97.9 million, ten-year mortgage.[15] Prospect Ridge won't talk about where the other $43 million came from, but it's no secret in the Portland real estate community that much of it came from OZ investors looking for a very low-risk tax break: a nearly completed, brand-new building for which a major corporation had already signed a twenty-year lease.[16] The city issued a certificate of occupancy on February 4, 2020. In March, NW Natural moved in.

Even among fans of OZs in the real estate business, that maneuver is troubling. "I think Opportunity Zones are largely a good program," says prominent Portland landowner-developer Greg Goodman. "But if someone said, 'Pick something that's wrong with Opportunity Zones,' I'd say, 'You shouldn't be able to roll your gains into a building that's already done except a certificate of occupancy.' That's the type of thing that makes a policy I like look like somebody got away with something. The point of the program is to spur development that hadn't already occurred." The Treasury and IRS received complaints about the certificate-of-occupancy loophole. But at the end of 2019, the agencies rejected suggestions that they tighten the rules, arguing that to do so would "introduce additional complexity and uncertainty" because local governments' procedures for issuing certificates of occupancy vary so much it would be hard to devise "a uniform standard."[17]

Of course, 250 SW Taylor was just one example, an egregious one. I kept looking.

THE PLAYERS

Real estate tends to build family empires, in large part because passing property to one's heirs avoids capital gains taxes (thanks to what's known as a "step-up in basis" at death). Portland's real estate aristocracy all know each other; several have been in the businesses for two or even three generations. It was this group that was best placed to take advantage of the surfeit of OZs in town.

Yet word about Opportunity Zones seeped out slowly among them. In May 2018, Owen Blank, a partner at one of Portland's largest law firms, Tonkon Torp, got an email from EIG that summarized OZs. Blank, who has an unruly head of gray hair and plays catcher on the local attorneys' softball team, emailed the link to several clients.

Among them was Greg Goodman. Goodman's grandfather started a parking business in Portland in 1955. His dad expanded it. In 2012, the family—now Greg, his brother, and Greg's two sons—sold the parking business but kept the land. By 2018, they had built a real estate business with stakes in more than 1.5 million square feet of retail, office, and warehouse space. Among their holdings were twenty-four parcels in Portland's downtown Opportunity Zones. (As real estate giant Trammell Crow's Portland honcho, Steve Wells, once said at a breakfast for the local real estate crowd: It's good to be a Goodman.)[18]

Another longtime figure in Portland real estate is Vanessa Sturgeon. Her grandfather dropped out of school in ninth grade, became a professional boxer, built and sold a chain of movie theatres, and, at age seventy-three, started a real estate business, which she inherited. Sturgeon now runs the firm from the twenty-second floor of its downtown office tower, which offers a spectacular view of the city and the hills beyond.

Sturgeon discovered OZs in a July 2018 article in *Forbes*, one that featured a photo of Sean Parker and Tim Scott standing in front of an abandoned building in South Carolina that once housed Scott's elementary school.[19] "I thought, 'Well, this is really interesting.' And then Oregon's Opportunity Zones rolled out, and there were two projects that we had been considering doing and both of them were very tight in terms of the numbers, right on the edge."

A few months later, a developer from another Portland real estate family, Paul Brenneke—who worked for his father's property management company for a few years out of college and then went out on his own—began hearing about OZs from his investors. Brenneke already was using the web to draw investors to a conventional income-producing fund that lends money to real estate projects. Doing the same for investors looking for OZ tax breaks wasn't much of a leap.

"It was about the time the maps came out, and we decided, in the areas we were active, it might be a pretty compelling way to raise capital," he tells me over breakfast at—only in Portland—an Icelandic restaurant near his new offices in an Opportunity Zone on the city's rapidly changing Eastside.

Others were contemplating Opportunity Zones, as well. On the eastern outskirts of Portland, Brad Ketch runs a local community development outfit in Rockwood, home to many of the area's recent immigrants. Ketch, who had been looking for ways to expand Rockwood's woefully inadequate supply of affordable housing, read about OZs—he can't recall where—and it all clicked. He started his own OZ fund, Oregon Community Capital, one of the first in the state, in July 2018.[20]

A three-hour drive further east, in Bend, Doug Layman, an industrial engineer who started and sold two companies, moved to France to do rock climbing for a time, and is now a venture capital/angel investor, heard about OZs from another local venture investor. He realized that a company in which he was about to invest—Lora DiCarlo, which makes high-tech vibrators for women—was in an OZ and qualified as an Opportunity Zone business. He alerted the founder, Lora Haddock DiCarlo.

Meanwhile, Sayer Jones, director of mission investing at the Meyer Memorial Trust—a $775 million Portland foundation created by the founder of the Fred Meyer grocery chain to "contribute to a flourishing and equitable Oregon"—heard about OZs at an Aspen Institute conference in January 2018, just a few weeks after the Tax Cuts and Jobs Act passed. "All anyone could talk about was Opportunity Zones. Sessions for Opportunity Zones were standing room only," he recalls.

A CPA, Jones knew something about New Market Tax Credits and how complicated they could be. And he worried that OZ designation could accelerate gentrification in Portland, already a concern of his. "I came out of the meeting more anxious than hopeful about what it could mean for our community." When Jones got back to his office, he called Nick Batz at Business Oregon to get a sense of how the state was thinking about OZs.

Over the next few years, these players would try to make the law work best for their purposes, which ranged from strictly commercial to socially beneficial. Their experiences would be starkly different, which says a lot about what OZs have accomplished in Oregon so far.

THE LANDOWNER: GREG GOODMAN

Greg Goodman's highest profile venture began about ten blocks northwest of 250 SW Taylor. The Ritz-Carlton, Portland, or the Block 216 project as it's known locally, is rising on what was once a Goodman parking lot. More recently, the land was the site of one of the largest collections of food carts in the city—about sixty, offering everything from gourmet bratwurst to Northern Chinese crepes.[21]

Early in 2017, Goodman began talking about the site with Walt Bowen, a local developer who made his fortune acquiring and developing assisted living facilities. Bowen, who had previously bought a couple of Goodman's parcels, signed a seventy-five-year ground lease for the land in May 2018, and in July 2019 he broke ground for a thirty-five-story building. The biggest building to go up in Portland since 1983, it will have eleven floors of a Ritz-Carlton, Portland's poshest hotel. Above the hotel will be fifteen floors of Ritz-Carlton-branded condos, starting at $1.6 million for a one-bedroom and going above $7 million for the eight penthouse units, marketed as pieds-à-terre for folks whose big house is somewhere else. When construction is complete in 2023, by which time Bowen is counting on both COVID-19 and the street protests being history, there also will be ten thousand square feet of retail (including a food hall, an homage to the food carts) and 165,000 square feet of Class A offices.

The $600 million project meets the letter of the law, but the Ritz-Carlton seems unlikely to uplift down-and-out communities in Portland. Nor is that its focus. A slick brochure Bowen is using to raise money says the project "offers investors the ability to enjoy substantial tax benefits while also investing in an institutional-quality real estate investment."[22]

Bowen filed plans with the SEC to raise $120 million from OZ investors (minimum investment $100,000) in July 2019[23] and, presumably because he'd raised that, he filed in March 2020 for another $50 million offering (minimum investment $50,000).[24] Much of that will come from wealthy OZ investors, many recruited by Baker Tilly Capital, a Chicago-based firm with a specialty in finding investors for OZ projects.

Bowen refused to meet with me or even to talk by phone, but in written answers to my questions, he says, "Without an Opportunity Zone designation, it would have been a greater challenge, if not impossible, to make a project of this magnitude pencil out."

Across the country, Portland's Ritz-Carlton is now a symbol of everything that's wrong with OZs. The heart of downtown Portland isn't the sort of left-behind place the EIG boys, Cory Booker, and Tim Scott talk about. As Bowen's brochure describes it, the project is in "an irreplaceable location, steps away from shopping, entertainment, and nightlife."[25] There's no mention of any social impact.

Bowen, by local ordinance, will have to either set aside some units with rents low enough to be deemed "affordable" or, more likely, pay into a fund devoted to building affordable units elsewhere. He also notes the building will pay over $10 million a year more in property taxes than Goodman was paying on the lot, and the hotel will, of course, employ a lot of people.

But if the Ritz-Carlton is just another chapter of a years-old property boom in downtown Portland, the Tax Cuts and Jobs Act did change one long-standing practice. For decades, owners like Goodman generally didn't sell properties and pay taxes on the profits the way investors in the stock market do. Instead, they conducted what are known as like-kind exchanges (or 1031 exchanges, 1031 being the relevant section of the tax code), the tax break I heard about at the OZ Expo in Las Vegas.

Here's how it works: Sell a building and put all the proceeds into another building. That's a "like-kind exchange," which defers capital gains taxes on the profits. Do this repeatedly and you can defer capital gains taxes until you die. And, under current tax law, your heirs won't have to pay capital gains taxes on the profits ever. But you have to put *all the proceeds* into a new building. In just one of the ways the EIG boys and their allies added a little extra juice to the OZ tax break, to get favorable OZ treatment you have to put only your *capital gains* (that is, the *profits* of your sale), into an OZ fund, freeing up the rest of your untaxed dollars for something else.

That changed Goodman's calculus. In November 2019, he sold a century-old building in which his offices are located, the stately Power and Light Building, for $67 million to another local developer and put the profits into an Opportunity Zone fund of his own. Goodman points out that taxes on his initial capital gains on the sale of the Power and Light Building are deferred, a valuable benefit, but he will have to pay state and federal capital gains taxes in 2026 (unless proposals to change the law and delay that date are approved by Congress).

Well before OZs surfaced in Washington, Goodman's family firm began work on another large project on one of its downtown parking lots, this one about a block from the new Ritz-Carlton. Eleven West—so named because it's at the intersection of SW 11th Avenue and SW Washington Street and near a building called Twelve West—is described by the developer as "the highest-end multifamily project in Portland."[26] A $230 million project, Eleven West will have one floor of retail, six floors of offices, seventeen floors with 222 residential units, and an outdoor swimming pool on the eighth floor. This being Portland, there will be underground parking for 365 bicycles, but for only 258 cars.

Goodman rolled about $57 million of his capital gains into Eleven West. Another $57 million in equity came from Cresset Partners, a Chicago outfit that began raising money for its first OZ fund in December 2018. By the beginning of 2020, the fund had topped up with $465 million. Nearly all the investors were rich enough to put in at least $250,000; some invested millions.

Eleven West was the second of the seven high-end real estate projects in which the Cresset fund eventually invested. Portland is particularly appealing to real estate investors looking at holding a property for ten years, says Cresset's Nick Parrish. It's a fast growth market, drawing millennials from all over. It's cool. It's in between the increasingly expensive high-tech boomtowns of Seattle and San Francisco.

It's hardly surprising that businesspeople, developers, and fund managers would take full advantage of Portland's most promising OZs—some even had fiduciary responsibility to do so. But even some of those people who stood to profit from OZs sounded stunned by the opportunity dropped in their laps. Cresset's Parrish described designating downtown Portland, just a block and a half from the trendy Pearl District, as an OZ as "unbelievable."

The Ritz-Carlton, 250 SW Taylor Street, and Eleven West are just three projects, but each was extremely profitable for developers and real estate aristocracy. Even though they probably would have happened without OZs, they were certainly made more attractive by the tax break—without necessarily providing much by way of additional benefits to the region's poorer communities. Nonetheless, Goodman and others in the industry were playing by all the rules.

Don't blame the players, blame the game.

THE DEVELOPER: VANESSA STURGEON

In the spring of 2018, one of Coni Rathbone's partners at the local law firm of Dunn Carney had to admit, when a client asked about them, that he didn't know what Opportunity Zones were. Rathbone saw an opportunity and studied up. So she was ready when Vanessa Sturgeon called and asked the lawyer to prepare documents that would allow her to raise up to $330 million from OZ investors.

I meet Rathbone in her law firm's offices in the very early days of the COVID-19 scare, just days before the lockdowns. We avoid a handshake and Rathbone warns me against a fist bump: on each hand she wears two rings, each with large, very spiky stones. Sturgeon's offering launched in November 2018, early in the OZ timeline. It was a heavy lift.

"Part of the complication is that she insisted on being first out," Rathbone says. "Which means, we didn't have any regulations at all when we started, and so we were doing guessing based on what the legislation itself said. And she's doing a $330 million offering. And so it's a full-blown securities offering, with a big private placement memorandum. You can imagine drafting the risk factors for a law that doesn't have any regulations yet."

That $330 million proved aspirational. As of the beginning of 2021, Sturgeon had raised about $26 million from wealthy West Coast investors, some referred to her by local accountants, others investors in or employees of high-tech companies who had sold stock at big profits. Sturgeon is using the money for equity for two projects she had been eyeing long before the tax bill passed.

The first project, on Portland's Eastside, brought an unusual challenge: a long-term lease to a gay bathhouse, which boasted of the only patio in town where one could smoke marijuana in the nude.[27] That eccentricity had scared away another developer, but Sturgeon took a risk and bought the property for $3.5 million in September 2019. After some legal spadework, she discovered the club was in violation of its lease; it didn't have a building permit for the notorious deck. She cut a deal with the club owners. They agreed to leave.

Sturgeon is now building an eight-story office building made of cross-laminated timber: layers of lumber that are glued, heated, and pressed into panels. The OZ fund put up half the money; she got a construction loan for the rest. Because she doesn't personally have any capital gains, she hasn't any equity stake, but her personal balance sheet guarantees the loan.

Sturgeon says she probably would have been able to raise money for a building on the Eastside without the OZ. But because the money likely would have come from institutional investors instead of wealthy OZ investors ("institutions take a layer of fat," she says), the building probably would have required a cheaper design. Cross-laminated timber is cool, a marketing edge for a landlord eager to get high-tech tenants, but it's more expensive than other materials.

Sturgeon's other project is forty-five miles south in the state capital of Salem, on the site of a dilapidated 1950s parking structure that was demolished despite a campaign to save it as a historically significant representation of mid-century urban design. In its place will be a $40 million, 123-room hotel, half regular rooms (for guests with government per diems) and half larger suites with kitchenettes (for lobbyists).

A suburban Portland construction company owned by Chris Duffin bought the property in March 2018, and initially talked about paying Sturgeon's firm a fee to develop it; she wouldn't have had any stake. The project became more attractive to her once she discovered it was in an Opportunity Zone. Duffin sold the property to Sturgeon's OZ fund and sheltered his profits from capital gains taxes by investing in her fund.

"The OZ legislation was a stroke of luck," Sturgeon says. The numbers on the hotel project weren't promising without the juice of an OZ tax break. What would have happened if not for OZs? A cheaper building, perhaps multifamily housing, she speculates.

Like the rest of Oregon, Salem is in the midst of a housing crisis. If Sturgeon had built a cheaper residential project, perhaps it would have been more socially beneficial than the hotel for lobbyists that OZ money made possible. But Sturgeon and other developers are using OZs as the law and regulations provide: to attract capital to tracts designated as tax havens no matter what the purpose.

Don't blame the players, blame the game.

THE ENTREPRENEURIAL DEVELOPER: PAUL BRENNEKE

Paul Brenneke made his first money in the real estate business three decades ago, buying property from banks and other distressed sellers crippled by the savings and loans crisis of the 1980s and 1990s, in which nearly a third of the nation's savings and loan associations failed. He since has built a diversified real estate and financial services firm under the umbrella of Sortis Holdings. His biggest project when I met him was converting an eight-hundred-thousand-square-foot Macy's in downtown Seattle into office space for Amazon, plus some retail stores and an event space.

Brenneke's firm is small and nimble. It makes money by taking fees for investing other people's money. Prior to the creation of Opportunity Zones, Brenneke had been successfully recruiting retail investors for a $100 million income-producing fund that lends money to real estate projects. When Opportunity Zones came along, creating an equity fund for OZ investors was the obvious next step. In November 2018, he and his partners launched Sortis Opportunity Fund. They marketed it primarily to West Coast investors, buying search terms on Google to draw business.

The public goal for the fund is $100 million, but it only takes money as it identifies projects. When we first met in November 2019, Brenneke was talking about doing one project each quarter. But even before COVID-19 hit, he was paring that back, worried about rising construction costs, the possibility of a recession, and uncertainty over the presidential election. The fund didn't do any deals in the fourth quarter of 2019 and didn't do much more business during 2020.

By March 2020, Brenneke's OZ fund had raised about $35 million from more than forty investors, some of it through an online platform that uses technology he licensed from a local firm, Crowdstreet, a website that matches investors to money managers. "Some guy in Florida can put $50,000 in our fund in fifteen minutes," he says. In early 2021, he had taken in only a couple of million dollars more. The constraint wasn't investors—the strong stock market of 2020 gave many of them substantial capital gains to shelter—it was finding building projects that made sense and for which someone would lend money. Deals that looked promising when I talked to him in March 2020—using OZ money to lease equipment to an Eastside winery, and a marijuana dispensary that rents space in an Eastside OZ—had fallen through when we speak later.

About half of Brenneke's OZ fund went to a 204-unit senior living development in Tukwila, Washington, about ten miles south of Seattle. And about half a million dollars went to a young OZ business—an app called medZERO, which allows employers to offer employees advances from their Health Savings Accounts—that moved from Kansas City to office space near Brenneke's on Portland's Eastside. At the beginning of 2021, he was eyeing possible OZ deals involving empty Macy's stores, including one in the sole OZ in Boulder, Colorado. "You'd never imagine that would be an Opportunity Zone," he says of the Boulder property. Google's ever-expanding offices are right next to it.

About $18 million of OZ money is headed for a $150 million project on land now occupied by one-story, light industrial buildings on Portland's Eastside: two connected buildings with three hundred thousand square feet of offices and labs (and a 148-car automated garage) for the city's expanding life sciences industry ostentatiously named the New Industrial Revolution Center. The original plan was to build one building immediately and the second later, but demand for lab space—fueled by COVID-19 research and an exodus from the pricey San Francisco real estate market—led the developers to advance plans for the second building.

How much difference did OZs make for this project?

"That's a loaded question," Brenneke tells me. "Could we have raised that money without OZs? Probably not. It was a catalyst. It leveled the playing field between us and the big guys. Could that deal have been done by someone else? Yes, probably."

His partner on the project, a local high-tech entrepreneur and real estate developer, Chris Marsh, isn't so sure OZ money was crucial. The demand for lab space is so strong that the project could have been financed anyhow, though he says the OZ designation "made it a little easier to raise equity."

This underscores how hard it is to evaluate OZs: it's not only about how much money went into OZ funds, it's whether the program is generating investment (at a cost to US Treasury revenues) in low-income communities that wouldn't have otherwise occurred.

But, in general, the OZ tax break isn't driving Brenneke's investment strategy. Instead, he usually starts with an appealing project and then decides whether it makes sense to finance it through his OZ fund or other avenues. In early 2021, the OZ option wasn't particularly appealing. After COVID-19 disrupted the real estate business, Brenneke got approval to be a Small Business Administration (SBA) lender of Paycheck Protection Program loans; he made some loans but was frustrated by the SBA's refusal to approve his plans to create an online loan portal. So he launched Sortis Rescue Fund "to capitalize on the dislocation and market stress caused by the COVID-19 pandemic and subsequent economic fallout," buying distressed properties (a Portland hotel, for instance) and businesses on the cheap. Through that fund, not the OZ fund, he invested in three businesses that had filed for bankruptcy protection—Bamboo Sushi, Blue Star Donuts, and Rudy's Barbershop chain—and kept them operating. And he decided against using OZ money to finance his latest idea: condos in the state's university towns that alumni can use when they come back for big games and rent out, Airbnb-style, at other times. He had enough investor interest to proceed without dealing with the strings of structuring the project as an OZ investment.

To Paul Brenneke, who is not an "impact investor" out to change the world, OZs are just one more way to attract investors who want to make money—and, for the moment, not a particularly appealing one.

Don't blame the players, blame the game.

THE COMMUNITY ORGANIZER: BRAD KETCH

Rockwood is only fifteen miles east of downtown Portland, but it's a world apart—single-family homes built in the post–World War II boom. A neighborhood within the city limits of Gresham, Rockwood is a community of about ten thousand, many of them immigrants, Hispanics, and Black people who can't afford Portland rents. One in four residents of Rockwood lives below the poverty line.

Brad Ketch is no third-generation real estate developer, and his office is not in a glass-clad tower but in what once was a Mexican restaurant and later a strip club. It has terra-cotta tiles on the roof and garish colors on the walls inside and out. A Rockwood native with an MBA from Northwestern University's Kellogg School, Ketch spent twenty-five years in the telecommunications hardware business, ending with the collapse of his company, Rim Semiconductor, in the Great Recession.

Ketch is a committed Christian who practices what he preaches. In 2011, he took his wife and the youngest of his sons to the Philippines and became CEO of International Care Ministries, which provides meals, schooling, health care, and microcredit to the poor. He returned to Rockwood in 2012 and, with his wife, started the Rockwood Community Development Corporation (Rockwood CDC) in January 2013 to organize and assist the poor folks in the community. Ketch, by his own account—he shared an 84,000-word memoir with me—has had conflicts and confrontations with nearly every local politician and bureaucrat, as well as with leaders of affordable housing organizations, but he doesn't discourage easily.

Ketch can't recall how he first heard of OZs, but he saw them as a potential end run around the "cabal" of affordable housing nonprofits and government agencies with whom he often spars. He spotted the Business Oregon website and put in a pitch for Rockwood. His board approved his plan to create Oregon Community Capital as an OZ fund that would invest in Oregon's poorest communities, beginning with Rockwood. He had some in-house expertise: Scott Gillis, a twenty-eight-year veteran of the real estate side of AIG (the insurer that figured prominently in the 2008 financial crisis) who had overseen a portfolio of multifamily housing units, and had moved to town to be near his grandchildren. For some reason, perhaps because he'd registered a generic-sounding name for his OZ fund, Ketch says he began getting calls from people who wanted to have coffee to pick his brain about OZs.

One day Gillis suggested they get all the inquisitive folks together. Since, as usual, the Rockwood CDC was low on money, they decided to charge: $79 a ticket. The first get together was on Friday, September 14, 2018. About 50 people showed up.

Several more conferences, some with paying sponsors, followed: seven in all.[28] They raised Ketch's visibility and spread the gospel about OZs. But ticket sales for a December 2019 conference were so lousy that Ketch cancelled it. In the end, the conference business proved more successful than the OZ fund. By early 2021, Ketch hadn't raised much OZ fund money—six figures, he says—and he told me he was planning to return the money to investors.

Not much OZ money has found its way to Rockwood, though it's precisely the sort of community the program was supposed to help. Across the street from the old Mexican restaurant, on a city-owned parcel empty since a Fred Meyer grocery store closed in 2003, construction is underway on a $70 million complex that will have office space, a workforce training center, and a food hall featuring the cuisine of the community's many ethnic groups. Half the financing comes from local developer Richard Kim, and half from city and state funds and New Market Tax Credits. None is OZ money.

"Rockwood is in a truly distressed community, not like downtown or the Pearl District," Kim wrote in an email. "Rents are low, so returns are low. Investors in O Zones are looking for higher returns, which are not available at Rockwood. For Opportunity Zones to truly provide capital to rural and distressed communities, the structure as designed does not work—unless you have an investor in need of tax deferral that is also a philanthropist willing to take a very small return."

The executive director of Gresham's urban renewal agency, Emily Bower, tells me she knows of no OZ projects in the town. I stumble onto a couple: Chris Marsh, Brenneke's partner in the Eastside project, has put some of his capital gains into an OZ fund of his own to finance a $28 million, 104-unit, three-story apartment building about a mile from Ketch's offices. And a Portland outfit, Community Development Partners, which specializes in affordable housing and is a heavy user of the Low-Income Housing Tax Credit, put some of its own capital gains into a $50 million, 224-unit workforce housing project called Rockwood 10. OZ incentives weren't key to either project.

"In order for a program like this to be effective," says Josh Fuhrer, a Rockwood native and real estate developer who ran Gresham's urban renewal agency for six years, "it needed to level the playing field between places like the Pearl District and places like Rockwood."

It didn't.

Don't blame the players, blame the game.

THE DO-GOODER: SAYER JONES

At the Meyer Memorial Trust, Jones's biggest concern about OZs was that the state "would plunk down a bunch of OZs that would exacerbate the problems we've had for the past twenty years," namely gentrification that drives up rents and pushes renters to the outskirts of town. His conversations with Nick Batz at Business Oregon were frustrating: the state was looking at demographic data—lots of it—but to Jones's taste, Oregon wasn't thinking creatively or holistically about how to use OZs. Batz met with Jones and leaders of community groups, and solicited feedback through the agency website, but Business Oregon (unlike similar agencies in some other states) wouldn't share the map showing designated zones until it was final.

"At the end of the day, the map, for our purposes, wasn't bad," Jones says. Designating downtown tracts as OZs had its advantages: The affordable housing there was owned by nonprofits that wouldn't sell. The city's inclusionary zoning rules meant anyone who built condos would have to provide some affordable units. And any new building would fatten the city's property taxes, which account for more than three-quarters of general revenues.

Portland would attract money, Jones was sure. The challenge would be channeling some money to other parts of the state. Left alone, the market wouldn't do it. So Meyer joined with two other local foundations and hired Stephen Brooks in May 2018 to create a clearinghouse of sorts for marrying prospective investors with community projects across the state in need of funds. Brooks, who started out as a tax lawyer and had been consulting on economic development and financial projects for years, knew the terrain. He took the assignment with enthusiasm and visited with local officials all over Oregon.

Brooks and the foundations assumed someone else would be aggregating money from people with capital gains; their clearinghouse would bundle a set of projects, each of which was too small for any OZ fund but which together would be attractive. Business Oregon, which hadn't much of a strategy for promoting OZs once it picked the zones, enlisted in the ambitiously named Oregon Opportunity Zone Initiative. "We were hoping if we could get some kind of scale, we could create momentum," Brooks says.[29]

It was a flop. Identifying promising projects in smaller communities across the state proved difficult. And finding pools of investors who had money and were looking for projects was no easier. Some funds had lots of ideas and ambitious fundraising targets, but not much money. Other investors had their eyes on particular real estate projects. After several months, the foundations pulled the plug.

Don't blame the players, blame the game.

THE ENTREPRENEUR: LORA DICARLO

Lora Haddock DiCarlo spent a couple of years working on her product, a high-tech sex toy that promises blended orgasms (both clitoral and G-spot), with an accelerator lab at Oregon State University in Corvallis. She launched her company, called Lora DiCarlo, in 2017 and then got publicity money can't buy. The organizers of the huge Consumer Electronics Show (CES), the Consumer

Technology Association, told the company in October 2018, quietly, that its first product had been awarded a Robotics Innovation Award. A month later, the award was withdrawn. According to DiCarlo: "They claimed they had made a mistake and that, due to the nature of our product (their exact words were 'profane,' 'immoral,' and 'obscene'), [it] should never have made it through judging."[30]

In January 2019, DiCarlo issued an outraged press release: "Men's sexuality is allowed to be explicit with a literal sex robot in the shape of an unrealistically proportioned woman and VR porn in point of pride along the aisle. Female sexuality, on the other hand, is heavily muted if not outright banned."[31] To the press, the story was irresistible. "Robotic Dildo Barred from Top Tech Showcase, Prompting Sexism Claims," said the *Guardian*.[32] In May, a red-faced CES changed its mind, again, and reinstated the award.

Thanks to the CES controversy, the brand got established well before the product. The company's "invest@LoraDicarlo.com" mailbox was overwhelmed with thousands of inquiries from prospective investors—ranging from a New Hampshire housewife to a French billionaire playboy.

Lora DiCarlo contracts with a Chinese manufacturer to make its products, but design, prototyping, and administrative functions are in a small, three-story, red, clapboard building in Bend, Oregon. A block away is a marijuana dispensary named Tokyo Starfish (it was conceived by a group of friends on a snowboarding trip to Japan), which boasts of the town's only "Bud-n-Breakfast" apartment, a cannabis-friendly two-bedroom unit that rents on VRBO for around $200 a night. Across the street is an old box factory, a remnant of the area's logging past, that was bought and renovated by yet another Portland family real estate firm in 2013 and now houses several local enterprises, including AVID Cider Company, River Pig Saloon, and The Bend Tour Company.

Near the foothills of the spectacular Cascade Mountains, Bend is popular with outdoorsy tourists—mountain bikers, hikers, anglers, skiers. Its resident population has doubled since 2000. It's also increasingly prosperous: house prices in the county are rising faster than in any of Oregon's other thirty-five counties.[33] As people fled big cities to work remotely during the pandemic, a headline in the local newspaper declared Bend was going "from Boomtown to 'Zoom town.'"[34] However, Bend is also home to enough poor people in census counts that it was eligible to be designated an OZ.

Doug Layman was ready. He had registered Oregon Opportunity Zone LP with the state in May 2018. (Such registrations are public records. As a result, Layman got calls in 2018 from twenty or thirty real estate developers looking for OZ money for their projects.)

Even before the Consumer Electronics Show controversy, Layman had raised $1.1 million in seed capital for DiCarlo through his OZ fund. He pulled in another $2 million in May 2019 after the rescinded award raised the company's profile. A big chunk of that came from a friend of his, Toronto investor Richard Kado, who was impressed with the business plan but isn't getting any OZ tax break—he pays taxes in Canada.

Still, the OZ approach did offer some advantages. It was a way for the entrepreneur to maintain control; since Layman is the general partner in the OZ, he votes for all the outside shareholders on the company's board. And the valuation of the company—which shipped its first product in January 2020—was higher than it would have been had it turned to traditional venture capital investors. For Layman's personal finances? "I won't pay taxes for a couple of years, which is awesome," he says.

To be sure, Layman reminds me, DiCarlo did create jobs in Bend: twenty-two of them. But there's a reasonably good case to be made that all that would have happened without the OZ tax break.

Don't blame the players, blame the game.

THE SKEPTIC: TODD GOODING

Not everyone in Portland's real estate crowd found a pot of gold at the end of the OZ rainbow. At ScanlanKemperBard, known as SKB, Todd Gooding, the president, fashioned a three-part strategy for the firm a couple of years ago: Build mixed-use developments in suburbs near mass transit. Renovate old factories into multi-tenant space for modern manufacturers doing R & D, testing, and proto-typing. Exploit Opportunity Zones.

"We went all in," he tells me, putting a Google map of Portland on a wall-mounted TV screen in his conference room and pointing out parcels he owns. "Turns out we had seven assets in our existing portfolio that were in Opportunity Zones. And we decided, 'Let's take our existing portfolio first and see what we can mine and recap-italize and do an Opportunity Zone deal.'"

It was a bust. Gooding, who has been in the real estate financ-ing business for three decades, discovered that OZ investors weren't like other real estate investors. "It has to be a safe haven. You can't put my money at risk," they told him. And tenants in his urban manufacturing properties sign five-year leases. Asking investors to lock up their money for ten years wasn't going to work because they worried about the risks of finding a tenant for the second five years.

So SKB dropped the OZ plank of its strategy to focus on the other two, accepting OZ investors in projects only if the projects made economic sense for reasons other than the OZ tax break. In Tigard, about ten miles south of SKB's Portland office, the firm is building a 219-unit apartment building with ground floor retail space on a vacant lot near a Walmart, a Costco, and an abandoned Babies R Us at the intersection of a couple of highways, near a planned light-rail stop. This is not the Ritz-Carlton or Eleven West. It's the sort of unglamorous mixed-use project near mass transit that

SKB is looking for. To make it work, the city chipped in $1 million and the state offered a ten-year property tax break. To finance the $70 million project, SKB borrowed some, put in $12 million of its own, and made a deal with an OZ fund organized by Canyon Partners, a Los Angeles asset manager, which chipped in another $24.4 million in equity.[35]

"The big difference between what we're doing versus what's happening here in downtown Portland is that this is a catalytic project. This project is happening because the city really wants it to happen, made some concessions, got the state behind it—and then the Opportunity Zone provides for the perfect mixture for us to get this done versus…"

I interrupt: So you're saying it wouldn't have been done without OZ money? "Correct," he replies, tersely, but he has a point to make. "…versus: You look at the Goodmans. There's nothing wrong with the Goodmans' projects. There's nothing wrong with the Northwest Natural Gas deal. They're great projects. The Ritz-Carlton is a great project. But is it gonna change the neighborhood? Is it going to make a material change in how people think or operate, or have the impact that an Opportunity Zone investment is supposed to have? I don't think so."

Don't blame the players, blame the game.

THE POLITICIAN: NANCY NATHANSON

A similar logic struck state Representative Nancy Nathanson, a Democrat who has represented the college town of Eugene since 2007 and chairs the House Revenue Committee. She had heard and long questioned the argument that "if we give a tax break to people everything will be better," and was alerted to OZs by Oregon progressive groups, who highlighted the choice of zones in Portland and the Ritz-Carlton project to attack OZs.[36] As is so often the case, an egregious example of someone taking advantage of a tax break stirred political opposition.

Nathanson introduced a bill that would have blocked Oregon taxpayers from taking advantage of the OZ tax break on their state tax returns. After all, she and her allies argued, Oregon taxpayers could invest in out-of-state OZ funds and get a state tax break with no benefit to the state at all. (Limiting the tax break to investments in Oregon, she says, probably violates the US Constitution.)

Real estate interests objected vociferously. Mayors, city councilors, and county commissioners told her the provision was essential to encourage investment in their communities. Her response: "Wouldn't they have done it anyways? The value of the Oregon credit is pretty small compared to the value of the federal credit. And we know for sure that there are some projects that were literally already in the works. Because of this poorly written tax bill, projects that were already going to happen got a windfall bonus."

In the face of political resistance, she diluted her bill. Taxpayers would be allowed to defer their initial capital gains tax, but when they sold their OZ investment after ten years or more, they'd owe Oregon half of what they would have owed otherwise (or 4.95 percent at current rates). In addition, any OZ fund that was investing in Oregon or had Oregon investors would have to disclose that to the state "so we can study these and figure out what is real and what is pie-in-the-sky thinking."

The bill never came to a vote. The Oregon legislature's 2020 session disintegrated over the governor's cap-and-trade climate change bill when Republicans walked out, denying the Democrats a quorum. The session ended abruptly in early March.

So what's the bottom line on how Opportunity Zones played out in Portland? Without much effort from local or state governments, OZ money is flowing, saving some wealthy people—Oregonians and others—some money on their capital gains taxes. It's making it easier and, in some cases cheaper, to finance construction projects in downtown Portland and the Eastside. But it's hard to find a project in Portland that would not have been built if not for Opportunity Zones. Meanwhile, in Rockwood, precisely the kind of community that proponents of Opportunity Zones said they were trying to help, OZs aren't doing much at all.

Don't blame the players, blame the game.

CHAPTER ELEVEN

Baltimore: Waiting to Be Asked to the OZ Dance

B ALTIMORE IS THE SORT OF PLACE OPPORTUNITY ZONES WERE supposed to save, and local leaders did everything they could to attract OZ dollars. But getting a city all dressed up and ready for the prom doesn't do much if no one asks it to dance. With so many other designated Opportunity Zones more attractive to investors, Baltimore hasn't had very many dates.

The city has some advantages. It sits along the prosperous New York–Washington corridor, about a fifty-minute drive north from the US Capitol. It has a rich history and vibrant neighborhoods, downtown tourist draws like the National Aquarium and Camden Yards baseball park, pockets of gentrification and entrepreneurial activity, a world-class university medical center, and a busy cargo port. But those are islands of prosperity in a stormy sea. In contrast to Portland, I didn't see much dirt being moved or many cranes swinging when I drove around Baltimore. I did see a lot of empty row houses, overgrown vacant lots, and street corners with men hanging out, smoking, drinking, and talking.

In investing terms, Baltimore has a lot of unrealized opportunity. More bluntly, it has nowhere to go but up.

The city's woes can be measured in its population numbers, which have been falling for decades. In 1950, its 950,000 residents made it the sixth-largest city in the United States. As of July 1, 2019, its population was down to 593,490, lowering it in the rankings to number 30.[1]

The one fact about Baltimore that hit me hardest is this: even as the city razes more than a thousand empty houses a year or turns them over to nonprofits for renovation, so many other homes are abandoned that the number of vacant properties—nearly seventeen thousand—has barely budged for a decade.[2]

Baltimore's national image doesn't help entice investors. It was forever shaped by *The Wire*, the HBO series about the city's drug scene, cops, and politics that had more than four million viewers in its first season. And, as the series dramatized, the city is plagued by violence—it records more than three hundred murders a year.[3] Among big US cities, only Saint Louis had a higher per capita murder rate in 2019. On New Year's Eve, the city's new mayor led other city leaders in an online virtual vigil to read the names of each of the 334 victims of homicide in 2020. It took more than an hour. A local line of apparel features the gallows humor line "Baltimore, Maryland. There's more than murder here!"[4] Adding to the air of dysfunction, two of the last four mayors were convicted on corruption charges and left office.

In 2015, seven years after *The Wire*'s last episode, Baltimore drew more negative national attention when Freddie Gray, a twenty-five-year-old Black man, died a week after suffering a spinal injury while being transported in a police van without a seatbelt, his hands and ankles shackled. His death triggered protests, sometimes violent, that were a precursor to 2020's nationwide protests over police brutality against Black people.

Gray's tragic story was intertwined with the decades-long struggle to improve the lives of Baltimore's poorest people. He was from Sandtown-Winchester, a neighborhood on the west side of Baltimore that was the target of a $130 million revitalization effort to increase homeownership, employment, and school achievement in the early 1990s. Led by James Rouse, the developer of Baltimore's Inner Harbor, the effort succeeded in increasing homeownership, but is largely remembered today as a case study of how hard it is to turn around a troubled Baltimore neighborhood—even if you spend a lot of money.[5]

These challenges are compounded by a distinct pattern of segregation in Baltimore that traces back to strictly enforced early-twentieth-century ordinances.[6] A local public health professor, Lawrence Brown, was the first to describe the demographic map of the city as a Black Butterfly: a mostly white, more prosperous L-shaped stripe down the middle with two wing-shaped majority Black and poorer neighborhoods on either side.[7] Money follows these boundaries, too. Baltimore neighborhoods that are less than 50 percent Black receive more than three times as much public and private investment as neighborhoods that are predominantly Black, according to the Urban Institute.[8]

Well before Opportunity Zones appeared, Baltimore had been trying all sorts of economic development incentives to turn around its poorer neighborhoods and its downtown. The city's waning political power at the state capital and the current governor's focus on suburban growth has forced the city to rely more on its own resources and on the federal government.[9] Because property taxes in Baltimore are significantly higher than in the surrounding jurisdiction (confusingly named Baltimore County), almost every significant successful real estate project seeks—and usually gets—a decade's worth of tax relief from the city.

What is clear is that the city's struggling neighborhoods need more than that. By EIG's ranking, the city is among the ten cities in the United States with the largest number of people in economically distressed zip codes.[10] One in five of its residents, and nearly one in three of its children, lives below the official poverty line. And that data predate COVID-19, which, as of April 2021, had infected more than 45,000 residents and killed more than 900 while scores of local businesses went under.[11]

In short, it isn't hard to find parts of Baltimore in need of the lift OZs were supposed to provide, and the city was prepared to welcome OZ money. It has forty-two Opportunity Zones, mostly well chosen. Many have so many empty buildings or vacant lots that displacing residents isn't much of an issue. The state of Maryland supplemented federal tax incentives with additional tax breaks, including tax credits for hiring. And to fully exploit Opportunity Zones, a local foundation paid for the city to hire an idealistic, energetic OZ coordinator to connect outside investors to locals looking for financing. It seems a great test case of the OZ concept.

So I went to Baltimore to answer a few questions. Was the tax break generous enough to lure money to Baltimore, with all its disadvantages, or would the money end up in less risky, more promising OZs elsewhere? Were investors in OZs reaping the tax break for projects that probably would have been done anyhow?

By identifying as many OZ-funded projects as I could, I hoped to gauge the early impact Opportunity Zones have had in Baltimore. But the search itself was instructive: it is striking how few OZ projects there are in the city. I heard a lot of talk about OZs. Some full of hope, some dripping with skepticism. I found out-of-state real estate developers who had looked at Baltimore, and then looked away. (One told me Baltimore resembles Newark, another troubled city near a big, prosperous one. "I prefer Newark," he said.) But I found only a handful of projects with OZ capital. And even those were bolstered by layers of other government subsidies, several of which offered developers and their investors a tax break for projects that almost surely would have been undertaken even if OZs had never been invented. And I found some very disappointed people.

MATCH.COM FOR OZs

Baltimore pounced early on OZs. Bill Cole—then head of the city's economic development agency, the Baltimore Development Corporation—got a call at the beginning of 2018 from Mayor Catherine Pugh (who later would land in prison after pleading guilty to corruption charges). Pugh had heard about OZs at a West Coast conference and she wanted Baltimore to move quickly. Cole tracked down the EIG boys to find out more and, with city officials, began studying the data and city maps. They were ready to move when the governor's office asked local governments to nominate OZs from among the state's 589 eligible tracts. The law said the governor could pick up to 25 percent of those for the tax break.

The city saw 168 of its 200 census tracts were eligible—more than the state's total allotment. City officials offered the governor forty-one, figuring that Baltimore's fair share was about a quarter of the state's eligible tracts. (It ended up with forty-two.) The city officials tried to be strategic. Given the tight deadlines the law set for investors interested in taking advantage of the tax incentive, Cole said, the city looked for places that were most likely to draw money, places where deals were already in the pipeline, mostly commercial and industrial areas as opposed to residential.

As the governor was finalizing the list of OZs, a Jimmy Carter–era HUD official, former local school board president, and former city housing commissioner named Bob Embry was paying attention. Since 1987, Embry has been president of the locally focused Abell Foundation, which was created by the family that once owned the

Baltimore Sun. He was skeptical that OZs would amount to much and disappointed the law didn't require investors to declare that they wouldn't have invested in a project "but for" the OZ tax break. "But it was the only federal player on the field, and if it could be used, we ought to have someone focused on it," he says. His foundation decided to give the Baltimore Development Corporation $100,000 a year for a couple of years to hire an OZ czar for the city.

Ben Seigel got the job. Seigel is a slim, bearded Baltimore native in his mid-forties, a Swarthmore grad who, after stints in local government and nonprofits in Portland, Oregon, and New York City, worked for Barack Obama's labor secretaries. After the 2015 Freddie Gray protests, Valerie Jarrett in the Obama White House asked Seigel to run a federal task force on Baltimore. The task force drew Seigel back to Baltimore professionally—he later got a job running a Johns Hopkins University urban research and outreach center—though he still lives in a Maryland suburb just outside DC.

In October 2018, Seigel became one of the nation's first local OZ coordinators, a role other foundations tried to replicate in other cities. He calls himself "the Match.com of Opportunity Zones," linking out-of-town investors with potential projects in the city, cajoling investors to take a look at Baltimore, and nurturing not-quite-ready-for-prime-time development projects in town. He has a PowerPoint that extols Baltimore's potential and, in the trunk of his blue 2019 Hyundai, a poster-sized map of the city with OZs shaded in green. He talks to OZ funds, big and small, and to local developers and entrepreneurs, big and small. He gives OZ funds a single point of contact in Baltimore, no small thing given the complexity of doing any project in any city. He speaks at OZ conferences—or he did when they were still hot—and checked in frequently with EIG and the Trump White House.

The White House didn't return the favor. Though Seigel is an easy-to-find liaison for OZ promotion in Baltimore, the Trump administration failed to consult him when it used the city as a backdrop to promote the program. The result was a PR debacle. It began in July 2019 after Trump—in a dispute with Elijah Cummings, a thirteen-term African American Democratic congressman from Baltimore—tweeted that the city was "a disgusting, rat and rodent-infested mess." Several days later, HUD Secretary Ben Carson, who had been at Johns Hopkins before going to Washington, came back to Baltimore to mend fences and promote Opportunity Zones. The night before, his staff alerted the *Baltimore Sun*. They didn't call Seigel.

Carson tried to hold a televised press conference in a vacant lot owned by Morning Star Baptist Church of Christ. A church member chased him off, saying HUD hadn't asked permission and, besides, the church didn't want to provide a venue for a photo op. "Why wouldn't they include a stakeholder like us that's been in the neighborhood for nearly one hundred years?" asks Cynthia Neverdon-Morton, seventy-six, a lifelong member of the primarily African American church. The press conference was hastily moved to an alley about thirty yards away. A HUD spokesperson said at the time that the site was in an Opportunity Zone; it actually is just outside an OZ boundary.[12]

Trump did not reinforce Carson's make-nice efforts. In September 2020, in tweets endorsing a Republican congressional candidate from Baltimore, the president said: "You have been ripped off for years by the Democrats & gotten nothing but poverty and crime... Baltimore is last in everything.... the WORST IN NATION." (The candidate lost.)

THE OZ IN THE PARKING LOT

In addition to President Trump's public excoriation of Baltimore, Ben Seigel also had to overcome a negative local perception of OZs, largely the result of one very high-profile case that severely stretched the definition of Opportunity Zone. Indeed, if you mention the words "Opportunity Zone" in Baltimore, you're likely to hear "Port Covington" in response.

South of downtown on the Middle Branch of the Patapsco River, just off heavily traveled I-95, Port Covington was once a port and railroad terminal. It was largely abandoned in the 1980s, leaving a couple hundred acres of postindustrial land that was disconnected from the city. The site was later home to a Sam's Club and a Walmart, both long gone. The Baltimore Sun building stands nearby. For the past few decades, the area has been largely a wasteland.

In 2011, long before OZs were conceived, Kevin Plank—founder of Under Armour, the Baltimore-based sports apparel firm—quietly began buying the land. In 2015, he unveiled what he said would eventually be a $5.5 billion mix of offices, housing, and shops adjacent to land where the company planned to move its headquarters. Plank and his partner, developer Marc Weller, have big ambitions for a mini-city at Port Covington. They've already turned an old city garage into an incubator space for start-ups and opened a rye whiskey distillery, an echo of the site's pre-Prohibition history. Their grand vision for the site, which covers the equivalent of forty-five city blocks, includes office, retail, and residential buildings to be built over the next ten to fifteen years.

In 2016, the city government agreed to borrow up to $660 million in Tax Increment Financing (TIF) bonds to pay for roads, utilities, and other infrastructure, pledging to pay bondholders back with increased future property taxes from the project (which means that added tax revenue isn't available to support other city services for many years to come).[13] As part of their deal with the city, the developers agreed to affordable housing set-asides and promised millions for job training, scholarships, and economic development aid for six low-income neighborhoods on the other side of the Patapsco

River. Port Covington also got various tax credits for cleaning up a brownfield site. Weller says construction costs in Baltimore are as high as in other nearby cities, but rents and building values aren't, so any major building project requires substantial public subsidy.

In September 2017, as Under Armour's business deteriorated, the project got a boost from Goldman Sachs. In the past several years, Goldman's Urban Investment Group has invested more than $9.6 billion into low-income communities around the country, in part to meet Community Reinvestment Act requirements that accompanied Goldman's change of legal status to a bank holding company during the 2008 financial crisis. (The Community Reinvestment Act, enacted in 1977, requires federal regulators to make sure banks meet the credit needs of the communities in which they do business.)

The group is run by Margaret Anadu, who joined Goldman right out of Harvard in 2003 and became a partner fifteen years later. Unlike many other deep pocket investors, she thinks Baltimore has a shot at achieving its potential. "Once you get past the perceived negatives, Baltimore is a great city," she says. "It's a classic mid-Atlantic market with 'eds' and 'meds,'" she says, referring to the city's universities and hospitals.

Goldman initially invested $233 million to buy the land—some land from Plank, the Under Armour founder, some from others—and build a forty-acre park, fix up the riverfront, and pay for utilities and rail transit. Goldman has a 75 percent interest in the project; Plank and Weller have the rest.

All of this was before Opportunity Zones. None of the $233 million Goldman invested initially is OZ money. In fact, almost no one thought Port Covington would ever be in an OZ. The city put several nearby tracts on its wish list, but not Port Covington. Bill Cole says the city's economic development organization didn't consider it because the tract didn't appear to be eligible.

As word of OZs began to spread, though, lobbyists for Port Covington got a meeting with the governor's top staff in February 2018, eager to get an OZ designation. That appeared to be an uphill battle. The census tract (24510230300) didn't have many people; it encompassed a gentrifying area, so its median income was too high to qualify; and it didn't fit under the contiguous tract provision because incomes in immediately adjacent tracts also were too high. A deputy chief of staff to the governor, Sean Powell, put it unequivocally in an email: "Opportunity zone... Port Covington does not qualify."[14]

Days after that meeting, the Treasury sent governors lists of all the census tracts eligible for OZ designation under the law. The federal government confirmed that Port Covington wasn't considered eligible, but the effort to get onto that list still wasn't dead. Three weeks later, the Treasury issued a revised directory—adding 168 tracts across the country to the list of certified low-income communities that it said had been "inadvertently" excluded previously. Port Covington was among them. How? The corrected list adjusted for an obscure provision in the OZ law that defined "low-income community" to include tracts with fewer than two thousand people that were "within" the boundaries of Clinton-era Empowerment Zones.

A Baltimore-based reporter for investigative journalism site ProPublica was surprised at the choice and started poking around. He wrote that the tract's inclusion stretched the boundaries of OZs to near the breaking point:

> Port Covington wasn't actually within an empowerment zone, but it is next to one. So how did it qualify? The area met the definition of "within" because the digital map files the Treasury Department used showed that Port Covington overlapped with a neighboring tract that was designated an empowerment zone, Treasury officials told ProPublica. That overlap: the sliver of parking lot beneath I-395. That piece of the lot is about one one-thousandth of a square mile.[15]

The issue turned on the definition of "within." The Treasury decided that any overlap with an Empowerment Zone was considered "within" that zone. An outdated mapping tool the Treasury's CDFI office used put the parking lot within that Empowerment Zone; other maps showed it wasn't. There's no indication anyone at the Treasury realized the significance of this to Baltimore, but the overlap, considerably smaller than a football end zone, put Port Covington over the line. And the decision was final.

Soon thereafter, Maryland governor Larry Hogan knocked three tracts off Baltimore's list of proposed sites and added four others— one was in downtown Baltimore (which Bill Cole says was "a bit of a shock"), another in Port Covington. None of this got much notice until the June 2019 ProPublica report, which indelibly stained the image of OZs in Baltimore.

A couple of days after the report, Marc Weller, the developer, fired back on the op-ed pages of the *Baltimore Sun*, which had reprinted the ProPublica story. "The assertion that Port Covington's designation as an Opportunity Zone is in some way inappropriate or not in the spirit of the legislation" is "unfair," he wrote.[16]

In an interview, Weller adds, "If you're not making this a site, then there's no point in the program. This is the quintessential OZ site." He insists the governor—eager to locate the state's OZs in places with shovel-ready projects—had decided to nominate Port Covington even before the developer's team made its plea. There is no question the governor's office made it happen.

Jay Brodie, who was president of the Baltimore Development Corporation for sixteen years until his retirement in 2012, winced: "I raised an eyebrow when Port Covington was designated," Brodie said. "Do they really need this designation on top of the city support?"

"If they're eligible, who isn't eligible?" he wonders.

On the western wing of the Black Butterfly, Jeffrey Hargrave also is frustrated. Hargrave grew up across the river from Port Covington, went to a local technical high school, and worked as a carpenter until founding his own general contracting firm, Mahogany, Inc., in 1991. The company—located in a west Baltimore OZ, in a squat brick building across the street from the B&O Railroad Museum—employs about fifty-five people.

Hargrave is president of the Presidents' RoundTable, an association of seventeen Black Baltimore-Washington area entrepreneurs, which hosted an OZ seminar for minority businesses in 2019. Nothing has come of it. Opportunity Zones, he says, are like other federal incentives. "The wealthy benefit while the poor get left out. It's been very slow going. People who actually live here in Baltimore are left on the outside looking in or hoping they're not left out on the outside looking in," he said.

Port Covington will undoubtedly be a huge boost for South Baltimore—if it lives up to the developers' dreams. Construction work began at the end of 2019, was suspended when COVID-19 hit, and resumed in January 2021 on the first five buildings—two office and three residential—which will cost an estimated $550 million.

But, given all the other public subsidies, how much does the project turn on the OZ tax breaks? Although Goldman's first $233 million, and $40 million it kicked in later, come from its ample corporate coffers without any OZ kicker, the firm is raising another $154 million in OZ money, most of that from its wealthy clients, to help finance those five new buildings. And Alexandria Real Estate Equities, a large publicly traded real estate investment trust, is planning 170,000 square feet of laboratory and office space targeted at life sciences companies.[17] Alexandria's plans were a vote of confidence in Port Covington amid uncertainty surrounding COVID-19 and Under Armour's sagging business, which led Plank to resign as CEO and the company to scale back its plans for a new corporate headquarters on the site. Alexandria won't talk about the financing of the deal, but local officials say they've been told some of the money will come from OZ investors.

Weller, not surprisingly, argues that the OZ tax break—on top of the other subsidies—is essential to drawing big-bucks investments from out-of-town institutional investors or family offices for a project of this scale. Never mind that Goldman invested a quarter of a billion dollars before OZs were created. "Bringing the cost of capital down in situations like this allows a deal to start to pencil. I don't know what we would have done without Opportunity Zones. I don't know that you'd get that money with all that's going on in Baltimore—all the instability—with all the other places to invest. It's safe to say that the Opportunity Zone is giving us the opportunity to do this. I certainly know that it has enhanced it." (The developer made much the same argument for the city subsidies.)

But would Port Covington have happened without Opportunity Zones? "Of course," says Goldman's Anadu. "It would take a lot longer and it would look different. And that matters as communities have been waiting a long time. That matters. With OZ capital, I think we will start more buildings than we would have, and we will have more impact and affordability on site than we would have."

BEN SEIGEL MAKES A MATCH

I kept looking.

On West North Avenue, on the west side of Baltimore, a few blocks from a CVS that was burned down in the Freddie Gray violence (and since rebuilt), there's a block of brick row houses, all vacant except for one that hosts a barber shop and a bail bondsman. All but the occupied one are to be demolished to make way for a mixed residential and business development. This is one project that squarely fits the OZ objective of rescuing a patch of burned-out urban blight.

Brendan Schreiber, a small-scale developer who describes himself as anti-racist and mission oriented, plans to build ground floor commercial space—five units of just seven hundred square feet each—with somewhere between fourteen and seventeen units of workforce housing upstairs. Some of the units are intended to be "live where you work" units for owners of the ground floor businesses. Schreiber figures the neighborhood needs more decent housing, but it really needs commercial space to be economically vibrant. Living above the shop will save on commuting costs, he reasons.

Although this project will surely give the neighborhood a needed boost, it's very small—just $4.5 million. But even raising that sum was challenging. Finally Ben Seigel connected Schreiber with Woodforest National Bank, a Texas bank that has a $22.5 million OZ fund and uses projects like this one to meet Community Reinvestment Act requirements.[18] It invested $1.1 million in OZ money on the condition that Schreiber promise to spend the money quickly, which he was happy to do. "We literally just got lucky," Schreiber says.

That's true, though this is an example of Seigel doing his job: Woodforest's partner in the OZ fund, CEI-Boulos Capital Management, contacted him in September 2019 and explained their criteria for OZ investments. Seigel offered them projects but nothing fit until he told them about Schreiber in July 2020.

Even with OZ capital, though, the project only pencils (as they say in the real estate business) with city and state subsidies. Schreiber is grateful for the investment—and for Ben Seigel's matchmaking—but skeptical that OZs as currently structured will deliver for Baltimore. "You still have to convince investors to invest in a community they don't want to invest in," he says. The tax break just isn't big enough to overcome the litany of obstacles to investment that trouble Baltimore. "What do you do when you have an entire city that needs subsidies? You have a fight for scarce resources," he says. "Ben," he fears, "is fighting a losing battle."

THE DISAPPOINTED REVEREND

Rev. Donté Hickman was an early and high-profile fan of OZs. In 2018, the entrepreneurial pastor invited Trump to visit East Baltimore to see how his four-thousand-member Southern Baptist Church has harnessed government subsidies to build a sixty-one-unit senior housing project, a building that was half built when it was burned during the April 2015 Freddie Gray uprising. The structure was rebuilt from the ashes and opened in February 2016.[19] The church is like a fortress amid blocks of vacant lots and brick row houses, some occupied, many not. Hickman has ambitious plans to put a $27 million health center—with Johns Hopkins as an anchor tenant—and eighty-eight units of workforce housing on nearby vacant lots. With the project located in an OZ, Hickman was hopeful he could attract capital looking for a tax haven.

In December 2018, plans for a Trump trip to Baltimore were scuttled at the last minute, so Hickman went to the White House and stood at the president's side as he signed an executive order creating his OZ-coordinating council. Notably, both the Democratic mayor of Baltimore and Republican governor of Maryland declined to attend. With Trump standing over his shoulder, Hickman said, "Our area has been federally designated as an Opportunity Zone, and this bipartisan legislation can leverage public and private funding towards community revitalization."[20] Hickman went on to tell the president, "Your influence on federal agencies and private entities through this executive order will enable distressed communities, like Broadway East in Baltimore, to obtain investment needed to capitalize and bridge funding gaps to create sustainable health, wealth, housing, educational, recreational, grocery, and employment opportunities."

Two years later, despite his elbow-rubbing with the president, Hickman was still waiting for the first OZ dollar. "What we have learned about Opportunity Zones and their investors is that they really are a challenge to work with in the severely distressed areas that they are meant for," he said.

"It's easy to get the kind of yields that OZ investors want in areas like Port Covington or Yard 56 [a retail development across the street from a huge Johns Hopkins medical center]. But when you look at the really distressed communities that have been financially repressed for more than three decades, it takes a lot of subsidy and investment to make those deals worth it," he said. Hickman doesn't resent Port Covington's designation—it'll benefit adjacent areas, he figures—but he thinks projects like Port Covington should be required to partner with "a really distressed community."

"What we need is more mission-minded investors," he says. "The Opportunity Zone investments are nothing more than a monetary play. It's all about money. I'm not down on the investors. I just think that...more public spending has to come to the table." Indeed, every OZ-financed project I identify in Baltimore also benefits from several other local, state, or federal subsidies.

FROM FACTORY TO SHOPPING CENTER: WOULD HAVE HAPPENED ANYWAY

With Hickman's words ringing in my ears, I scouted a few other, smaller projects in Baltimore that have landed OZ money. I wanted to see whether the OZ incentive was pivotal or just one more way for investors to shave their tax bills on an investment that, most likely, they or someone else would have made otherwise.

Yard 56 is twenty acres next to the working-class, eastern Baltimore neighborhood called—officially since the late 1980s—Greektown. It's across the street from the world-class, 130-acre Bayview Medical Center, where Johns Hopkins has invested hundreds of millions of dollars over the past four years. For nearly one hundred years, Yard 56 was home to a porcelain plant that, among other things, made the distinctive orange tiles for Howard Johnson's rooftops. The plant closed in 2007. Production moved to Alabama, idling ninety workers and leaving behind environmentally contaminated land. Walmart was said to be interested in the site but backed off after community opposition.[21]

David Bramble's real estate firm bought the land in April 2014 for $3 million. Bramble grew up in Baltimore, went to Princeton and got a law degree from Penn, practiced corporate and real estate law for a while, then moved into commercial real estate lending, and now is a full-time developer. He spent years getting approvals and arranging financing for a mixed-used development at Yard 56. Construction finally started in 2018, and Streets Market grocery store, an enormous (34,000 square feet) LA Fitness, Chipotle, Starbucks, and a branch of Fulton Bank (which lent money for the project) opened in 2020. Construction on an office building that will house a nonprofit health center was slated to begin in the summer of 2021. The development would be unremarkable in most suburbs; here, the freshly paved parking lot and the new brick retail structures contrast with the shabby storefronts along a nearby avenue.

The price tag for the first phase—plans for a second include residential—was around $77 million, about half equity (including several million dollars from Bramble himself) and half debt. Half the equity (roughly $19 million) came from Prudential Financial. The insurance giant had been talking with Bramble about putting money into the project as one of its social impact investments before

OZs popped up. With fanfare (and, according to Bramble, lots of time spent with lawyers and accountants), the company in January 2019 made Yard 56 the first investment of its OZ fund.[22] In other words, Prudential harnessed OZs to get a tax break for itself and its clients for a project it already was eyeing. (In a sign of how tainted OZs have become, Prudential refused to talk to me, though it did eventually email a short statement that said the Opportunity Zone tax break was "a material factor in our decisions to invest in Yard 56." If it has made another OZ investment, it hasn't said so publicly.) Like so many other developers in Baltimore, Bramble also tapped New Markets Tax Credits (a program the EIG boys criticize) for some of the debt and got brownfield tax credits from the state. In other words, the OZ incentive was just one of several government subsidies that made this project work.

Bramble is an OZ fan. "I think the OZ legislation is awesome," he tells me. "Not because it's a panacea. It's helping deals over the finish line. It is making things possible that haven't been looked at before." He's frustrated at the bad publicity the program gets and readily accepts invitations to talk on panels, webinars, and conference calls. "If we don't go out there and say, 'We did this deal. We cleaned up a brownfield site. We created jobs,' then all people will hear is about the guy who built a condo in Miami. If we let that be the narrative, people who care about community development lose an arrow, and we need all the arrows we can get."

He complains that impatient OZ critics don't understand how long it takes to get a project done, a fact of life that makes many ambitious urban renewal projects incompatible with the tight deadlines in the OZ law. (Indeed, Bramble hopes to raise OZ money for another project on land once occupied by a Baltimore housing project infamously known as "murder mall." It was held up for months because Amtrak has an unused underground right-of-way for a tunnel on the site.) The test of Opportunity Zone investments, he says, is whether the bulk of money is "moving the needle on community development," as he is. That is, he concedes, a question that can't be answered definitively given the scarcity of public data.

Bramble's bottom line on the importance of OZs to Yard 56? He says Prudential didn't make a final commitment until it could take account of the benefits of the tax break. But given that he owned the land, he allows that he almost surely would have found some other way to finance the project if Prudential hadn't come through.

THE TRAIN STATION: TOO SOON TO TELL

Amtrak's one-hundred-year-old Beaux-Arts railroad station north of downtown Baltimore is encircled by a maze of overpasses and parking lots with little connection to surrounding blocks or nearby public transit. It has a single retail establishment. For decades, there's been talk of turning Penn Station, as it's known, into a mix of shops, offices, and hotels that might spark development of the neighborhood. After all, the boosters say, planned high-speed rail service to Washington could someday be appealing to commuters who are priced out of the DC housing market.

The first attempt in 2012 at designating a master developer for the site flopped, so Amtrak tried again in 2017 with a larger-scale plan. In 2019, the pieces finally began to fall into place. City officials put the Penn Station census tract on their OZ wish list because, they said, "the area is identified for transformative reinvestment," and the governor complied. In addition to $90 million for a new passenger concourse and railroad improvements, Amtrak said it would put $50 million toward a $75 million plan to turn the current rail station into restaurant, retail, and office space. The state and federal governments chipped in about $6 million in historic tax credits. All of that had no OZ angle. A hole of about $19 million was left for the developers to fill. Early in 2020, one of the final pieces of the financing jigsaw puzzle came through—an equity investment from an OZ fund sponsored by an outfit called Blueprint Local. (Blueprint won't disclose the size of its investment; its SEC filings indicate the initial tranche was less than $10 million.)[23] The local press celebrated this as the second OZ investment in Baltimore, after Yard 56, and this was more than two years after the law passed.[24]

Blueprint Local was founded in early 2019 by Ross Baird, a venture capitalist and self-described "impact investor." He is hoping to build a series of local funds that'll match investors looking for projects with "measurable" social impact with developers and business entrepreneurs looking for capital. Blueprint is concentrating its activities in a few cities—Austin, San Antonio, Houston, Richmond, and Baltimore. "Blueprint could exist in the absence of OZs, but they really accelerated it," Baird says.

To raise money, Blueprint teamed with a money manager with Baltimore roots, Brown Advisory, which is both an investor and an operational partner. The Baltimore fund has twenty-two investors. Half, which include banks seeking projects that'll satisfy Community Reinvestment Act requirements, are mission-driven, though they welcome the tax benefit. The other half showed up primarily because of the tax break.

But would the Penn Station project be happening if not for Blueprint's small OZ investment? I put that question to Bill Struever, the longtime Baltimore-based developer who is one of the lead players on the project. I didn't get a "yes" or "no," which is reasonable because real estate deals—like so many things in life—are rarely that black and white. "I think it's important," he allowed. But he is confident he and his partner in the project were capable of doing the centerpiece of the project—the renovation of the old train station—without Opportunity Zone funds. But the true test of OZs is yet to come: will the tax break lure other investors to put up office buildings adjacent to the station, perhaps a corporate headquarters?

Blueprint's man on the ground in Baltimore, a city native with a Stanford MBA, Chris Grant, said the firm hoped—and still hopes—to invest in small businesses within a ten-block radius of the station. Even before COVID-19, that was proving more challenging than he anticipated; the potential projects just aren't ready for Blueprint-caliber equity investments. "I've had to reset my expectations," he says.

If you're keeping score, I'd found one small project, Schreiber's, that was very close to what the EIG boys and Tim Scott talked about. I'd found one huge, already subsidized development that squeezed itself into an Opportunity Zone; it offers wealthy investors a juicy tax break for a real estate deal that is, with Goldman Sachs's backing, relatively low risk. And I'd found two significant projects—Yard 56 and Penn Station—that probably would have happened without OZs. I kept looking.

PROSPER ON FAYETTE: FILLING A HOLE

Jill Homan is an OZ evangelist. She grew up in suburban Baltimore, worked for one of Maryland's Republican congressmen, got a master's degree at Duke with a thesis on how small revitalization programs affect residents of a community, and dived into real estate in the mid-2000s. She heard about OZs around the time the Tax Cuts and Jobs Act passed at the end of 2017 and was sold almost instantly.

Homan decided to focus all her energy on Opportunity Zones—raising money from OZ investors, advising others on how to invest and attract OZ money, and sending a weekly email "designed to highlight the positive change Opportunity Zones are making throughout the United States" to a couple of thousand people. "My family wishes I'd quit talking about it so much," she says.[25]

In Baltimore, she did more than talk. For years there were dreams of replacing the vacant buildings and empty lots that sit between the University of Maryland, Baltimore campus and the decaying Lexington Market, a food hall that dates to 1782 and is now being rebuilt. The first plan to fill the site with apartments for students flopped in 2014. "We struggled because Baltimore struggles," says the master developer for the site, Shaffin Jetha.

In early 2018, Homan joined a reconfigured version of the project. She and her partner, a student housing developer called RISE: A Real Estate Company, raised $20 million from individual OZ investors to finance a $50 million "luxury student housing" project, as the construction banners on the site proclaimed. It has fully furnished units for 314 students and retail on the ground floor. Prosper on Fayette—"Don't just live, *prosper*," the ads say—boasts a fitness center, roof top terrace and lounge, outdoor courtyard, and kitchens with granite countertops and stainless steel appliances. Occupancy was slated for Summer 2021.

"I jokingly say we're gentrifying cars because we're buying a parking lot, and we're displacing the cars," says Homan.[26]

To finance an adjacent $30 million Marriott SpringHill Suites hotel, the lobby of which will incorporate a 125-year-old bank building, Jetha talked to several potential equity investors; most weren't interested. Once the financing for the housing was set, he took the hotel project to Atlanta's Peachtree Hotel Group, which began raising money for its OZ fund in the fall of 2018. "In those early days of Opportunity Zones," he says, "funds raised a lot of money and had to place it relatively quickly." The hotel project found favor with OZ investors because, he says, it wasn't in a terrible neighborhood but on the border between a "reasonably good" neighborhood and a bad one. The project also got a lift from reduced property taxes from the city.

So would it have happened without the OZ tax incentive?

At Peachtree—whose $200 million OZ fund has invested in a dozen hotels in second-tier cities like Baltimore, Indianapolis, and Saint Louis—Executive Vice President Brian Waldman says the Baltimore deal worked because investors understood they have to hold it for ten years. (A ten-year hold means accepting a lower rate of return than investing in a new hotel project that can be sold a couple of years after it's finished. The tax break compensates for that.) Compared to other OZ investments he has seen, the Baltimore hotel is the best example of OZs doing what they're supposed to do: spur investment in a blighted neighborhood that just needed a nudge.

Says Jetha: "There's a high likelihood—let's say an 80 percent chance—it wouldn't have happened without some more public subsidy, and that's what OZs are. There was a lot of attention placed on locations like this one because of the law."

Prosper on Fayette obviously won't be providing affordable or workforce housing for Baltimoreans, and the hotel, though it'll create jobs, won't either. But in this case, the OZ tax break seems to have come closer to the stated objectives: it has led to development on an abandoned site in a decayed neighborhood on the cusp of renewal.

Of course, the pitch for Opportunity Zones going back to the Bernstein-Hassett white paper and the EIG talking points was that *this* tax break would be different from all its predecessors because it would seed all sorts of businesses that would create jobs for people who live in OZs. Indeed, in an interview, Sean Parker volunteers Baltimore as an example. He says he hopes the OZ tax incentive will persuade Johns Hopkins biotech experts to establish and grow their start-ups in Baltimore instead of taking them to biotech centers such as Cambridge, Massachusetts, or Bethesda, Maryland. So I went searching for OZ businesses in Baltimore.

SURGICAL ROBOT START-UP: ICING ON THE CAKE

Galen Robotics, founded in 2016 to commercialize technology licensed from Johns Hopkins, is developing surgeon-controlled robots that eliminate even slight hand tremors during delicate otolaryngological and spinal surgery. Think power steering for surgeons.

Galen was doing fine in Redwood City, California, though the company had strong ties to Baltimore and was recruiting Johns Hopkins engineering grad students. Ben Seigel heard about the firm from a Johns Hopkins administrator and called the CEO.

"Ben said, 'Would you be interested in moving to Baltimore?' There were twenty of us and we said, 'Fat chance, but send us a proposal,'" says CEO Bruce Lichorowic. Seigel outlined various subsidies Maryland offers to encourage businesses to move to the state. "We said, 'What's California giving us?'" Lichorowic says. The firm and its executives moved to Baltimore in 2019—without any serious attention to the OZ tax break.

Lichorowic wanted space where the rent was low and there wasn't much of a crime problem. After a brief stay at a local incubator, Galen landed at 1100 Wicomico Street, a then largely empty, hulking eight-story brick structure built in 1915 for a Lithuanian immigrant's burgeoning wholesale business—with elevators, conveyers, interior driveways, and railroad tracks. (One elevator is big enough to hold a Mini Cooper, the developer boasts.)

The building, which shares a parking lot with the Baltimore Ravens football stadium about half a mile away, happens to be in one of the city's Opportunity Zones. That allows Galen to qualify as an OZ business. If the firm makes it big, any new investors will be able to escape capital gains taxes on their profits, provided they hold on for ten years. Galen drew a small slice of its initial $10 million in capital from an OZ fund launched in late 2019 by Len Mills, a College Park, Maryland, economist and former Fannie Mae portfolio manager who is now trying his hand as a money manager. On top of the federal OZ tax break on capital gains, Maryland offered Mills a state income tax credit for half of his investment (up to $250,000 a year) targeted at investors in early stage biotech companies located in OZs. As of February 2021, Mills's fund had raised a total of about $2.5 million, much of it from family and friends—not Silicon Valley scale.

Lichorowic is enjoying the PR glow that accompanied the OZ status, and fans of OZs talk as if almost anything that happens in an Opportunity Zone is solely because of the program. "Galen Robotics Shows How the Opportunity Zone Program Can Fund Startups," said one headline.[27] "This Tech Company Is the First to Get a Boost from Moving to a Baltimore Opportunity Zone. Are More Coming?" asked another.[28] "From Silicon Valley to Baltimore: Opportunity Zone Lures Surgical Robot Maker and Opens New Investment," said a third.[29] Not surprisingly, the firm got a shout-out in a May 2020 report on OZs from Trump's White House Opportunity and Revitalization Council.[30]

But state tax incentives—the old-fashioned kind that states use to lure out-of-state companies—and the Hopkins-trained workforce were key to Galen's decision to leave California, Lichorowic says. The OZ tax incentive? "It was basically icing on the cake."

FROM THE NFL TO ANIMATION: GETS ME IN THE ROOM

Trevor Pryce's fledging animation studio is an Opportunity Zone business by accident. After fourteen years as an NFL defensive lineman—five with the Baltimore Ravens—Pryce successfully transitioned to business.[31] He was an investor in an online music business and turned his children's books about an army of frogs into a Netflix cartoon series called *Kulipari*. In February 2019, the forty-three-year-old launched a new project—an animation studio called

Outlook OVFX—in space leased from Baltimore's Maryland Institute College of Art (MICA).

The college was not in an OZ, and Pryce says that when he finally heard about Opportunity Zones he didn't understand them. Then MICA decided it needed his company's space and kicked Pryce out. He found an ideal replacement in a 135-year-old brick building that once housed a lithography business—it went bankrupt in 1981—and was being renovated. It also happened to be in an OZ on Baltimore's east side. "It was pure, dumb luck that we happened to be an Opportunity Zone," he says.

Fortune or not, being in an OZ did make it easier for him to find investors. "They don't understand what we are doing, but they do understand that we're an Opportunity Zone business. I get into rooms that I wouldn't otherwise get into," he says. Pryce has raised money from three OZ investors, including from Len Mills, who was introduced to Pryce by the Blueprint Local folks. Pryce won't say how much he has raised, but it's enough to expand his payroll from thirty-three in October 2020 to forty-five in March 2021.

Nonetheless, Pryce isn't entirely an OZ fan. Too much of the money is going into real estate and not enough into operating businesses. "It seems like it's just a place for rich people to hide their money," he says.

Pryce understands real estate's appeal: there's a ceiling on how much you can make on a building, but there's also a floor—you always have a physical asset. With a start-up business there's no ceiling, but there's also no floor: you can lose everything. But delivering opportunity to people who live in an OZ requires more than "plopping money down for a piece of real estate," he says.

Perhaps there are more OZ-funded deals soon to arrive in Baltimore. In the rapidly gentrifying, once industrial neighborhood of Canton, a couple of miles east of the Inner Harbor, veteran local developer Mark Sapperstein is putting his own capital gains into a five-story office building (made of cross-laminated timber like the one Sturgeon is building in Portland) on a vacant lot. He says he is enjoying the tax break for a project he would have done anyhow.

But if there are other consequential OZ projects in Baltimore, I couldn't find them—and I looked. In the fall of 2020, the state of Maryland said all the state's OZ projects of which it was aware—undoubtedly an incomplete list—added up to just $150 million, which is roughly what OZ investors have put into *a single building* in downtown Portland. The OZ tax break hasn't, at least so far, drawn a lot of money to Baltimore for projects that meet Bob Embry's "but for" test or projects that will turn around troubled neighborhoods.

Baltimore is not, at least not yet, an OZ success story. After dozens of interviews in the city, Sandra Newman of Johns Hopkins and Michael Snidal, a Baltimore resident who is a graduate student at Columbia University, concluded that the Opportunity Zone incentive "is stimulating investment conversations and local government capacity, but it is failing at . . . changing development outcomes."[32]

"In Baltimore," says Blueprint's Ross Baird, "there was a lot of buzz and attention to Opportunity Zones. There was a lot of hype. There was a lot of excitement. A lot of people said we are going to get a lot of investment in Baltimore. Then there was a high-profile project that wasn't the intent of the program—Kevin Plank and Port Covington. There was a little bit of a backlash."

"The fear of tax havens creating waves of gentrification? There hasn't been money that's going into that yet. There are green shoots of really positive programs across the city," he added. "The city is obviously struggling. Opportunity Zones didn't turn it around overnight."

Ben Seigel still thinks OZs "could really make a difference in Baltimore," coupled with other public subsidies. But he says to do so in a big way will require major changes to the law, such as offering bigger tax breaks for those who invest in the worst-off zones.

He isn't giving up, though. At the start of 2021, he secured another year of funding from the Abell Foundation to keep trying to find Baltimore a date for the prom.

CHAPTER TWELVE

No Guardrails

Let's talk about his Opportunity Zones

The $100 billion lie this motherfucker proposed

Saying he'd pour the money into the hood, but, you know, the thing about money is we can track where it actually goes

At best, it's been invested in expensive student housing

But the rest of where he's spending it is even more astounding

When a man can claim he's spreading out the national wealth by pouring it in storage units and his high-rise hotels

—DAVEED DIGGS, INSTAGRAM, SEPTEMBER 20, 2020

THE POINT OF OPPORTUNITY ZONES, CONGRESS AND THE Treasury said repeatedly, is "to encourage economic growth and investment in designated distressed communities." As a goal, that's clear. However, nothing in the statute that created Opportunity Zones nor in the regulations that implemented them even defines, let alone requires, that OZ funds pursue that objective. The only criteria are geographic—with just a few exceptions.

Lifting a provision from the New Market Tax Credits statute, the OZ law does bar the tax break for investments on a very specific list of what are colloquially known as "sin businesses."[1] So, you can't enjoy a capital gains tax break for investing in a golf course, country club, massage parlor, hot tub facility, tanning parlor, racetrack, casino, or liquor store. Almost anything else goes.

Legal cannabis businesses offer one example of just how far anything goes. Presumably they would have been included on the NMTC's list of sin businesses along with liquor stores. But since such businesses didn't exist in the 1990s, the NMTC law doesn't mention them. As Treasury Secretary Mnuchin told a Senate hearing, in his view, putting money into cannabis businesses "is not the intent" of the OZ law, but he couldn't cite anything in the rules prohibiting that.[2] Without any ban, the inevitable happened. In January 2019, a real estate company called Canna-Hub announced to prospective investors that its biggest development—with sites for growing and other cannabis-related businesses—is within an Opportunity Zone in Williams, California, a small town fifty miles north of Sacramento, home of what is reputedly the world's largest tomato paste factory.[3]

A more common practice, investing in high-end apartment buildings for college students, is allowed—as Daveed Diggs, who played Jefferson and Lafayette in the original production of *Hamilton*, so accurately rapped in his forty-five-second get-out-the-vote Instagram post in the fall of 2020. Self-storage facilities, which create practically no jobs, are likewise kosher. So are big data centers or server farms—as seen in Storey County, Nevada—which do generate local property taxes and revenues for the local electric utility, but hardly any jobs.

Sean Parker, Tim Scott, and the EIG boys wanted and delivered an incentive with only a few guardrails. Their pitch: restrain the bureaucracy and let investors and the market identify the most promising investments. They got their wish. But while some money did flow to designated communities, it didn't necessarily invest in real estate or businesses that would do much for the poor neighborhoods and people who live in them—as Rev. Donté Hickman discovered in East Baltimore. Self-storage and high-end student housing illustrate the downsides of a no-guardrails approach.

THE FOUR Ds

The American self-storage industry, according to industry lore, dates to Texas of the late 1960s, when entrepreneurs began renting prefab garages to people who had more stuff than their homes could hold. The business model, namely building cheap structures on cheap real estate—vacant land, infill sites, parking lots near the periphery of populated areas—caught on.

The chief executive of the biggest company in the industry once said demand is driven by the four Ds—death, divorce, disaster, and dislocation.[4] And there's almost always plenty of the four Ds to create demand. Thanks to a boom in self-storage construction that began in 2016, there are today 1.7 billion square feet of self-storage in the United States. That's 5.4 square feet per person and almost three times the land area of Manhattan.[5] One in every eleven households rents a unit. More than $4.5 billion a year was spent building new self-storage facilities in each of the past three years.[6]

Although the business is dominated by a few large, publicly traded companies, there are scores of small investors in the facilities, which, when well-managed, can throw off lots of cash. Self-storage facilities can fill an empty lot or make a vacant warehouse useful, but they create next to no jobs and do not encourage economic growth. Yet they fit cleanly within the OZ rules.

As word about OZs spread, the self-storage trade press—yes, there is one—was sprinkled with headlines about the potential benefits of OZs. A typical example from *Inside Self Storage*: "Opportunity Zones: A New Self-Storage Investment Option with Great Benefits."[7]

In July 2018, Jimmy Day, a businessman who is also a competitive bicyclist in the sixty-plus category, sold fifty Aaron's rent-to-own franchises to the parent company for what he says was about $80 million, giving him a $15 million capital gain—and a potential tax bill of about $3 million.[8]

"As I looked around for how to shelter that income, an attorney mentioned something very new coming on the scene called Opportunity Zones," Day recalls. "So I did some research and I found that it was legitimate—that I could defer, not abolish, the tax for a period of time." He looked around to see where OZs were located and discovered one was in South San Antonio, encompassing a 1,300-acre mixed-used development going up on land that until 2011 was Brooks Air Force Base.

Day called the head of the city-run Brooks Development Authority, Leo Gomez, and asked what the community needed most. Self-storage, Gomez told him. Day did some checking and discovered that the only self-storage facilities in South San Antonio were outmoded, 1970s-style. So he created his own OZ fund and spent $12.5 million of his capital gains to buy a nine-acre parcel and build a three-story, climate-controlled facility with some additional "flex space" that may be used for a day care center. He expects about 60 percent of the units to be rented by households with stuff to store and 40 percent by small businesses. The local newspaper celebrated it as "Texas' First 'Opportunity Zone' Investment Under Trump Tax Bill."[9]

Day acknowledges that self-storage facilities don't create many jobs, which is one of the stated intents of the program. "Perhaps it was a mistake to write the law that way," he said. "And I think they're thinking about changing the law, but they should rethink that a little bit."

"Although I'm not a big employer there, I am bringing something very nice to the citizens that otherwise they would not have had. And isn't that also the purpose of the law?" he added, without even the slightest hint that he realized how absurd this sounded. "Should these 500,000 people be sentenced to impoverishment and denied the nicer things in life that they have in the better suburbs? No, they should not. This law brings them this nice storage facility. Yes, it did. That seems like a legitimate social purpose to me."

Whether it's self-storage or luxury hotels:

Don't blame the players, blame the game.

Mike Wagner used to be a physical therapist who dabbled in real estate on the side. Now he owns a few self-storage sites outright and runs an advisory business called The Storage Rebellion, coaching would-be investors in self-storage in exchange for a stake—perhaps 15 or 20 percent—if they go into the business.[10]

In August 2018, he and his wife sold a self-storage facility for a profit and expected to face a significant, for them, capital gains tax bill. In December of that year, he heard about OZs. Wagner bit. He formed his own OZ fund (perfectly legal) and, with the 180-day clock ticking (this was before the IRS extended the deadlines during the pandemic), he looked around for an OZ property in the Carolinas, where he already had holdings, that he could convert into self-storage. He spent $260,000 to buy two vacant warehouses in Dillon, South Carolina, in a neighborhood that appeared to be taking a turn for the better.

Converting existing buildings into self-storage is particularly well suited for OZs because of the requirement that investors spend at least as much on improvements as on the initial purchase. The Dillon conversion proved to be, as Wagner puts it, "a project and a half" with unanticipated structural problems. He spent about $1.2 million and opened Dillon Storage Center in July 2020.

How many workers will he employ? I ask. None, Wagner tells me. He says the facility is completely automated and all transactions are done online.

Don't blame the players, blame the game.

There's no way to know how much OZ money has gone into self-storage. West of Dallas, a developer with millions of dollars in OZ money is putting up a Texas-sized facility with 1,255 units.[11] In Florida, Jeanine Warhurst Blake, whose family founded and sold the PODS (portable self-storage units that can be parked outside your house) business, started an OZ fund that's investing in a self-storage facility off the interstate in Fort Myers. In Los Angeles, Kevin Staley, a prominent real estate developer, is using OZ fund money to demolish an old industrial building and build a 109,000-square-foot "state-of-the-art self-storage facility." An OZ fund organized by former New Jersey governor Chris Christie and a real estate company run by one of his longtime allies raised $45.5 million as of August 2020.[12] One of its first investments: a four-story, 100,000-square-foot CubeSmart brand self-storage facility in a strip mall along I-95 in New London, Connecticut.[13]

Shay Hawkins, the former Tim Scott aide, tells me he regrets not adding a line to the OZ law that would have added self-storage to the sin businesses list.

But Scott doesn't see the need. The federal government doesn't need to tell local governments what should or shouldn't be built in their communities, he says. "They shouldn't have to depend on the federal government to say this is a good business or this is a bad business."

BED-BATH PARITY

In college towns across the country, billions have been invested in high-end, privately owned apartments for students. The properties usually are leased by the bed as opposed to by the apartment. They often boast state-of-the-art gyms, game rooms, and roof-decks. Managing the properties can be a challenge—these are college kids, after all—but parents generally guarantee the rent, owners can raise the rent nearly every year, and promoters of student housing as an investment routinely deem it to be "recession proof," though that was before COVID-19.

Since 2010, the industry has added four hundred thousand beds, most near big state universities. Even before the pandemic disrupted higher education, some industry analysts were warning of an over-supply; others see the pandemic creating new demand for students to avoid crowded dorms. In any event, student housing is now large enough to be considered what investment pros call an "asset class" of its own. Industry estimates say more than $10 billion a year go into developing, buying, and selling these buildings.[14]

Before OZs, Jackson Dearborn Partners, a Chicago developer, had been planning to build student housing on the site of what had been a nursing home adjacent to the fifty-thousand-student University of Illinois flagship campus in Urbana-Champaign. The university and local officials began redeveloping the neighborhood's commercial district, known as Campustown, about twenty years ago; there's been a student housing building boom there since 2012, Jackson Dearborn tells prospective investors.

One day someone mentioned to Ryan Tobias, a partner and co-founder of the firm, that the property was in an Opportunity Zone; he can't recall when or whom. "Opportunity Zones found us," he says.

Jackson Dearborn already had experience raising money from wealthy investors and family offices (as opposed to big institutional investors), so shifting to OZ-fundraising looked like an easy step. The firm started Campustown Opportunity Fund I to raise equity for the student housing projects in early 2019 and had no trouble hitting its $10 million goal by June of that year, even though the Treasury Department hadn't issued the final regulations yet. That $10 million came from just eleven investors. It projected a 16 percent annual rate of return on their initial investment.[15] A second fund was launched in April 2020 and raised another $8.5 million for student housing nearby.[16]

Construction is now underway at 309 East Springfield Avenue on a six-story, 276-bed building with what is known in the business as "bed-to-bath parity," which means every student gets his or her own bathroom. Amenities include a fitness center, a lounge, a business center, fast internet, and a second-floor deck with an outdoor grilling area. The building is to be ready by the start of the 2021–2022 school year. The Campustown OZ fund is also investing in three similar buildings going up nearby, each of which advertises granite countertops and stainless steel kitchen appliances, among other amenities.[17]

Tobias says Jackson Dearborn has a few other OZ projects—an upscale seventy-six-unit apartment building and retail space in downtown Lafayette, Indiana, and an affordable housing project in Madison, Wisconsin—that better fit the law's goal of boosting distressed communities. But these?

"Campustown really shouldn't be an Opportunity Zone," he says. "It's student housing. There's a flurry of development there without any incentives. It looks like a low-income tract because it has a lot of kids with zero income."

Don't blame the players, blame the game.

Jared Hutter, another small player in the student housing business, signed a contract for a property near the University of Louisville in

Kentucky in January 2018. As his firm, Aptitude, was going through the permitting process, he discovered the site was in an Opportunity Zone. After consulting lawyers and accountants, he pitched the OZ option to investors. Some weren't interested; some were. So he restructured the project, created an OZ fund, and says between 40 and 45 percent of the equity capital for the deal is OZ money. The fund is structured so Aptitude doesn't have to hold the building for a full ten years but can sell it and put the money in another OZ project and still get the tax benefits.[18]

In October 2018, Aptitude broke ground on The Marshall Louisville, which it describes as a ten-story "luxury student living complex" with a fifty-inch TV as well as a washer and dryer in every unit, indoor parking, a twenty-four-hour gym, a rooftop terrace with views of the university's stadium, a courtyard with a large projection screen for outdoor movies, and "game rooms for students to relax with unobstructed views of the iconic Churchill Downs."[19]

Don't blame the players, blame the game.

Similar OZ funds popped up across the country. For instance, Alpha Capital Partners, a Pittsburgh real estate firm, discovered that 40 percent of the student housing it already owned was in an OZ. In October 2018, it launched an OZ fund to invest up to $250 million in student and multifamily housing—and claimed it had $95 million in funding lined up at the start. Among its first projects was the $12.5 million purchase of a rundown apartment building linked by a pedestrian bridge to the campus of the University of Louisiana in Lafayette. Rehab of the building was "supported by significant capital that would not have been possible without the Opportunity Zone program," Alpha's CEO says.[20] As with many OZ projects, this one also won local property tax abatements.

The 342-bed student housing facility includes "a swimming pool with LED lighting, cybercafé with free printing and a host of other amenities," the firm says. That project won Alpha the White House seal of approval: the site was a stop on an August 2019 tour of OZ projects led by Scott Turner, the former NFL player turned director of the Trump White House Opportunity and Revitalization Council.[21]

THE BACKLASH

Opportunity Zones, by design, allowed investors to put money into almost anything in an Opportunity Zone and get the tax break. The EIG boys and their allies excluded any government entity (other than local zoning authorities) from any approval or oversight. Empowered government bureaucrats and intermediaries, they argued, were the reason the New Markets Tax Credit and the Low-Income Housing Tax Credit had failed to transform left-behind communities. But capital mostly flows to where it can earn the highest return, not to where it has the greatest social impact—namely places where it would, as OZs are supposed to, encourage economic growth and investment in designated distressed communities.

Claiming OZ tax treatment for self-storage and luxury student housing is clearly legal. But headlines and rap songs decrying the use of the tax break for property and businesses for which public subsidies seem either inappropriate or unnecessary led to calls for narrowing the scope of OZs.

Michael Milken's Milken Institute suggested to the Treasury that it add private prisons to the sin businesses list. "Given that a significant number of residents of Opportunity Zones suffer from mass incarceration, providing tax benefits to enterprises (i.e., private prisons) that profit from these activities would be in direct conflict with the spirit of Opportunity Zones," it said in a comment letter to the IRS.[22]

Ron Wyden, now chair of the Senate Finance Committee, has proposed banning the OZ tax break for future investments in self-storage and sports stadiums and limiting investments in rental properties to those in which more than half of the tenants have incomes below 50 percent of the area's median income. Joe Biden's campaign platform said he would "direct" the Treasury to "review" OZs to make sure the investors provided "clear economic, social, and environmental benefits to a community, and not just high returns—like those from luxury apartments or luxury hotels—to investors."[23]

CHAPTER THIRTEEN

Doing Good

E VEN AFTER WITNESSING THE OZ EXPO IN LAS VEGAS, immersing myself in stories from the OZ-fueled student housing and self-storage "asset classes," and sitting with the OZ-financed developers of downtown Portland's biggest new buildings, I figured somebody someplace must be exploiting the tax break as intended. There are 8,764 Opportunity Zones; surely a few must be in struggling neighborhoods that got investments that benefit the people who live there—investments that wouldn't have been made otherwise. In short, I looked for projects like the ones Tim Scott and Cory Booker talk about.

I did find some. Whether they represent the bulk of OZ projects or the admirable minority is another question, one made infinitely harder to answer by the lack of reporting requirements. Either way, examples of Opportunity Zones done right are a part of the bigger narrative—affordable housing in South Los Angeles, a wealthy Chicago couple with a windfall to invest, a family in rural Indiana resuscitating a small-town Main Street, a partner of a slain rap artist promoting OZs as a way to bring investment to impoverished communities, and an ambitious business-led effort to rescue downtown Erie, Pennsylvania.

SOLA IMPACT

In Los Angeles, Martin Muoto of SoLa Impact is a justly celebrated exemplar of what OZs can be.

Muoto grew up in Nigeria, the son of a Nigerian father and a Polish mother; his parents met while his dad was studying at a Polish medical school. In 1989, Muoto followed his older brother to the United States, went to the University of Pennsylvania's Wharton School on a scholarship, and spent several years working in private equity on deals like Priceline and Fandango. His job then took him to Los Angeles where, in 2006, he began buying and renovating, primarily on nights and weekends, small apartment buildings in the Venice and Echo Park neighborhoods. Around 2008, he turned his attention to South LA, figuring the community had a lot of undervalued, overlooked properties that could potentially deliver good returns.[1] Largely Black and Hispanic, South LA—which includes the South Central, Watts, and Compton neighborhoods—is a mix of aging mom-and-pop storefronts, stucco homes with security gates, the remnants of manufacturing activity, and very few hints of gentrification. With his own money, Muoto bought several South LA properties and managed them himself.

In 2012, Muoto and an acquaintance, Gray Lusk—who migrated to LA immediately after graduating from East Carolina University and ended up in real estate—started a property management firm. They discovered landlords were reluctant to maintain and improve the buildings they owned, so the pair started to buy their own. In 2014, their outfit, SoLa Impact, raised $10 million from wealthy friends and family—enough to buy and renovate thirty-five buildings. The basic investment thesis was that the stigma of South LA depressed real estate prices and frightened away potential landlords, even though there were plenty of reliable tenants.

"Our goal was to rent to the best tenants in difficult neighborhoods," says Lusk. "In reality, the vast majority of tenants are reliable. However, there is a small percentage that are inconsistent, and many landlords deal with it by painting everyone with a broad brush." Two-thirds of SoLa's tenants get federal Section 8 rent subsidy vouchers; half have been homeless at some point in their lives. In 2017, Muoto and Lusk stepped up their operation, raising $55 million from a wider net of about thirty wealthy investors and family offices over nine months. That paid for another 130 buildings, nearly all of them built in the 1960s or before and ranging from eight to thirty units each. According to SoLa, most of these units are rented to local residents; nearly all the tenants are racial minorities. When SoLa buys a building, most tenants end up staying, although the company has been criticized by groups who claim it is overly strict about building rules and pet policies.

Up to this point, Muoto and Lusk had never tapped any federal incentives, not the Low-Income Housing Tax Credit nor the New Markets Tax Credit, and they hadn't heard much about Opportunity Zones. That changed when Jeremy Keele, the impact investor from Jim Sorenson's orbit in Utah, heard about SoLa from a friend of a friend and went to LA to see what Muoto was doing. "I remember showing him the OZ map and superimposed his target market over it and it was a clean fit," Keele says.

Muoto and Lusk weren't interested. "We said, 'Don't bother us right now. We are heads down and in the middle of deploying capital. And we haven't gotten much help from the government, so this probably won't apply to us,'" Lusk recalls.

Keele was persistent. He called back a while later and said, "You're idiots if you don't do this." This time, they took his advice and hopped aboard the OZ train, crisscrossing the country to speak to potential investors in a never-ending road show. "It was like being on the first date over and over again," Lusk says. But it was a providential decision. In just twelve weeks in 2019, SoLa raised $115 million[2]—$15 million more than their goal—from OZ investors, Keele's Catalyst Opportunity Funds among them.[3] Given that it had taken them nine months to raise less than half of that sum, Muoto and Lusk were awed. "I don't think we've gotten more articulate or better looking," Lusk says.

Most of the OZ money has gone to new construction. By mid-December 2020, they'd deployed about $90 million of it and had almost a dozen buildings under construction. The plan is to build more than 1,200 affordable housing units in buildings between twenty-five and ninety units each; any larger and construction triggers time-consuming zoning and environmental reviews. About 10 percent of the OZ money is going to renovate 92,000 square feet spread across six red brick warehouses, dubbed The Beehive, to house embryonic businesses, including an Afro-Caribbean, women-led café and a Black-owned craft beer brewery.[4]

SoLa is more than a landlord; it has a "social impact" staff of ten that counsels tenants, partners with other organizations to offer social services, and, through a nonprofit affiliate, offers scholarships. All this has brought it a measure of celebrity—it got a $1 million contribution from Oprah Winfrey's foundation—and more funding from corporations and banks.[5] The operation drew a visit from HUD Secretary Carson and White House OZ czar Scott Turner, but Muoto and Lusk have yet to meet Sean Parker.

Muoto is now a combination cheerleader and conscience for the OZ crowd. "A lot of the narrative out there is that Opportunity Zones are just a tax break for the rich. In reality, OZs have the potential of bringing billions of dollars to communities that have been starved for capital—these are often urban, Black and brown communities," he says. At first, he was pleased to be thrust into the limelight by the OZ crowd, as it gave him a chance to talk about what OZs could do. He still enjoys the attention, but since has realized they were more interested in getting him publicity to soften the image of OZs than in following him. When his firm began offering training to workers laid off due to the pandemic, he hoped other OZ-financed real estate investors would join him. "I wasn't looking to lead the effort. I was looking to hear from others, 'Look, we understand we're getting a tax benefit. We're all doing something—a food drive, a tech drive, helping your tenants find financial assistance.' But no one bellied up."

"It is unfortunate that a lot of OZ funds appear not to focus on true social impact," Muoto says. "Some investors are skeptical that you can have both social impact and market-rate returns. We strongly believe socially responsible investing actually improves returns."

Muoto's preaching drew SoLa attention from mayors across the country eager for help in replicating its enterprise and, following the rise of the Black Lives Matter movement, from some financial institutions looking to put money behind their promises (and Community Reinvestment Act requirements) to invest in Black and brown communities. So in December 2020, SoLa announced plans to raise a $500 million OZ fund to invest in cities across the country, plus a $500 million fund to invest outside of OZs. "Sometimes a part of a community should be an OZ and isn't," Lusk says, noting that only one-third of South LA is designated as an OZ. "And sometimes the building across the street from an Opportunity Zone is a better deal." (As of March 2021, SoLa had commitments for $150 million in investments for the two funds.)

The plan, with its audacious $1 billion goal, is to invest the money over three years, starting in Los Angeles, Oakland, and San Diego, and then in the Pacific Northwest and beyond. SoLa says 13 percent of the asset appreciation and fees will go to a new nonprofit, the Black Impact Community Fund, that will, among other things, offer social services and build condos and townhomes to sell at cost to local residents. "We are focused on finding ways that wealth is created for the residents in the Opportunity Zones, not just for investors."

THE BILLIONAIRE PHILANTHROPISTS

In Chicago, Jim Casselberry manages money for 4S Bay Partners, the family office for wealthy philanthropists Steve and Jessica Sarowitz.[6] The Sarowitzes became billionaires after taking their payroll-processing company, Paylocity, public in 2014, but maintain a down-to-earth lifestyle. They own one house, Steve drives a slightly dented Toyota Camry, and they have pledged to give away at least a billion dollars. Casselberry puts it simply, "I work for a family who is interested in philanthropy and wants to manage its tax liability."

Casselberry, a University of Chicago MBA who has been in the investment management business for thirty-five years, first heard about OZs in June 2018 from an OZ enthusiast, Aron Betru of the Milken Institute, at a conference of social impact–focused Black venture capitalists and money managers. OZs seemed a perfect fit. At his urging, the Sarowitzes created their own OZ fund. Casselberry figured it was a no-brainer: "If nothing else, I defer my taxes. If it works, great. If not, I can donate the land or something."

Here's one example: The Chicago Cook Workforce Partnership, which coordinates workforce training programs in the area, was looking for a new home for offices and classrooms. Steve Sarowitz offered to donate money to buy a vacant building in the largely Black Chatham neighborhood, on the city's South Side. But, Casselberry says, nobody wanted to accept the money and take responsibility for owning the building. One day something clicked: the Sarowitzes' OZ fund bought the building for about $2 million, invested another $1 million to finish construction, and is renting it to the partnership—but not to get a market rate return. If the rent is sufficient to cover the property taxes, that'll be enough, Casselberry says.

In July 2020, 4S Bay Partners invested in another Opportunity Zone project, this time buying four adjacent two-story office buildings in the Baldwin Hills neighborhood in South LA.[7] However, Casselberry has had trouble finding other groups willing to favor socially beneficial projects over profits. "The biggest surprise and disappointment—I thought we'd find aligned investors to invest with us," he says. "We have not. It comes down simply to this: people who have advisers who are stuck on maximizing financial return, not economic return," the latter encompassing the broader benefits to society.

AN INDIANA WINDFALL

Mick and Jenny Wilz have lived for forty-five years in the softly rolling hills on the southeastern edge of Indiana. Over much of that time, they've been boosters of the nearby town of Brookville, where they opened Third Place—a combination shared workspace, tavern, and event hall. In spring 2018, when they heard about Opportunity Zones, Mick and his brother already were planning to sell their majority stake in the family business—Sur-Seal, an industrial-seal manufacturing company—to a private equity firm. At the instigation of their accountants, the Wilzes decided to create their own OZ fund to shelter their seven-figure capital gain and began looking for local investment opportunities.

Brookville prospered in the nineteenth century as a gateway to the Northwest Territory, but its fortunes have declined since the mid-twentieth century. Commerce in downtown largely dried up when an interstate highway bypassed Brookville in the 1960s. In the 1970s, the Army Corps of Engineers created a reservoir in nearby

Lake Brookville, which draws millions of boaters, anglers, and other tourists, but the town sees few of those tourist dollars. While visitors have to drive down Main Street to get to the lake, they rarely stop, except perhaps at McDonald's or to fill their gas tanks. The town's population peaked in 1980 and has steadily declined since then. Today, there are about 2,500 residents, only a few hundred more than in 1890, though the surrounding area has grown as a bedroom community for Cincinnati.

Brookville's downtown, untouched by urban renewal, features well-preserved nineteenth century, three-story brick structures laid out on a precise grid of Midwestern streets. Across Main Street from the stately county courthouse and a small park sits one such building, the Valley House Hotel. Built in 1852, the hotel went out of business soon after the Greyhound bus station closed in 1976. It was shuttered for decades, ending up on the list of the state's ten most endangered historic landmarks.[8]

Around 2014, Bruce Rippe, a venture capitalist and manufacturing executive from nearby Batesville, began trying to put together a deal to buy the historic hotel and build an annex behind it with apartments for "active adults 55+." He planned twenty-seven units of affordable housing financed by Low-Income Housing Tax Credits and Historic Tax Credits and twenty market-rate apartments with conventional financing. However, the banks balked and Rippe had to cut back plans to add a fourth floor; he also settled on ten instead of twenty market-rate apartments.

Four years later, in 2018, the state designated downtown Brookville as one of the 156 OZs in the state. Mick and Jenny Wilz already had a connection to Valley House. For years, Mick had secretly, and without anyone's permission, repaired leaks in its roof. In May 2019, the housing project became their first OZ investment after they agreed to invest $2.2 million in what's now called Valley House Flats. Their money allowed Rippe to add back the fourth floor to his building plan. The town chipped in with a ten-year, 100 percent property tax abatement. The state says Valley House was the first OZ deal in Indiana.

The Wilzes' OZ adventure was just beginning, though. One day in October 2018, the three owners of the local weeklies—the Brookville Democrat and the Brookville American—came to the Wilzes' restaurant and asked if they wanted to buy the struggling newspapers along with two others that serve nearby communities. Mick Wilz was interested; he had long been unhappy with the papers' coverage. For $500,000 from their OZ fund, they bought the businesses and three buildings on Main Street.

Mick said the investment probably will be profitable in the long run. "Like drive-in movies," he says, "these little newspapers are going to come back." It is, though, he acknowledges, "more a labor of love." Like many other local papers, Brookville's struggled during the COVID-19 pandemic and got a federal Paycheck Protection Program loan to help it survive.

The Wilzes weren't done. Late in 2018, Jenny Wilz told the local economic development authority's consultant, Nick Lawrence, that the couple might be interested in investing in a hotel. Even though the area draws a lot of tourists for outdoor recreation, there are no hotels within fifteen miles of Brookville. At the time, Jenny says, it wasn't clear the Valley House deal was going to go through; the couple needed to find somewhere to invest their OZ money to meet the law's deadlines. Lawrence told her the authority already had done a feasibility study for a hotel and had been talking to the Cobblestone Inn & Suites chain.

In December, Lawrence took the Cobblestone team around Brookville. Mick Wilz was the last appointment on the agenda. He stunned Lawrence and impressed the Cobblestone delegation by laying out a detailed plan, including the piece of land in an Opportunity Zone that he was ready to buy for the hotel. Everything clicked. The Wilzes put up about $1.1 million of their capital gains for a 68 percent stake in the $5 million project; a local bank lent the rest. The forty-five-room hotel opened in October 2020.

"I knew they were great community partners," Lawrence says of the Wilzes. "I didn't imagine they'd be investors in so many projects. We caught lightning in a bottle." There aren't any OZ projects in Franklin County besides the Wilzes'.

Would Mick and Jenny Wilz have done all this even without the OZ tax incentives? No, Mick says. "We love our community, but I don't think we would've tackled three projects. Maybe the newspapers. Maybe the hotel. But, no, we could not afford to tackle all three." OZs made it financially easier for the already civic-minded couple to pursue their social goals.

"What I tell people is this," Mick says. "The retirement money— we could have held on to it and then our kids could have given it away after we died. This Opportunity Zone gave us the chance to live our dream. So we get to spend the money and see the vision come true."

A RAP STAR'S LEGACY

David Gross grew up on the streets of Los Angeles. Nearly every other male in his family was in a gang; his older brother is in jail and his younger brother was killed in a gang fight. Gross escaped to Cornell, got an MBA from NYU and a master's degree in real estate development from Columbia, and went to work on Wall Street and in real estate. He came back to LA in 2016, but lives in Santa Monica because he didn't want his kids to grow up in South Central LA. Yet Gross was committed to doing something for his old neighborhood.

Shortly after the Tax Cuts and Jobs Act passed, real estate developer Gross read about Opportunity Zones in the *New York Times*.

"I thought I wasn't understanding it correctly. This is the most substantial tax incentive I've ever heard about," he says.

He looked up EIG and saw some big names there. Among them was tech angel investor Ron Conway, who is a mentor to several NBA players. Gross called a friend in the NBA who connected him to Conway, who, in turn, connected him to Sean Parker's office and eventually to John Lettieri.

"I was pretty candid with him," says Gross. "This could be transformational, but you are going to have a pretty big PR problem. On your website, I don't see anyone familiar with the inner city. You've got no diversity.... You created a law for people outside cities to buy up these neighborhoods. When Vox or *Washington Post* writes the take-down piece, it's going to be pretty damning. You can't go and build something in the inner city without having community buy-in." (The EIG website hasn't changed. Except for the photos of Tim Scott and Cory Booker, all the faces—and all its staff—are white.)

Gross was a friend and business partner of Nipsey Hussle, a rap star and entrepreneur who was determined to lift up the LA neighborhood in which he had grown up. The pair opened Vector 90, a coworking space designed to be a small business incubator, in the largely African American Crenshaw neighborhood. Hussle (who was born Ermias Asghedom) also had been selling his popular clothing brand, Marathon, from a store located between Baba Leo's Fish Shack and Princess Insurance in an L-shaped strip mall.

Hussle and Gross bought the mall, a ten-minute drive from Vector 90, for $2.5 million in early 2019. For years they had been talking about what Gross calls "a domestic emerging-market fund" to encourage residents to invest in their own neighborhoods. For popular consumption, they called it "Buy Back the Block" or, as Hussle put it in a song, "All Money In."[9] Opportunity Zones seemed a good fit. They began the process of forming an OZ fund. (In an example of the irregularities caused by census tract borders, the strip mall itself is not in an OZ; the other side of the street is.)

On March 31, 2019, Hussle, thirty-three years old, was shot and killed in the parking lot of the strip mall he and Gross owned. A twenty-nine-year-old man with whom Hussle had argued was arrested and charged with the murder a few days later. The Marathon Store closed in May 2019, though the business survives online. Gross put aside the OZ fund paperwork for a time.

But OZ promoters knew a good thing when they saw it. As a successful Black man who'd escaped LA's poverty and gangs and succeeded at Ivy League universities and Wall Street before returning to invest in his old neighborhood, Gross was exactly what Opportunity Zones were supposed to be about. He became a celebrity on the OZ circuit as Hussle's surrogate. Gross was invited to *Forbes* OZ "summits," appearing on stage at a conference in Newark with radio host Charlamagne tha God and rapper T.I., who had been talking to Hussle about replicating his LA projects in Atlanta.[10]

"It's not a new concept: doing it for self, investing in your own, empowering your own people, hiring your own," says Charlamagne tha God. "But it's something that sometimes a lot of us tend to get away from. And [Hussle] he was a person that never got away from it and he showed and proved through actions and deeds so that's just the type of people that I vibe with."

Added T.I.: "One of my buddies who happens to be a reverend, he said this to me, he said, 'Hey, man, why is it that the answer to the problems in our community is always for us to get rich and move out and never come back?'"

As Gross had predicted, though, OZs were soon splattered with bad publicity: Amazon's decision to put its HQ2 in Long Island City, Scaramucci's hotels, the *New York Times* allegations about Michael Milken. "I didn't want to be the person writing the op-ed and using Nipsey's legacy in response to Mnuchin and Milken getting together," Gross told me. "Sean Parker needed to call out the bad actors. I genuinely believe this is a pretty robust potential tool for good, but you can't be Anthony Scaramucci saying we're going to build eight hotels."

Gross had invested in the New Orleans hotel project but pulled out when Scaramucci got in. "He is corrupting the intent of the program," Gross says.

His OZ fund hadn't taken off by the time this book went to press.

CAN A RUST BELT DOWNTOWN BE SAVED?

Erie, in the far northwest corner of Pennsylvania, holds a few unwanted titles. It is home to the poorest zip code (16501) in the entire United States—the median income in 2018 was just $11,049.[11] It has been declared "the worst city for Black Americans" based on racial economic disparities—and 16 percent of its residents are African American.[12] The city's population is around one hundred thousand, about 40 percent below its 1960 peak. Nearly 30 percent of the remaining residents live below the poverty line. A 2016 comprehensive plan found 4,700 vacant housing units; half of the city's residential properties were on blocks where at least one nearby property was "visibly distressed."[13] Acres of commercial and industrial sites were empty.

Erie is an archetypal Rust Belt community struggling to recover from the decline of American manufacturing—with one big advantage: for the past five years, downtown Erie has been the focus of a business-led economic revival initiative spurred by the city's largest employer, Erie Insurance. The company has three thousand employees in the downtown, and importantly, its CEO, an Erie native, made saving the city one of his priorities when he took over in 2016. In 2017, the insurance company and other local institutions raised about $3 million to create the Erie Downtown Development Corporation (EDDC) and an allied, for-profit $27 million fund that offers patient capital (long-term investing without expectation of a quick profit), first- and second-loss guarantees, and bridge financing for the EDDC to buy and renovate downtown buildings. All of this happened before Opportunity Zones arrived.

In 2017, as the Tax Cuts and Jobs Act was moving through Congress, John Persinger—who ran, unsuccessfully, for mayor as a Republican in 2016—and his colleague Matthew Wachter were practicing tax law at a local law firm. Wachter was poking around the text of the bill, noticed the Opportunity Zone provisions, realized that the incentive might help fund Erie's redevelopment, and ran into Persinger's office saying, "Read this. This is for us."

After checking with his brother, also a lawyer, Wachter called the newly elected mayor—a former banker—and their state legislators, explained the provision, and pitched Erie's downtown for designation. They claim to be the first locality to contact the governor's office about OZs. The beleaguered city ended up with eight of the state's three hundred OZs.

Persinger and Wachter left the law firm to become president and executive vice president of the Erie Downtown Development Corporation. They knew they were going to need more money—a lot more money—if they were going to pull off Erie's economic revival. With the funds they had, Persinger says, "it would take us twenty or twenty-five years to revitalize the downtown core, and we don't have twenty to twenty-five years."

Their effort drew attention from organizations like Accelerator for America (a group started by LA mayor Eric Garcetti that offers technical assistance to other cities) and policy wonks interested in helping troubled cities, including EIG. The Accelerator crew invited Persinger to dinner at Sean Parker's Los Angeles mansion in July 2018. After listening to what other cities were doing, Persinger came home convinced that Erie needed a polished prospectus to woo investors.

Later that year, the pair were invited to an EIG meeting in Washington where they met Jonathan Tower, a Harvard MBA and private-equity veteran who founded Arctaris Impact Investors in 2009 to direct investment to businesses and infrastructure in underserved communities. It would turn out to be a providential encounter, an example of the networking that an OZ designation has generated in some communities. As an Urban Institute team concluded in a somewhat skeptical "early assessment" of Opportunity Zones: "OZs are helping spur the evolution of a new community development ecosystem, engaging both project developers and investors who have limited historical engagement in community development work."[14]

While Erie is exactly the sort of place Parker, the EIG boys, Tim Scott, and Cory Booker describe when they talk about Opportunity Zones, Persinger and Wachter immediately recognized those features don't make it an easy sell to out-of-town investors.

"One of the things I've enjoyed the most about this is watching how different people sell their projects," Persinger says. "I was listening to a presentation by an Opportunity Zone fund in Colorado Springs. And I'm sure they didn't mean it this way, but by the time they got done selling the project, any reasonable person would say, 'Why the hell is this an Opportunity Zone?' They were selling the Garden of Eden."

Wachter, who joins my conversation with Persinger, chimes in: "We've taken the opposite approach. We realized very quickly we couldn't hide from the challenges, so we have what we've called essentially the litany of horribles that we will list." But then they quickly follow up with the pitch that goes something like this: Yes, the current appraisal value on this property is very low, but over the next ten years, it's going to go up because we're investing $100 million in this neighborhood—and we're going to "de-risk this for you" by subordinating our investment to yours.

The first dollop of OZ money came from Erie Insurance. The company is unusual: although it's a Fortune 500 company listed on the New York Stock Exchange, *all* the voting shares are still held by descendants of the man who founded it in 1925. It is a family with deep roots in Erie. The company's chairman and former CEO, Thomas Hagen, who married into the family and is number 213 on the Forbes 400 list (estimated wealth: $4 billion, more than Sean Parker), says there was talk thirty years ago of moving the headquarters to Pittsburgh, but "fortunately there were some of us around who felt more strongly about Erie."[15] With his vocal encouragement, the company began actively promoting and investing in downtown renewal well before OZs materialized. (Most other Rust Belt cities don't have a resident billionaire to supercharge their OZs.) Erie Insurance's interests are obvious: its offices are actually in one of the city's OZs and its ability to recruit and retain employees is linked to Erie's success.

The insurer has committed $75 million of its nearly $900 million investment portfolio to OZ funds that will invest in Erie, including $25 million through Arctaris.[16] In turn, Arctaris has pledged to put $50 million into Erie, a chunk of which is going to fund local building or business projects selected in a competition. Erie Insurance also has allocated $6.5 million to a new downtown food hall, where nine local women and minority vendors will have stalls; $1.2 million in Whitethorn Games, an Erie-based developer of "wholesome" video games; and an undisclosed investment in a new plastic-recycling plant.

Erie Insurance was a big winner in the Tax Cut and Jobs Act, thanks primarily to the cut in the federal corporate tax rate, its tax bill, as reported on its financial statements, fell by 30 percent in 2018.[17] Some of the savings went to cover $2,000 bonuses to nearly all of its employees.[18] The company still books more than $75 million in taxes a year. Its OZ investments will help keep that down.

Christina Marsh, the insurer's economic development chief, sees the OZ tax incentive as a welcome addition to the economic development tool kit, but says the OZ program's biggest impact wasn't financial. Rather, OZs put a spotlight on some of the city's poorest neighborhoods, galvanized energy around revitalizing them, and helped to persuade skeptical residents that the business-led downtown renewal campaign will work for them, too.

Persinger, though, says the import of OZ capital to the Erie project is that, by law, it is patient capital that has to wait ten years before cashing out if it wants the full OZ tax break. And that's the only way investing in downtown Erie makes any sense. The standard line among the real estate crowd is that OZ tax breaks won't make a bad investment good but can make a good investment great. In Erie, Wachter says, "We're making palatable investments good. But that's okay, that's enough."

ROCKEFELLER AND KRESGE TEST THE WATER

Foundations were initially skittish about Opportunity Zones, much to the frustration of the EIG boys who complain that, despite their lofty mission statements, foundations were reluctant to put billions from their endowments into socially beneficial investments. For their part, the foundations were suspicious of OZs: Why should an organization with the mission of expanding opportunities for low-income people get involved in a capital gains tax break for rich people? Foundations had experience with existing place-based tax breaks and programs for low-income communities, but OZs had none of their rules. Almost no one in the affordable housing community had been involved in developing the OZ law. Finally, the architects of OZs were, in effect, accusing the anti-poverty establishment, foundations included, of failure.

A couple of hundred-year-old foundations did take the plunge, though. The Kresge Foundation (with an endowment of $3.6 billion) and the Rockefeller Foundation ($4.4 billion) sought to steer OZ funds to make investments that would, as they put it, "create high-quality jobs and further opportunity for people with low incomes."

"No one who is seriously in our world—community development—took this seriously...until it appeared in the markup," says Aaron Seybert, who came to Kresge in 2016 to help manage its social investing after six years working on tax breaks for community development at JPMorgan Chase. "Nobody knew who these guys at EIG were. They aren't from our world."

The OZ tax break was draped in the clothing of community development, he says, but it didn't have any oversight beyond the IRS, there were no guardrails, and there was no clear articulation of the social benefit investors would provide in exchange for a tax break. However, the OZ notion of attracting equity investment to poor neighborhoods was intriguing; nearly all other government efforts focused on helping projects borrow money.

In June 2018, Kresge and Rockefeller launched what Seybert calls "a fishing expedition," advertising their interest in subsidizing OZ funds that "seek deep, positive community impact" to see who would bite.[19] Seybert thought there was a 10 percent chance of finding a project the foundations would support. They were startled to get 141 responses, ranging from a small town in rural Nevada that wanted to renovate an old gas station to multinational banks.[20]

Kresge picked two funds, offering to absorb initial losses to folks who invested in OZ funds organized by Jonathan Tower's Arctaris ($15 million in first-loss protection) and Community Capital Management of Fort Lauderdale ($7 million). Both companies already had a tradition of "impact investing," that is, investing for both social and financial returns. The foundations hoped these projects would help set standards for the new marketplace, for public reporting as well as for directing investments. Community Capital's plans to invest in affordable housing and sustainable agriculture were disrupted by the COVID-19 pandemic. Arctaris was more active. (See below.)

Seybert's thinking on OZs has evolved: "I started out being very curious and mostly optimistic that this was going to be good for the people we care about. I have migrated to being openly skeptical. I am not ready to say, 'Burn it down!' yet because it has the bones to be very powerful, but it's too dangerous to have no transparency and no accountability."

He challenges the Trump administration's view that any money flowing into an impoverished community is better than no money; it depends what the money is going there for. And he would prefer that local authorities and community groups had more say about where an OZ fund puts its money; in other words, he'd make OZs more like the New Markets Tax Credit the EIG boys criticized.

"Capital is going to flow to the lowest-risk, highest-return environment," he says. "Perhaps 95 percent of this is doing no good for people we care about, perhaps it is. We don't know."

Kresge also allocated $390,000 for technical assistance to five nonprofit organizations to help them exploit OZs. Only one came close to working out. Robert Jenkins is a former administrator of the DC public housing authority who now runs a firm that specializes in NMTCs. Jenkins helped create an OZ fund, Renaissance HBCU Opportunity Fund, that invests in real estate around historical Black colleges and universities, college towns that often lack the amenities that surround richer schools in bigger cities.[21]

"When people go to college, they're not looking only for dorms and classrooms," he says. "They're looking for a pizza parlor where they can talk about professor so-and-so's class, a restaurant to take mom and dad to." Half the nation's historically Black colleges and universities are in OZs.

The initial plan was to invest in four or five mixed-use projects and a couple of teaching hotels, where students can learn the hospitality trade. COVID-19 nixed the hotels, so the fund focused instead on mixed-use projects around Stillman College in Tuscaloosa, Alabama; Norfolk State University in Norfolk, Virginia; and—the one most likely to materialize first—the University of the Virgin Islands on Saint Croix. (More than a fifth of the Virgin Islands' residents live below the poverty line, so this qualifies as an OZ, but a Saint Croix headline isn't what the EIG boys longed for.)

"Raising money has been much more difficult than people thought," Jenkins said. "The OZ incentives are not creating the avalanche of investment capital that many people thought they would initially."

Jenkins also says lots of OZ projects, including several in Washington, DC, would have happened without the tax break. "That was frosting on the cake that would have been baked anyhow."

That didn't discourage Jenkins from trying to use OZs as a tool, though. With the help of Kresge-financed consultants, the fund's private placement memorandum was finished in late 2019. He delayed raising money for a few months, in part because he wanted to be sure the projects in the pipeline were ready to go and in part because of COVID-19–related delays. As of December 2020, he still hadn't raised any.

Rockefeller took a different approach than Kresge. It gave about $1 million each to Atlanta, Newark, Oakland, Saint Louis, and Washington, DC, to fund full-time OZ coordinators—positions similar to the one Ben Siegel holds in Baltimore—and pumped some money into an "OZ Academy" to offer technical advice for several other cities. Those efforts didn't bear much fruit, though. And by mid-2020, in the wake of the devastating impact of COVID-19 on small businesses, the foundation was "pivoting away" from OZs to focus on Black- and brown-owned businesses.

IMPACT INVESTORS

Arctaris Impact Investors has been investing "with the aim of delivering above-market investment returns alongside positive social impact" since 2009. When Jonathan Tower first heard about OZs from Utah's Jim Sorenson, his reaction was simple: "That's a really neat idea, but Congress isn't going to pass anything like that." He was pleased to be proven wrong, and soon decided that "the OZ incentive was better than all of the other economic development tools in the shed combined."

With Kresge's backing, Arctaris started an OZ fund consistent with its principles. "Fundamentally," Tower says, "Opportunity Zones are a tax incentive with very few requirements that you actually do anything good, and very little reporting." His biggest concern was that OZs would encourage investments that hurt families living in designated zones, pushing people out of their homes as rents rise.

Fundraising was disrupted for a couple of months during the spring 2020 COVID-19 panic, but then picked up. By the end of 2020, Arctaris had raised $200 million from institutional investors like insurance companies, foundations, and wealthy individuals (minimum investment $1 million).

Among its early investments was financing a management buyout of Recaro Automotive, a maker of premium car seats. The company wasn't initially in an OZ, but the new owners moved it to an OZ in Clinton Township, just north of Detroit, where it employs 125. Despite strong support from the mayor of Detroit, the company couldn't find a one-hundred-thousand-square-foot factory available in time within the city limits.

Recaro is now an Opportunity Zone business, which means its investors won't face any capital gains taxes if they sell it after ten years. Arctaris also invested $60 million in broadband fiber infrastructure in OZs, leasing it to internet service providers and municipalities, providing a steady stream of income—and juicy depreciation deductions—for its investors.[22]

MEASURING SOCIAL IMPACT

A luxury hotel in an already thriving downtown versus a workforce training center in a low-income African American neighborhood—sometimes it's easy to distinguish OZ projects that are socially beneficial from those that aren't. But those are rare contrasts. And, in almost all cases, accurately measuring the social impact of OZ investments—whether they actually create jobs and lift the fortunes of people who live in OZs—is difficult. This is both because these effects are hard to measure and because there's so little data on OZ projects to analyze.

EIG's Lettieri bristles at the suggestion that every OZ is supposed to be strictly defined as an "impact" investment. "We don't say only impact investors are benefitting a community," he tells me. "I want OZ investments to have an impact. The trick is to get people to behave as impact investors even if they are not. The first principle here is getting a functioning economy."

Some other government initiatives do attempt to quantify successes. The EB-5 program—the one that offers visas to foreigners who invest in US businesses—requires an estimate, usually produced by an economic model, of the number of jobs that'll be preserved and created, or can be expected to be created within a reasonable time, though the estimates are squishy. The EB-5 rules require an immigrant show they will create at least ten jobs.

In part because of the peculiar parliamentary rules of the Senate, Opportunity Zones require nothing of the sort. There are, though, proposals in Congress that would require OZ projects to estimate the numbers of jobs created and otherwise beef up their reporting requirements. In the absence of legislation, Cory Booker, unsuccessfully, urged the Treasury to come up with "a rigorous list of positive and measurable community-development outcomes to evaluate Opportunity Funds' performance" and require funds to commit to some of these outcomes.[23]

In the absence of any required reporting, several organizations tried to persuade OZ funds to do voluntary reporting. The Beeck Center at Georgetown University and the US Impact Investing Alliance, for instance, built a scoresheet for funds or developers who want to disclose how their investments affect the communities in which they're located, including the number of jobs and the number of affordable housing units created.[24] The Urban Institute developed an online tool to assess the potential social impact of OZ projects.[25] The District of Columbia government requires developers to score highly on the Urban measure before getting city money or local approvals, an example of ways state and city governments can influence the shape of OZ projects.[26]

One of the most elaborate tools—trademarked as the Impact Rate of Return,[27] a play on the more traditional financial Internal Rate of Return—was developed by Howard W. Buffett, grandson of legendary investor Warren Buffett and an evangelist for "social value investing."[28] It's an algorithm that, somewhat subjectively, allows investors, developers, and local officials to compare the impact of alternative projects from the start.

Why should OZ funds go through the trouble? Buffett offers several reasons. First, calculating an Impact Rate of Return upfront helps build trust with neighbors, lessening the chance of community blowback. Second, tracking data from the start is easier than doing so retroactively. Third, Opportunity Zones have gotten lots of bad press; projects with impact data will be better prepared to defend the tax break. Finally, if additional accounting is mandated by the government, projects with Impact Rate of Return numbers will be well placed going forward.

A third-party administrator firm, NES Financial, embraced Buffett's measure and offered it as standard on the information dashboard it sells to OZ funds. But it turns out most funds don't want to share the social impact score with investors. Once an OZ fund starts talking about the social benefits of an investment, it seems, prospective investors assume they'll have to settle for a lower financial return—and, as Jim Casselberry learned, that's a turn off.

CHAPTER FOURTEEN

The Bottom Line

T HE BOTTOM-LINE QUESTIONS AROUND OPPORTUNITY ZONES are easy to state: Do they spur economic development and job creation in poverty-plagued, left-behind communities as Sean Parker, Cory Booker, Tim Scott, and the EIG boys promised? Or do they merely provide a lucrative capital gains tax break to the wealthy who make investments, largely in real estate, they would have made anyway? Is the no-guardrails, no-oversight, let-the-market-allocate-capital design unleashing a flood of money to the nation's worst-off neighborhoods? Or does the design instead allow real estate developers, promoters, and investors to exploit a tax break sold as a way to help poor folks without actually helping very many of them?

More than three years after Donald Trump's signature turned Sean Parker's brainchild into law, definitive answers to these questions are elusive. Opportunity Zones are still young. Reliable data are nearly nonexistent. Final regulations weren't issued until December 2019, and, economically, the year 2020 ranked somewhere between bad and disastrous. But I've learned a lot since my trip to Mandalay Bay in the spring of 2019.

FOLLOW THE MONEY

On the ground, it is clear that a lot of money went to places, like downtown Portland, that didn't need added incentives. A lot of money went to gentrifying neighborhoods that already were attractive to investors. A lot of money went to luxury condos, shiny office towers, self-storage facilities, and high-end student housing—projects that won't do much to boost the economies of truly distressed communities or to help low-income families who live in them. Yet money did flow to create affordable housing in South Los Angeles, to sow seeds for the revival of downtown Erie, to replace a vacant block of row houses in Baltimore, to fund a Black-owned animation studio, and to turn a long-vacant hotel in rural Indiana into senior housing.

But how much OZ money went to the first sort, and how much to the second?

Well, we know where the big bucks went: to high-end apartments, condos, office buildings, and mixed-use buildings in attractive markets. And why not? Nothing in the law or regulations required anything different or offered any extra kick to investors who took risks in the worst-off, most capital-starved communities. While most of the tracts that governors chose to be Opportunity Zones were relatively low-income, high-poverty places, money was always going to flow to the best-off zones—to those that were particularly appealing to investors because of governors' (deliberate or foolish) choices, or because college students were counted as low-income, or because outdated demographic data made some already blooming neighborhoods look poor enough to qualify.

Even without a full accounting of OZ dollars, I can see a pattern by looking at where some of the larger OZ funds invested. Cresset, a Chicago money manager that raised $465 million for its first OZ fund, is one of the biggest and admirably transparent. The company lists its first seven OZ investments on its website: the Eleven West high-end apartment-office building in downtown Portland; a 300-unit top-of-the-line apartment building in Charleston, South Carolina ("three elevated courtyards with grills and a resort-style pool, and a rooftop deck offering Bay views"); and others in Denver ("the only development site within an Opportunity Zone in downtown Denver"), Omaha ("apartments, condos, retail, a beautifully land-scaped boulevard, a boutique hotel, and office space"), Houston, Nashville, and just outside DC in Silver Spring, Maryland ("average household income within 5 miles is $117, 328").[1] Not exactly what proponents describe when they talk about OZs.

Or take Bridge Investments, which has raised an impressive $1.3 billion for its OZ fund. It has twenty-six properties in seventeen markets across the United States, mainly multifamily residential buildings in fast-growing second-tier markets such as Salt Lake City. The firm does have a substantial affordable housing business—one largely targeted at banks looking for ways to meet Community Reinvestment Act requirements—but it finds Opportunity Zones are unsuited for those. The firm says the required ten-year hold isn't compatible with other affordable housing incentives. As a result, one of the biggest players in the OZ universe doesn't direct any of its OZ money to affordable housing.

Meanwhile, appealing, and much ballyhooed, "impact investments" like Martin Muoto and Gray Lusk's SoLa Impact or the downtown Erie renewal effort generate a lot of publicity per dollar, but, as best I can tell, draw fewer OZ dollars than the office towers, condos, and luxury apartments. And in many cases, OZ dollars are a small ingredient in a larger stew of federal, state, and local subsidies.

The track record of a big financial institution, PNC Bank, underscores the difference in scale between "impact" projects and the much bigger commercial ones. PNC is among the commercial banks investing their own capital gains in Opportunity Zones. It uses them to meet its Community Reinvestment Act quota and says it accepts much lower returns (between 3 and 5 percent) than other real estate investors. Through October 2020, PNC had put up $96.5 million in equity (plus additional money in loans) for eleven projects across its eastern US turf. Of that, $11 million went to finance the conversion of a long-vacant Birmingham, Alabama, office building into workforce housing. The other ten deals (none of which are in Baltimore, though the city is in PNC's domain) average $8.5 million in equity. In contrast, Cresset has invested an average of more than $40 million in equity for each of its projects. In short, the OZ money going to heavily celebrated, heart-warming projects appears to be a small percentage of total OZ investments.

THE TWO CHARLESTONS

While parts of South Carolina have drawn headline-making OZ investments, a glimpse at Tim Scott's hometown illustrates how the money flowed, at least initially, to real estate projects in areas that were already on the way up as opposed to those that were truly down and out. Scott is from North Charleston (45 percent Black, median household income around $45,500), which is the slightly less populous, much less affluent sibling of neighboring Charleston (22 percent Black, median household income $68,400). The state designated four census tracts in Charleston as Opportunity Zones and three in North Charleston.

In general, OZ money quickly gravitated to more prosperous and already gentrifying areas, often to projects targeted at well-off residents. One OZ is in the heart of the Charleston Peninsula, a major tourist draw and home to the city's poshest hotels (the five-star Dewberry and Hotel Bennett) and ninety-nine-dollar steak dinners. This zone is also home to the College of Charleston, whose students have little to no income, making the area appear poor enough to qualify for OZ status. That designation was so embarrassing the city tried to trade it for another tract, but it was too late. ("The outliers are bad, and they are obvious," Lettieri told the local newspaper, acknowledging that picking that tract was a bad decision. "It's...a zero-sum exercise so another community that needed that designation didn't get it.")[2] There's one OZ project in the designated tract: an old department store is being turned into a fifty-room hotel.

A bit further north, still within the Charleston city limits, is the trendy NoMo (for north of Morrison Avenue) neighborhood, where there was lots of construction activity before OZs surfaced. Now, more than half a dozen projects are drawing OZ money—some residential, some commercial—several of which were well along before OZs. Typical is The Merchant, a 231-unit apartment complex where a two-bedroom apartment goes for between $1,900 and $2,600 a month, out of reach for most residents of Tim Scott's nearby North Charleston (though by city ordinance, 10 percent of the units must be "affordable").

"The way Opportunity Zones work, they tend to attract investment to more expensive properties," says Ryan Johnson, North Charleston's economic development coordinator. There is nothing unusual about Charleston; this is the way the game is played across the country.

Still farther upstream is North Charleston. Though it's precisely the sort of struggling community OZs were supposed to help, it hadn't drawn any OZ money to its three designated census tracts as of early 2021—with one tantalizing exception.

The 1996 closure of a US Navy base in North Charleston was devastating to the local economy, costing thousands of jobs. In the decades since, the base has been the target of persistently unsuccessful (and costly for taxpayers) renewal efforts, one of which ensnared Donald Trump Jr.[3] William Cogswell Jr., a local developer and Republican state legislator who specializes in renovating historic buildings, raised about $15 million in OZ equity to finance his $75 million plan to turn part of the old base and its hospital into around three hundred apartments and, perhaps, stores.

Cogswell and his partner, Atlanta developer Jay Weaver, say they almost surely would have pulled off the project even without OZ money, but particuarly welcome OZ investors' willingness to make a ten-year commitment, longer than traditional institutional money. Local property tax breaks and state and federal historical rehabilitation tax credits, though, play a huge role in making the project's financing work, perhaps even more important than the OZ tax incentives. (In March 2021, the pair unveiled plans for a big mixed-use project on the old base. Weaver said it was too soon to know if it would draw OZ money.)

In June 2018, Scott took Parker to tour a North Charleston Opportunity Zone. The two posed for a *Forbes* photographer in front of a two-story red brick building that once housed a school Scott attended. The name, Chicora Grade School, is etched in stone above the entrance. The grounds are clean, but weeds grow through the sidewalk. The windows have been boarded up since 2012. Today, students go to the new Chicora Elementary, two miles away.

Forbes called Opportunity Zones "the most unbelievable tax break ever," but that hasn't done much for Scott's old school building.[4] Eyeing more traditional state and federal subsidies, a local nonprofit called Metanoia is raising money to turn it into an early childhood education center, office space, and artist studios; it hasn't drawn any interest from OZ investors.[5] "OZs will not work…if wealthy investors are the only ones making decisions about what might happen within the zones," says Metanoia CEO Bill Stanfield.

WHAT THE EXPERTS SAY

People who make money off Opportunity Zones have a perspective on OZs often quite different from that of Parker and the EIG boys. Many real estate developers and tax lawyers, most in private conversations, acknowledge their surprise and glee at the OZ tax break—and then criticize it.

"It's a way for the rich to get richer," a developer of student housing confided, and then begged me not to use his name. "No one is going into these communities and lifting them up. They're just extracting what they can from that space. No one is doing workforce housing. Institutional capital doesn't deal with blue-collar workers. Even our student housing doesn't uplift those areas. It doesn't improve the lives of those people. It doesn't really work the way it should be working. To me, it's another way of spurring more development without there being any consequences for improving the community or not displacing people who have lived in those communities forever."

Says Mark Falcone, founder of Continuum Partners, a Denver-based firm with lots of public-private partnerships (including a big parcel in Portland abandoned by a USPS mail-sorting facility): "You should have to make some kind of case for how your project would benefit the neighborhood, perhaps a competitive process administered by the state economic development authority."

Why does Falcone argue for more government oversight? "We are doing projects that are going to raise values in a neighborhood, but not benefit people who live there. That's fine, but I don't know that we should be getting a massive tax benefit for that." (Continuum has just one OZ project, an office building on the site of what used to be a produce warehouse in Los Angeles.)

Another class of experts, academic economists, is hobbled by a lack of data, but their preliminary analyses of OZs aren't encouraging.

Ed Glaeser, a Harvard urban economist, and graduate student Ji-afeng Chen (with my encouragement) compared the change in prices of single-family houses in Opportunity Zones to those in tracts that were eligible for OZ designation but didn't make the cut. Unlike some other exercises, this one isn't distorted by changes in the size or quality of the houses sold before and after OZ designation. The bottom line through 2019: OZs had "a negligible price impact" on houses.[6] In other words, at least in the first couple of years, OZs didn't move the needle as much as proponents hoped. Economists at Trump's Council of Economic Advisers did their own number crunching on house prices and found a bigger and thus more favorable effect: a 1.1 percent increase in home prices in tracts designated as OZs above what those prices would have been without OZs.[7]

Much of the action in OZ real estate was in commercial property. Economists from MIT, the University of Connecticut, and the University of Reading in England did a similar exercise with commercial real estate for a subset of tracts where commercial real estate changed hands through 2019.[8] They found that owners of vacant land and deteriorating buildings enjoyed a windfall, but not those who owned other buildings. If investors anticipated OZ designation would boost an entire neighborhood's economy, then the value of existing buildings should have risen, too, the economists reasoned. That didn't happen. But the stated goal of OZs was to lift entire neighborhoods, not simply fatten the wallets of people lucky enough to own a vacant lot or a rundown building.

Other researchers tried to ascertain whether employment increased in OZs relative to other similar communities. A couple of studies found little effect.[9] One found an increase in jobs, particularly in construction, in metro areas, but none in rural OZs, though it's too soon to draw any firm conclusions.[10]

In response to such criticism, EIG's Lettieri argues the initiative he helped give birth to should not be judged a failure, even if fully half of the 8,764 designated zones don't get any OZ money. This "experiment," as he calls it, was about giving those places a chance, particularly those that weren't drawing much private investment before. "This is about giving them a shot, but it is also dependent on what they do. How the market responds is not exclusively based on the federal incentive. It's contingent on a host of other outside economic factors and local leadership."

EIG IS A WINNER

One thing is clear: as a start-up think tank, the Economic Innovation Group is a runaway success. Its politically diversified strategy maneuvered Opportunity Zones into law, influenced Treasury rule writing, defended its baby against hostile publicity in the Trump years, and then protected OZs when Joe Biden became president.

EIG itself has prospered and expanded its agenda. The organization started 2020 with $2.5 million in the bank. John Lettieri (whose total annual compensation now exceeds $450,000) had an annual budget of more than $3 million and ten full-time staff. Besides nurturing and defending Opportunity Zones and making the case that Congress needed to help small businesses walloped by the COVID-19 pandemic, EIG was pushing "heartland visas" to bring skilled immigrants to communities that desperately need them, ways for low- and moderate-income Americans to save for retirement, and legislation to limit the use of noncompete clauses in employment agreements. Steve Glickman was advising OZ funds and cofounded a firm called Statt. Based in an OZ tract in Silver Spring, just outside DC (he says he couldn't find a suitable site in the city), it's a subscription-based software platform that will aggregate policy intelligence and analytics from around the country.

Sean Parker himself continues to be an active investor, putting money in a New York baby-nutrition firm and a Redwood City,

California, firm offering analytical software to nonprofits and political organizations.

But Parker has not invested any of his billions in an OZ fund. On one hand, he isn't putting his money where his mouth—and his lobbying—are, which doesn't show much confidence in the initiative he so vigorously promoted. On the other, he can't be accused of promoting a tax break just so he could save money on his own taxes.

"I went into this very, very clearly stating that I would do everything I could to promote Opportunity Zones, but that I would not invest in them or, certainly, would not create my own fund," he says, determined to draw a sharp distinction between his business investments and his philanthropic and political projects. He applies the same rule for his other advocacy interests: Despite the millions he spent on the campaign to legalize marijuana, he doesn't invest in cannabis businesses—or even use marijuana. And he says any money he makes on personal investments in companies working on cancer immunology goes back to the research institute he funds.

The EIG boys' dream that the OZ tax break would direct billions to start-up businesses in depressed neighborhoods, seeding the next Facebook or Apple in gritty parts of Baltimore or Chicago, is—so far—more fantasy than reality. In part, that's because the design was so much friendlier to real estate investors, who are well-practiced at harvesting benefits from tax incentives, than to would-be investors in small businesses. In part, it's because it took the Treasury and the IRS a while to issue relevant regulations. And in part, it's because requiring a ten-year hold does reward patient capital. It turns out a lot of investors in businesses aren't patient; they don't want to lock up their money for a decade. Perhaps some OZ real estate projects will end up housing some OZ businesses, like SoLa Impact's Beehive, but there's not much of that yet.

The talk, much of it generated by Kevin Hassett, that the OZ incentive would lead to big mutual fund–style venture capital funds that would direct money from lots of small investors to capital-starved neighborhoods—well, that was never realistic. OZs are not a game for small investors; they can't afford to play. Any tax break for which table stakes generally start at $100,000 in unrealized capital gains will be a game only the well-off can play.

Although the law, vaguely worded in parts, gave the Trump Treasury substantial leeway to scrutinize governors' choices of zones, to demand more information from OZ funds and their investors, and to limit ways in which the OZ tax break can be used, it chose in most instances to do less than it could have. That left the door open to some of the most outrageous ways OZs have been used.

I don't think Sean Parker, his congressional allies, Tim Scott and Cory Booker, and his field commanders, Steve Glickman and John Lettieri, are venal. They did not set out to make the rich richer. They really did intend to craft a tax break that would prod the rich to put their money into left-behind places that sorely need it.

They are, instead, idealistic, arrogant, stubborn, and naive.

Parker and the EIG boys were very focused on making sure the tax break was generous enough to get rich people to move their money. They thought hard about what would motivate wealthy investors but listened less to people who had designed and implemented earlier versions of place-based policies—and didn't take their advice. They were so eager to avoid the rules and bureaucratic processes that they thought restrained the effectiveness of earlier place-based policies that they underappreciated the value of those strings.

They overestimated the idealism of wealthy Americans, some of whom care about the social impact of their investments, particularly in their hometowns, but most of whom actually don't. They underestimated the energy and craftiness of tax lawyers, accountants, money managers, financial planners, and real estate developers who exploited the vulnerabilities of the OZ law and the taxpayer-friendly regulations the Treasury issued, and they disregarded those who warned that this behavior was inevitable. They didn't appreciate that clever lawyers would, for instance, discover how to use OZ tax breaks to buy an already completed building just before it got its certificate of occupancy (like the NW Natural Gas deal in Portland) and count the whole thing as a new investment. Overall, Opportunity Zones—conceived in the aftermath of the 2008 financial crisis—evinced a remarkable amount of faith in the social good of unleashing capital that is, generally speaking, agnostic.

Tim Scott and the EIG boys say they didn't anticipate—although it's hard to fathom why—that partisan gridlock in Congress coupled with Trump's bear-hug embrace of OZs would block even minor legislative fixes to the OZ statute. EIG supports several changes, including adding back reporting requirements stripped from the original bill, sunsetting some "specific high-income census tracts that do not meet the spirit of the incentive," and allowing for the creation of "feeder funds" (also known as "fund of funds") that will take money from investors and direct it toward smaller funds that invest, perhaps, in a single project.[11] The think tank now describes 2020 as "a 'proof of concept' phase for the policy." It adds, delicately, "The early results are promising but also suggest that further tweaks to the policy will be necessary."[12]

For his part, Sean Parker says he is neither surprised nor troubled by the evident shortcomings of the law he championed. "Nothing that's done on this scale can ever be perfect," he says. "We couldn't anticipate where all of the holes would be. Now, with hindsight, we can see where some of those holes are...or cracks, and where they should be tightened up." And despite all the EIG promotion about the impact of OZs, the plethora of industry conferences and newsletters since 2017, and incentives written into the statute to encourage investors to invest early, Parker argues the program is simply too young to be fairly judged. "I spent a much longer time thinking about this and advocating for it than the time that it's been law," he told me.

But Parker and the EIG boys didn't fully appreciate what veterans of targeted tax breaks have always known. One, pushing a tax break through Congress without sufficient scrutiny of the details by skeptics often will produce a flawed design too easily exploited by lawyers and accountants who are expert in finding the vulnerabilities of the tax code. And, two, a few bad examples on the front pages of national newspapers can taint the most well-intentioned initiative. Any law creating a new tax incentive should do more than the OZ statute did to minimize abuse—or assign a clear and inescapable mandate to the Treasury.

NOW WHAT?

The combination of the *New York Times*, ProPublica, and Bloomberg stories and Democratic antipathy toward anything Trump embraced turned some initially pro-OZ Democrats against the tax break—at least as long as Trump was in the White House.

In the House, members of The Squad on the left side of the Democratic caucus, Alexandria Ocasio-Cortez of New York and Rashida Tlaib of Michigan, proposed complete repeal of the provision. In May 2019, long before she joined the Biden ticket, Senator Kamala Harris said she, too, favored repeal.[13] (She spoke more favorably about OZs at least once during the 2020 campaign, though.)[14] The number three Democrat in the House, James Clyburn from Tim Scott's South Carolina (joined by, among others, Ohio's Marcia Fudge, who became Biden's HUD secretary), cosponsored a bill that would ban future OZ tax breaks for investments in private planes, skyboxes, parking lots, sports stadiums, self-storage facilities, and housing that isn't affordable for OZ residents. "From the start, I've raised concerns that the Opportunity Zone incentive would turn out to be a tax credit for rich investors with limited benefits for low-income communities," Clyburn said. "This program needs to be tweaked if it is to accomplish its stated purpose."[15]

Clyburn's bill, identical to one introduced by Senator Ron Wyden, now chair of the Senate Finance Committee, also would bar the tax break for future OZ investments in the contiguous zones— the ones adjacent to low-income areas—and would exclude zones in which most of the residents are college students.[16] Wyden says his intent is to fix, not kill, Opportunity Zones. He told me he wants to to apply two basic tests to an investment that takes advantage of the tax break: "Does it benefit low-income communities? And is it new investment?"

For all their flaws and bad publicity, though, OZs found a constituency among many mayors, state legislatures, and state economic development agencies hungry for any carrot with which to draw investment. Boston University's Menino Survey of 119 mayors found that 51 percent agreed OZs "effectively targeted areas of true economic need," 20 percent disagreed, and a substantial 29 percent said they weren't sure.[17] The Congressional Black Caucus called for *expanding* OZ tax breaks to people who live in OZs, offering a tax credit to folks who don't have capital gains to invest, as well as setting aside units in OZ-financed multifamily housing projects at affordable rents and reserving some construction jobs in any OZ project for local residents.[18] And in proof of the proposition that once a tax break becomes law it doesn't die but instead becomes a vehicle for members of Congress eager to do something—anything—when bad things happen to their districts, several members proposed expanding the list of tracts that qualify as OZs to automatically include those hit hard by hurricanes.

With Cory Booker talking up OZs among his fellow Democrats and Jared Bernstein working as an influential Biden insider, the Biden campaign proposed reform rather than repeal of the OZ tax break, to the relief of the EIG boys. Bernstein isn't the only friend of OZs in the Biden inner circle: Biden's White House chief of staff is Ron Klain. Previously a top lieutenant to AOL founder Steve Case in his campaign to move venture capital investment from the coasts to the heartland, Klain was an early (though not very active) member of EIG's "policy council" and thus sympathetic to the case for OZ-style place-based policies. And Chris Slevin, a former Booker aide, left his $250,000-a-year gig as number two to Lettieri at EIG to join the Biden White House office of legislative affairs. Parker himself recalls a favorable reaction from then vice president Biden when Parker described the OZ concept to him in "a footnote to a conversation that we had about cancer." (Both men are passionate about cancer research.)

What exactly President Biden will propose and what Congress will do is, at this writing, unclear. As part of his "racial equity" agenda during the campaign, Biden said he would "direct" the Treasury to "review" OZ benefits "to ensure these tax benefits are only being allowed where there are clear economic, social, environmental benefits to a community, and not just high returns—like those from luxury apartments or luxury hotels—to investors." But Biden stopped short of promising tough new restrictions, and his initial tax proposals were silent on OZs. It wasn't clear whether Treasury Secretary Janet Yellen—who had several more pressing issues to address her first several months on the job—would revisit regulatory decisions her predecessor made and tighten oversight of OZ funds.

Both Democrats and Republicans in Congress favor legislation to require more reporting from OZ funds. Some would require funds to give more detailed information only to the IRS; others want more information made public. OZ-friendly Democrats also want to appropriate money to help cities and states better exploit the OZ incentive, going beyond the Trump administration's moves to focus spending from existing federal programs on OZs.

Among money managers, investors, and real estate developers, there is hope that, in light of the economic side effects of the pandemic, Congress will go even farther than the IRS did in extending deadlines in the law. Citing the COVID-19 pandemic, the IRS waived the 180-day deadline for investors to put capital gains into an OZ, saying they could wait until March 31, 2021, to get the tax break for investing profits made as far back as October 2019. It also extended the amount of time OZ funds have to invest their cash.

But the IRS couldn't unilaterally make one change investors wanted: to let them defer paying capital gains taxes on their initial investment in OZ funds beyond 2026 for a couple of years, an idea EIG was pushing. They knew that because congressional scorekeepers estimate the cost of any tax law change over ten years, moving the projected capital gains revenue from one year to another within that new ten-year window would be a relatively easy change to slip into some big Biden-backed tax bill—just as OZs got into Trump's 2017 tax bill. And EIG will continue to celebrate examples of how the tax break is being used in left-behind communities, though even they don't know what share of OZ money has gone to such places.

Opportunity Zones, flawed as they are, are very likely to survive. Once launched, government programs and tax breaks tend to persist. This one now has a formidable constituency, not only in Scott, Booker, and Bernstein, but also in the wealthy Americans and real estate interests exploiting it, as well as in the big-city mayors and state economic development agencies who view it as one more tool in their kit. Given the egregious examples—the rich folks who got a tax break for an investment that didn't do much for its intended targets or investments that would have been made anyhow—the law probably will be tightened a bit. Investors may be required to at least assert ways in which their project will improve the target community and required to report on their results, perhaps in exchange for an extension of deadlines to pay taxes. And if Biden delivers on his campaign promise to raise capital gains tax rates, then the benefits of escaping taxes on OZ investments after ten years will be even more lucrative than they are already.

Whatever the evidence eventually shows about the outcomes, Opportunity Zones stand as a case study of how a clever, ambitious, and big-idea billionaire like Sean Parker can hire the right people and court the right members of Congress to turn an idea into reality even at a time of partisan gridlock.

But without substantial changes, either by law or regulation, Opportunity Zones look to me like a program with a worthy goal—connecting "struggling communities with the private investment they need" and "dramatically expand[ing] access to the capital and expertise needed to start and grow businesses, hire workers, and restore economic opportunity," to quote Booker and Scott from 2016—that is doing more to help wealthy investors and real estate businesses reduce their tax bills than to help residents of the neighborhoods it was supposed to revive.

BACK TO MANDALAY BAY

What about those people I met—long before COVID-19—at Mandalay Bay in Las Vegas?

Even before COVID-19 devastated Las Vegas's tourist industry, Clark County—which contains Las Vegas—had fielded only a few inquiries about potential developments in tract 68, where Mandalay Bay, Luxor, and the Las Vegas airport are located. Then came COVID-19, and for months nothing was formally submitted, according to Dan Kulin, the county's public information officer. In November 2020, though, a Southern California real estate firm, Shopoff Realty Investments, announced plans to raise $200 million from OZ investors to finance a $545 million, 450-room "luxury lifestyle" Dream Hotel and 42,000-square-foot casino on five acres of vacant land less than a mile from Mandalay Bay. (But the company's chief executive, Bill Shopoff, doesn't expect to make many more OZ investments. "For the most part, we have found QOZ [Qualified Opportunity Zone] land assets to be overpriced, driven up by the potential QOZ tax benefits, in inferior locations, or just not generally a good investment from a risk versus reward perspective," he said.[19])

Robert Whyte, the man in the cowboy hat, hadn't landed any OZ money when I last talked to him. He had planned to return to Las Vegas in the spring of 2020 to wear the hat again—until the organizers announced that the OZ Expo in June would be virtual-only due to COVID-19. Whyte said he was in the process of buying a 20,000-square-foot property surrounded by tattoo shops and massage parlors in an OZ in Long Beach, California, and was still optimistic about luring one or two people who had sold a company and had big capital gains to shelter. But he was frustrated.

"I know there are a lot of people with capital gains," he told me. "The problem is that these real estate funds don't work. They're asking someone to invest in a blind pool of $250 million...and they don't have one deal that they're looking at."

Cindy Leuty Jones decided not to sell the Warhol, even though it turns out to be much more valuable than she realized: in the neighborhood of $2 million. She decided investigating the right OZ fund would take too much time, so she plans to let her kids inherit the painting. They can sell the Warhol to pay estate taxes.

She did connect me to the friend who tried to recruit her to help run his OZ fund, Fred Hameetman. Although he began as an aerospace engineer, Hameetman grew wealthy investing his and other people's money in California real estate for the past fifty years. He and his wife live in an eleven-bedroom mansion around the corner from the house Sean Parker bought from Ellen DeGeneres, but his firm's offices in the Westwood section of Los Angeles are utilitarian, almost shabby.

Hameetman stumbled onto OZs. He was trying to sell a half acre of land in San Pedro, California. It was in the middle of the block and not particularly attractive. He was planning to ask $1 million and settle for $750,000, but his son, an attorney, discovered the property was in an Opportunity Zone and sold it for $3.5 million to a developer who flipped it to an outfit aggregating property for an OZ fund.

"Anything that makes me four times as much money as I expect.... There's got to be something there," Hameetman told me. "I studied it. It's an irresistible tax benefit, and tax benefits already are so beneficial to real estate."

Even before his OZ fund got off the ground, he invested some of his own capital gains to buy a nearly ten-acre site along I-95 in fast-growing West Palm Beach, Florida, where he plans a 375-unit apartment building called Paradise River Walk. "We like to be where gentrification is going," he says.

For six months, Jim Goldfarb did little besides spend time with his wife and two daughters and look at potential OZ deals—more than one hundred. "I've been in public stock markets for twenty-seven years, private equity deals for twenty-five years. I've never done real estate except for my house and some publicly traded REITs [real estate investment trusts whose equity is traded like shares of stock], and one of things I found during this process was that the real estate industry is full of criminals," he says. People said one thing, but the documents said another, and things like that.

He decided to stick to projects where there was some connection, a mutual friend perhaps, between him and the developer. "That's the power of LinkedIn," he says. His criteria included a project that would have been attractive without the OZ tax break, a deal with the developer—not a middleman—who had a stake in the project, and reasonable fees.

He had hoped to invest in refurbishing existing buildings because that's lower risk, but he couldn't find any he liked. Goldfarb ended up with four new-construction projects: a multifamily project in Los Angeles near the University of Southern California, another along the waterfront in Yonkers outside of New York City, a hotel in Lancaster, California, and an office building in Salt Lake City. (A fifth project in Miami made his original list, but the deal fell through.) About the Salt Lake City site, Goldfarb confesses, "I don't understand why that's an OZ. It's one of the less nice places in Salt Lake City, but to me it still seems pretty nice." But the hotel in Lancaster, north of Los Angeles, he suspects wouldn't have been done if not for the OZ incentives; most of the hotels there are along the freeway, and this one is about ten minutes away.

Proponents of OZs celebrate social impact investors, the ones willing to take lower returns in favor of some social purpose. Goldfarb is not among them. "I'm not doing these projects for the purpose of giving back to society. I'm doing these projects as an investment, though it's nice when some good can get done. Projects in the heart of the inner city aren't the first ones that are going to get done."

Arcis Real Estate's student housing projects are still drawing investors—and the industry weathered the COVID-19 storm—but the firm largely abandoned its OZ focus. Most ArcisRE deals soak up between $15 million and $40 million in equity. Most potential OZ investors were interested in writing checks of between $250,000 and $1 million. It couldn't raise enough OZ money to finance projects based outside of Seattle or in Reno, so it did them with other financing. "We have taken our foot off the pedal on OZ deals because it's just too much work for too little capital," Mohi Monem told me just eight months after the press release celebrating the firm's OZ focus. He has since left ArcisRE for another Atlanta real estate firm.

Jimmy Rose, the Utah developer, went back to Washington—actually to the IRS offices in Lanham, Maryland—in July 2019 to another IRS hearing. At this one, he spoke, suggesting the IRS use its website to make OZs easier for investors and developers to understand. "There could be more of the kind of Opportunity Zones for dummies kind of sections," he said.

He also offered another idea: Why not expand the eligibility for OZ capital gains tax breaks to anyone willing to lock up their money for ten years in a zone or OZ business, and drop the requirement that the money come from capital gains from selling an asset. "You may want to communicate that to the people who actually can change the law," Treasury tax lawyer Michael Novey replied.[20]

Rose had a few health challenges—bone cancer, then COVID-19—that set back his OZ fundraising. By June 2020, he and his wife and friends had put $3.5 million toward the $10 million he hopes to raise for the renovation of their properties in Saint George's historic downtown and were launching a campaign to raise more.

I tracked down Chulapamornsri, but he's no longer at Crop One and didn't want to talk about the company. That vertical farm the company was talking about building with OZ money in Texas? Never happened. A company spokesperson told me the OZ fund never got off the ground.

Despite the attention and the business cards Susan Iwamoto got at Las Vegas, she hasn't found an OZ investor for the property her family owns. She's convinced the parcel is a great place for a hotel catering to families of patients at a nearby hospital. Iwamoto is still frustrated at the local government's lack of interest in promoting OZs and even more frustrated by her unsuccessful search to find someone who'll buy her land.

"I call it a 'missed opportunity' zone," she told me.

Acknowledgments

My interest in Opportunity Zones was sparked by my Brookings colleague, Adam Looney, who combines a sharp analytical mind with an unusually strong capacity for outrage at how the tax code is shaped and exploited. He set me out on what proved to be a fascinating reporting journey.

Telling the story of Opportunity Zones was like putting together the pieces of a jigsaw puzzle without the benefit of the photograph on the cover of the box. At EIG, John Lettieri, Steve Glickman, and Chris Slevin were unfailingly helpful, even though they knew they wouldn't like everything I would write. Sean Parker was generous with his time. Several local reporters helped me find pieces of the puzzle and understand their communities: Doug Donovan in Baltimore, Carrie Porter in Los Angeles, David Slade of the *Post and Courier* in Charleston, and Chuck Slothower of the *Daily Journal of Commerce* in Portland. I was fortunate to have Akiko Matsuda chasing down facts and hard-to-get interviews for a few months after she finished the Knight-Bagehot Program at Columbia. Reporting by top-notch journalists Steven Bertoni at *Forbes*, Noah Buhayar at Bloomberg, Damian Paletta at the *Washington Post*, Richard Rubin at the *Wall Street Journal*, and Jim Tankersley at the *New York Times* provided useful guides for my reporting. The *Oregonian* kindly shared the fruits of its public-records requests to the state government. Brett Theodos at the Urban Institute read the manuscript carefully and offered many helpful comments, as did my brother Bruce. The Hutchins Center on Fiscal and Monetary Policy at the Brookings Institution is a terrific place to think and write about policy. My colleagues there, including Sophia Campbell, Jeffrey Chang, Kadija Yilla, and, especially, Haowen Chen, were unfailingly helpful when I asked for assistance. Dozens of people in real estate, money management, academia, community development, and state and local government answered my questions and provided details without which it would be impossible to tell a story like this. Several current and former congressional and Treasury staffers, some of whom I cannot identify, gave me valuable insights into how Washington really works.

As he has before, my agent, Rafe Sagalyn, frequently provided wise counsel through the process of conceiving and producing this book. From his outpost in New Zealand, Nathan Means offered skillful editing and turned up interesting tidbits for the narrative. At Public-Affairs, I had the good fortune to be reunited with John Mahaney with whom I worked on *In Fed We Trust*. His guidance and suggestions are reflected throughout the manuscript. Brittany Smail provided excellent copyediting and caught several mistakes. I alone am responsible for any remaining errors or omissions.

Book writing is hard on spouses. Naomi, my wife of thirty-seven years and the love of my life, was unfailingly supportive and patient as I droned on over dinner about the details of the tax code and the frustrations of reporting during a pandemic. For that, I am extremely grateful.

Notes

I CONDUCTED SCORES OF INTERVIEWS FOR THIS BOOK, WATCHED hours of video of public events and interviews, listened to podcasts, and monitored Twitter. Quotes, descriptions, and facts in the book come from that reporting unless otherwise attributed. These notes indicate where I have consulted the reporting of others and identify relevant websites and documents.

INTRODUCTION

1. Steven Bertoni, "An Unlikely Group of Billionaires and Politicians Has Created the Most Unbelievable Tax Break Ever," *Forbes*, July 18, 2018, www .forbes.com/sites/forbesdigitalcovers/2018/07/17/an-unlikely-group-of-billionaires -and-politicians-has-created-the-most-unbelievable-tax-break-ever/#71fc40 381485.

2. Organisation for Economic Co-operation and Development, *Revenue Statistics 2020: Tax Revenue Trends in the OECD*, 2020, www.oecd.org/tax/tax -policy/revenue-statistics-highlights-brochure.pdf.

CHAPTER 1: AND YOU DON'T HAVE TO DIE...

1. "2019 Opportunity Zone Expo Las Vegas," OpportunityZone.com, Opportunity Zone Expo, www.opportunityzone.com/conference/2019-opportunity -zone-expo-las-vegas/.

2. "Revenue Projections, by Category," Congressional Budget Office, April 2018 (.xlsx file), www.cbo.gov/data/budget-economic-data#7.

3. "About the EB-5 Visa Classification," US Citizenship and Immigration Services, US Department of Homeland Security, www.uscis.gov/working-in -the-united-states/permanent-workers/employment-based-immigration-fifth -preference-eb-5/about-the-eb-5-visa-classification.

4. Arcis Real Estate Capital, "Arcis Capital Partners LLC Spins Off Its Real Estate Investment Business into Arcis Real Estate Capital LLC," press release, June 3, 2019, www.arcisrecap.com/press-release.

5. US Census Bureau (2019), *American Community Survey 5-Year Estimates*, retrieved from "Profile Page for Tract 636.05, Orange, CA," Census Reporter, https://censusreporter.org/profiles/14000US06059063605-census-tract -63605-orange-ca/.

6. "Legislative History of IRC Section 1031," 1031taxreform.com, Federation of Exchange Accommodators, www.1031taxreform.com/1031history/.

7. Jim Tankersley, "A Curveball from the New Tax Law: It Makes Baseball Trades Harder," *New York Times*, March 19, 2018, www.nytimes.com /2018/03/19/us/politics/baseball-tax-law-.html.

CHAPTER 2: WIZARDS OF OZ: SEAN PARKER AND THE EIG BOYS

1. Sean N. Parker, "Initial Statement of Beneficial Ownership of Securities (Form 3) (May 17, 2012)," US Securities and Exchange Commission, sec.gov /Archives/edgar/data/1326801/000118143112030686/xslF345X02/rrd344417 .xml.

2. Steven Bertoni, "Sean Parker: Agent of Disruption," *Forbes*, September 28, 2011, www.forbes.com/global/2011/1010/feature-sean-parker-agent-disruption -napster-facebook-plaxo-steven-bertoni.html?sh=6460113f7c28.

3. "Sean Parker: The Picasso of Business," *Forbes*, September 21, 2011, video, www.youtube.com/watch?v=ppiLJeFP4n0.

4. Josh Constine, "Sean Parker's Brigade/Causes Acquired by GovTech App Countable," TechCrunch, May 1, 2019, https://techcrunch.com/2019/05 /01/brigade-countable/.

5. "Tom Steyer (D)," Opensecrets.org, The Center for Responsive Politics, www.opensecrets.org/2020-presidential-race/tom-steyer/candidate?id=N000 44966.

6. Dale Russakoff, *The Prize: Who's in Charge of America's Schools?* (Boston: Houghton Mifflin Harcourt, 2015).

7. Josh Constine, "Sean Parker's GovTech Brigade Breaks Up, Pinterest Acquires Engineers," TechCrunch, February 10, 2019, https://techcrunch.com /2019/02/10/brigade-pinterest/.

8. Erica Gonzales, "Meet Lady Gaga's New Man, Michael Polansky," *Harper's Bazaar*, August 27, 2020, www.harpersbazaar.com/celebrity/latest /a30756629/who-is-michael-polansky-lady-gaga-boyfriend/.

9. Bertoni, "An Unlikely Group of Billionaires."

10. Clifton Leaf, "Q&A: Sean Parker on Napster, Spotify, and His Federal Tax Law Triumph," *Fortune*, May 25, 2018, https://fortune.com/2018 /05/25/sean-parker-napster-spotify/.

11. Henry Blodget, "And, Speaking of Orgies, Who Can Forget the Star-Studded Bacchanalian Davosian 'Taxidermy' Party?" Business Insider, January 25, 2014, www.businessinsider.com.au/davos-parties-2014-1#the-coat-check-you -arrive-here-after-being-greeted-by-some-extremely-attractive-people-whose -sole-job-was-to-greet-you-1.

12. Felix Salmon, "Branding and Anti-Branding, Davos Edition," Reuters, January 28, 2013, http://blogs.reuters.com/felix-salmon/2013/01/28/branding -and-anti-branding-davos-edition/.

13. "Sean Parker Talks About Silicon Valley Support for Ro Khanna," Carla Marinucci, May 16, 2013, video, https://www.youtube.com/watch?v=F8QD0AwJNyw.

14. Economic Innovation Group Inc., "Return of Organization Exempt from Income Tax (Form 990) (2013)," IRS, US Department of the Treasury, retrieved from ProPublica, https://projects.propublica.org/nonprofits/organi zations/462450336/201413219349303606/full.

15. "Christen Krzywonski and Steven Glickman," *New York Times*, November 10, 2013, www.nytimes.com/2013/11/10/fashion/weddings/christen -krzywonski-and-steven-glickman.html.

16. Somini Sengupta and Eric Lipton, "Silicon Valley Group's Political Effort Causes Uproar," *New York Times*, May 8, 2013, www.nytimes.com/2013/05/09 /technology/fwdus-raises-uproar-with-advocacy-tactics.html.

17. Gregory Ferenstein, "Why Zuckerberg's Lobby Is Collapsing Like a 'House of Cards' Outside of DC," TechCrunch, May 12, 2013, https://

techcrunch.com/2013/05/12/why-zuckerbergs-lobby-fwd-is-collapsing-like
-a-house-of-cards-outside-of-dc/.

18. Josh Miller, "FWD.us Breaks Its First Promise: To Be Different,"
BuzzFeed News, May 1, 2013, www.buzzfeednews.com/article/joshmiller/fwdus
-breaks-its-first-promise-to-be-different.

19. Ellis Hamburger, "Facebook Acquires Link-Sharing Service Branch
for Around $15 Million," Verge, January 13, 2014, www.theverge.com/2014
/1/13/5303702/facebook-acquires-link-sharing-app-branch-for-15-million; In-
grid Lunden, "After Facebook Acqui-Hired Branch Media in 2014, Founders
Shutter Branch (and Potluck)," TechCrunch, June 3, 2015, https://techcrunch
.com/2015/06/03/bye-branch/.

20. Christian Oth and Mark Seliger, "Inside the Extravagant Wedding of
Sean Parker and Alexandra Lenas," *Vanity Fair*, August 1, 2013, www.vanityfair
.com/news/2013/09/photos-sean-parker-wedding.

21. Paul Rogers, "Tech Billionaire Sean Parker Settles Big Sur Wedding
Coastal Violations by Creating App for California Beachgoers," *Mercury News*,
December 13, 2018, www.mercurynews.com/2018/12/13/free-new-app-from
-facebook-billionaire-sean-parker-will-help-public-find-california-beaches/;
Eli Rosenberg, "How Does a Tech Billionaire Say Sorry for His Unauthorized
Wedding? There's an App for That," *Washington Post*, December 14, 2018, www
.washingtonpost.com/technology/2018/12/14/how-does-tech-billionaire-say
-sorry-his-unauthorized-wedding-theres-an-app-that/.

22. Paul Harris, "Sean Parker and Wife Spat on in Public as Part of Backlash to Lavish Wedding," *Guardian*, June 19, 2013, www.theguardian.com
/world/2013/jun/19/sean-parker-wedding-backlash.

23. Sean Parker, "Weddings Used to Be Sacred and Other Lessons About Internet Journalism," TechCrunch, June 27, 2013, https://techcrunch.com/2013/06/27
/weddings-used-to-be-sacred-and-other-lessons-about-internet-journalism/.

CHAPTER 3: THE BRAINS

1. Alyson Shontell, "Sean Parker and Fiancée Living in Plaza Hotel for 1.5
Years While Their $20 Million NYC Townhouse Gets Renovated," Business
Insider, May 16, 2013, www.businessinsider.com/sean-parker-and-his-fiance
-will-live-in-2013-5; Matt Lynley, "Check Out the Art in Sean Parker's Huge
$20 Million New York Mansion," Business Insider, May 4, 2012, www.busi
nessinsider.com/check-out-the-art-in-sean-parkers-huge-20-million-new-york
-mansion-2012-5.

2. "Donor Lookup: Sean Parker," Opensecrets.org, The Center for Responsive Politics, www.opensecrets.org/donor-lookup/results?name=sean+parker.

3. Alex Byers and Alexander Burns, "Parker's Next Mission: Politics," *Politico*, April 21, 2014, www.politico.com/story/2014/04/sean-parker-105852.

4. Damien Cave, "Cory Anthony Booker: On a Path That Could Have No Limits," *New York Times*, May 10, 2006, www.nytimes.com/2006/05/10/nyregion/10man.html.

5. "Donor Lookup: Sean Parker," Opensecrets.org.

6. Russ Choma, "Money Won on Tuesday, but Rules of the Game Changed," Opensecrets.org, The Center for Responsive Politics, November 5, 2014, www.opensecrets.org/news/2014/11/money-won-on-tuesday-but-rules-of-the-game-changed/.

7. Tim Scott, *Opportunity Knocks: How Hard Work, Community, and Business Can Improve Lives and End Poverty* (New York: Hachette Book Group, 2020), 70.

8. "Senator Tim Scott—2017 Kemp Leadership Award Dinner," Jack Kemp Foundation, December 9, 2017, video, www.youtube.com/watch?v=ZLtWk0vjpLU&feature=youtube&t=1206.

9. Stephen Moore, "Tim Scott: Meet the New Senator from South Carolina," *Wall Street Journal*, December 21, 2012, www.wsj.com/articles/SB10001424127887323777204578193322865708896.

10. Scott, *Opportunity Knocks*, 134.

11. Office of Tim Scott, "Senator Tim Scott Introduces Opportunity Agenda," press release, January 15, 2014, www.scott.senate.gov/media-center/press-releases/senator-tim-scott-introduces-opportunity-agenda.

12. Ed O'Keefe, "Cory Booker, Tim Scott Team Up for the First Time," *Washington Post*, April 9, 2014, www.washingtonpost.com/news/post-politics/wp/2014/04/09/cory-booker-tim-scott-team-up-for-the-first-time/.

13. Senator Tim Scott, "Our American Family," *Congressional Record* 162 (July 13, 2016): S5055, www.congress.gov/congressional-record/2016/7/13/senate-section/article/s5045-2.

14. Emma Dumain, "For Sen. Tim Scott and Chief of Staff Jennifer DeCasper, a Close Bond and 'Divine' Partnership," *Post and Courier*, May 5, 2017, www.postandcourier.com/news/for-sen-tim-scott-and-chief-of-staff-jennifer-decasper-a-close-bond-and-divine/article_669c6cce-3017-11e7-a4c2-235355f59ef8.html.

15. Economic Innovation Group Inc., "Return of Organization Exempt from Income Tax (Form 990) (2014)," IRS, US Department of the Treasury, retrieved from ProPublica, https://projects.propublica.org/nonprofits/display

_990/462450336/2016_01_EO%2F13-145302_20004_462450336; Economic Innovation Group Inc., "Return of Organization Exempt from Income Tax (Form 990) (2015)," IRS, US Department of the Treasury, retrieved from ProPublica, https://projects.propublica.org/nonprofits/display_990/462450336 /2017_02_EO%2F46-2450336_990O_201512.

16. EIG, "The Economic Innovation Group Launches to Engage Entrepreneurs and Investors in Addressing America's Economic Challenges," press release, March 31, 2015, https://eig.org/news/the-economic-innovation-group -launches-to-engage-entrepreneurs-and-investors-in-addressing-americas -economic-challenges-2.

17. Sean Parker, "Philanthropy for Hackers," *Wall Street Journal*, June 26, 2015, www.wsj.com/articles/sean-parker-philanthropy-for-hackers-1435345787.

CHAPTER 4: ONCE UPON A TIME ON THE ISLE OF DOGS

1. Sir Geoffrey Howe, "Liberating Free Enterprise: A New Experiment," Margaret Thatcher Foundation, speech, June 26, 1978, www.margaretthatcher .org/document/111842.

2. Timothy P. R. Weaver, "Neoliberalism by Design: Poverty and Plenty in London's Docklands," in *Blazing the Neoliberal Trail: Urban Political Development in the United States and the United Kingdom* (Philadelphia: University of Pennsylvania Press, 2016), 249.

3. Stuart Butler, *Enterprise Zones: Greenlining the Inner Cities* (London: Heinemann Educational Books, 1981), 95–97.

4. Butler, *Enterprise Zones*, 107.

5. Kiernan Larkin, *What Would Maggie Do?* Centre for Cities, February 28, 2011, www.centreforcities.org/wp-content/uploads/2014/09/11-03-02-Enterprise -Zones-1-pager.pdf.

6. Stuart Butler, *Enterprise Zone: A Solution to the Urban Crisis?*, Heritage Foundation, February 20, 1979, www.heritage.org/transportation/report/enter prise-zone-solution-the-urban-crisis; Weaver, "Neoliberalism by Design," 34.

7. Jack Kemp, *An Inquiry into the Nature and Causes of Poverty in America and How to Combat It*, Heritage Foundation, June 10, 1990, www.heritage .org/poverty-and-inequality/report/inquiry-the-nature-and-causes-poverty -america-and-how-combat-it.

8. Timothy P. R. Weaver, "Losing the Battle but Winning the War: The Story of the Federal Enterprise Zone Program That Never Was: 1980–1992," in *Blaz-*

ing the Neoliberal Trail: Urban Political Development in the United States and the United Kingdom (Philadelphia: University of Pennsylvania Press, 2016), 25–71.

9. Ian Pulsipher, "Enterprise Zones: Development for Distressed Communities," *LegisBrief* 13, no. 38 (October 2005), www.ncsl.org/documents/econ /EntZonesDev.pdf.

10. US Library of Congress, Congressional Research Service, *Empowerment Zones, Enterprise Communities, and Renewal Communities: Comparative Overview and Analysis*, R41639 (2011), www.everycrsreport.com/files/20110214_R41639 _b18ae5bf0fbe93505d7b6c2b13b744b76124b9ed.pdf.

11. David Neumark, "Rebuilding Communities Jobs Subsidies" in *Place-Based Policies for Shared Economic Growth*, ed. Jay Shambaugh and Ryan Nunn (Washington, DC: Brookings Institution, 2018), www.brookings.edu/wp-content /uploads/2018/09/PBP_Neumark_web_0926_2.pdf.

12. Community Development Financial Institutions Fund, US Department of the Treasury, *NMTC Qualified Equity Investment Report*, February 5, 2021, www.cdfifund.gov/sites/cdfi/files/2021-02/NMTC%20QEI%20Issuance%20 Report-February%202021.pdf.

13. Martin D. Abravanel et al., *New Markets Tax Credit (NMTC) Program Evaluation: Final Report*, Urban Institute, April 2013, www.urban.org/sites /default/files/publication/24211/412958-new-markets-tax-credit-nmtc-program -evaluation.pdf.

14. Matthew Freedman, *Teaching New Markets Old Tricks: The Effects of Subsidized Investment on Low-Income Neighborhoods* (unpublished manuscript, June 13, 2012), Cornell University, https://ecommons.cornell.edu/handle/1813/89085.

15. US Government Accountability Office, *New Markets Tax Credit: The Credit Helps Fund a Variety of Projects in Low-Income Communities, but Could Be Simplified*, GAO-10-334 (Washington, DC, 2010), www.gao.gov/products /GAO-10-334.

16. Jared Bernstein and Kevin Hassett, *Unlocking Private Capital to Facilitate Economic Growth in Distressed Areas*, EIG, April 2015, https://eig.org/wp-content /uploads/2015/04/Unlocking-Private-Capital-to-Facilitate-Growth.pdf.

17. "State Annual Personal Income, 2020 (Preliminary)," Bureau of Economic Analysis, US Department of Commerce, www.bea.gov/sites/default/files /2021-03/spi0321_3.pdf.

18. Olivier Jean Blanchard and Lawrence F. Katz, "Regional Evolutions," *Brookings Papers on Economic Activity* (Washington, DC: Brookings Institution,

1992), www.brookings.edu/wp-content/uploads/1992/01/1992a_bpea_blanchard_katz_hall_eichengreen.pdf.

19. Benjamin Austin, Edward Glaeser, and Lawrence Summers, "Jobs for the Heartland: Place-Based Policies in 21st-Century America," *Brookings Papers on Economic Activity* (Washington, DC: Brookings Institution, 2018), www.brookings.edu/wp-content/uploads/2018/03/AustinEtAl_Text.pdf.

20. William H. Frey, "Just Before COVID-19, American Migration Hit a 73-Year Low," Brookings Institution, December 15, 2020, www.brookings.edu/blog/the-avenue/2020/12/15/just-before-covid-19-american-migration-hit-a-73-year-low/.

21. Ellora Derenoncourt, *Can You Move to Opportunity? Evidence from the Great Migration* (working paper, December 31, 2019), www.dropbox.com/s/l34h2avpjomylrb/derenoncourt_2019pdf?dl=0.

22. Shankar Vedantam et al., "Zipcode Destiny: The Persistent Power of Place and Education," December 9, 2019, in *Hidden Brain*, National Public Radio, podcast, www.npr.org/2019/12/09/786469762/zipcode-destiny-the-persistent-power-of-place-and-education.

23. "The Opportunity Insights Economic Tracker: Supporting the Recovery from COVID-19," Opportunity Insights, https://opportunityinsights.org/.

24. "Opportunity Zones: The Early Evidence," Brookings Institution, February 24, 2021, www.brookings.edu/events/opportunity-zones-the-early-evidence/.

25. "Rethinking Economic Renewal," AtlanticLIVE, April 15, 2015, www.theatlantic.com/live/events/rethinking-economic-renewal/2015/.

26. "About Us," EIG, https://eig.org/about-us.

27. "Distressed Communities Index," EIG, https://eig.org/dci.

28. Nelson D. Schwartz, "Poorest Areas Have Missed Out on Boons of Recovery, Study Finds," *New York Times*, February 24, 2016, www.nytimes.com/2016/02/25/business/economy/poorest-areas-have-missed-out-on-boons-of-recovery-study-finds.html?searchResultPosition=1.

29. Claire Galofaro, "To Some, Trump Is a Desperate Survival Bid," Associated Press, July 18, 2016, www.ap.org/explore/divided-america/to-some-trump-is-a-desperate-survival-bid.html.

30. "Economic Recovery Boom Has Left Behind Poor Areas, Report Finds," *All Things Considered*, National Public Radio, February 25, 2016, www.npr.org/2016/02/25/468149454/economic-recovery-boom-has-left-behind-poor-areas-report-finds.

CHAPTER 5: A BILL IS BORN

1. "Walter Laidlaw," 1910 United States Census, Manhattan Ward 12, New York, New York, digital image, Ancestry.com, www.ancestry.com.

2. Paul Theerman, "The Public Health Origins of Census Data Collection," New York Academy of Medicine, February 3, 2020, https://nyamcenterfor history.org/2020/02/03/the-public-health-origins-of-census-data-collection/.

3. "Glossary," Census Bureau, US Department of Commerce, www.census .gov/programs-surveys/geography/about/glossary.html#par_textimage_13.

4. Clifton Leaf, "Q&A: Sean Parker on Napster, Spotify, and His Federal Tax Law Triumph," *Fortune*, May 25, 2018, https://fortune.com/2018/05/25 /sean-parker-napster-spotify/.

5. Brett Theodos, *A Tailored Opportunity Zone Incentive Could Bring Greater Benefits to Distressed Communities and Less Cost to the Federal Government*, statement before the Subcommittee on Economic Growth, Tax, and Capital Access, US House Committee on Small Business on October 17, 2019, https://smallbusiness.house.gov/uploadedfiles/10-17-19_mr._theodos_testi mony.pdf.

6. "Distribution of Long-Term Capital Gains and Qualified Dividends by Expanded Cash Income Percentile, 2019," Table T20-0152, Tax Policy Center, May 5, 2020, www.taxpolicycenter.org/model-estimates/distribution-individual -income-tax-long-term-capital-gains-and-qualified-44.

7. Lily L. Batchelder and David Kamin, "Taxing the Rich: Issues and Options," Social Science Research Network, February 1, 2020, https://papers.ssrn .com/sol3/papersscfm?abstract_id=3452274.

8. "Opportunity Zones: Tapping into a $6 Trillion Market," EIG, March 21, 2018, https://eig.org/news/opportunity-zones-tapping-6-trillion-market.

9. Blake Christian, "Five Hidden Gems in the Federal Opportunity Zone Program," *Accounting Today*, August 1, 2019, www.accountingtoday.com/opinion /five-hidden-gems-in-the-federal-opportunity-zone-program.

10. Office of Congressman Tim Burchett, "Burchett, Cueller Look to Extend Opportunity Zone Program," press release, February 11, 2021, https:// burchett.house.gov/media/press-releases/burchett-cuellar-look-extend-opport unity-zone-program.

11. *Investing in Opportunity Act*, HR 5082, 114th Congress, introduced in House April 27, 2016, www.congress.gov/bill/114th-congress/house-bill/5082 /cosponsors.

12. Office of Senator Cory Booker, "Senators Booker and Scott and Congressmen Tiberi and Kind Introduce the 'Investing in Opportunity Act,'" press release, April 27, 2016, www.booker.senate.gov/news/press/senators-booker-and -scott-and-congressmen-tiberi-and-kind-introduce-the-and-147investing -in-opportunity-act-and-148.

13. Mary Troyan, "Legislation Aims to Boost Investment in Economically Distressed Areas," *USA Today*, April 27, 2016, www.usatoday.com/story/news /politics/2016/04/27/legislation-aims-boost-investment-economically-distressed -areas/83554552/.

14. Andrew Yang, "How the Investing in Opportunity Act Could Help Distressed Communities," *Forbes*, April 28, 2016, www.forbes.com/sites/andrew yang/2016/04/28/investing-in-opportunity/?sh=2e9a11c41f1f.

15. John Avlon, "Cory Booker and Tim Scott's Bipartisan Plan to Wage a Smart War on Poverty," *Daily Beast*, April 13, 2017, www.thedailybeast.com /cory-booker-and-tim-scotts-bipartisan-plan-to-wage-a-smart-war-on-poverty.

16. Angela Rachidi, "Employability of Poor a Complicated Issue," *Montrose Daily Press*, May 8, 2016, www.montrosepress.com/opinion/employability-of -poor-a-complicated-issue/article_5834841c-14d1-11e6-bbf7-3bbf2454200f.html.

17. EIG, "The Economic Innovation Group Applauds Introduction of the 'Investing in Opportunity Act,'" EIG, press release, April 27, 2016, https:// eig.org/news/the-economic-innovation-group-applauds-introduction-of-the -investing-in-opportunity-act.

18. Evan Halper, "Napster Co-Founder Sean Parker Once Vowed to Shake Up Washington; So How's That Working Out?" *Los Angeles Times*, August 4, 2016, www.latimes.com/politics/la-na-pol-sean-parker-20160804-snap-story.html.

19. "The Millennial Economy: Findings from a New EY & EIG National Survey of Millennials," EIG, September 2016, https://eig.org/millennial#1473667707197 -bfde262a-83c9.

20. "Index of State Dynamism," EIG, May 2017, https://eig.org/index-state -dynamism.

21. Jack Kemp Foundation, "Return of Private Foundation (Form 990-PF) (2018)," IRS, US Department of the Treasury, retrieved from GuideStar, www .guidestar.org/profile/27-0856599.

22. "Think Tank Awards 2017: Who Won?" *Prospect*, July 14, 2017, www .prospectmagazine.co.uk/magazine/think-tank-awards-2017-who-won.

23. Halper, "Napster Co-Founder Sean Parker."

24. "A Transcript of Donald Trump's Meeting with the Washington Post Editorial Board," *Washington Post*, March 21, 2016, www.washingtonpost.com /blogs/post-partisan/wp/2016/03/21/a-transcript-of-donald-trumps-meeting -with-the-washington-post-editorial-board/.

CHAPTER 6: AN ARCHIPELAGO OF TAX HAVENS

1. Linda Qiu, "Donald Trump's Top 10 Campaign Promises," Politifact, July 15, 2016, www.politifact.com/article/2016/jul/15/donald-trumps-top-10 -campaign-promises/.

2. Victor Fiorillo, "Here Is the (Apparently Leaked) Agenda for the Republican Retreat in Philly," *Philadelphia*, January 25, 2017, www.phillymag.com /news/2017/01/25/republican-retreat-agenda-philadelphia-donald-trump/.

3. Lauren Thomas, "Read the White House Memo on President Trump's Proposed Tax Plan," CNBC, April 26, 2017, www.cnbc.com/2017/04/26/heres -the-white-house-memo-on-president-trumps-proposed-tax-plan.html.

4. Jared Bernstein (@econjared), Twitter, February 24, 2017, 1:16 p.m., https://twitter.com/econjared/status/835191700905734144?lang=en.

5. Quinn Scanlan, "Kellyanne Conway on Accusation Trump Is Racist: 'None of Us Would Be There If That Were True,'" ABC News, August 12, 2018, https:// abcnews.go.com/Politics/kellyanne-conway-accusation-trump-racist-us-true /story?id=57142582.

6. Dees Stribling, "Ja'Ron Smith Still Stands by Opportunity Zones, The Platinum Plan and Being a Black Trump Staffer," Bisnow, November 17, 2020, www .bisnow.com/national/news/opportunity-zones/former-deputy-assistant-to-the -president-jaron-smith-talk-about-ozs-106746.

7. Alan Rappeport, "5 Hurdles to the Adoption of Trump's Tax Plan This Year," *New York Times*, April 27, 2017, www.nytimes.com/2017/04/27/us /politics/white-house-tax-plan.html.

8. Donald Trump, "Remarks by President Trump on Infrastructure," White House, August 15, 2017, https://trumpwhitehouse.archives.gov/briefings-state ments/remarks-president-trump-infrastructure/.

9. Tim Scott (@SenatorTimScott), Twitter, August 15, 2017, 9:50 p.m., https://twitter.com/senatortimscott/status/897636621432102912; Tim Scott (@SenatorTimScott), Twitter, August 15, 2017, 9:47 p.m., https://twitter.com /senatortimscott/status/897635809280634880.

10. Shawna Thomas, "Sen. Scott Says Trump's Moral Authority Was Compromised by His Tues. Comments on Charlottesville," VICE News, August 17, 2017, https://news.vice.com/en_us/article/j5dab3/tim-scott-trump-charlottesville-race.

11. Scott, *Opportunity Knocks*, 4

12. Scott, *Opportunity Knocks*, 4

13. Seung Min Kim, "Top State Department Official Resigns in Protest of Trump's Response to Racial Tensions in the Country," *Washington Post*, June 18, 2020, www.washingtonpost.com/politics/top-state-department-official -resigns-in-protest-of-trumps-response-to-racial-tensions-in-the-country/2020 /06/18/e142e342-b181-11ea-a567-6172530208bd_story.html.

14. "Statement on President Donald J. Trump's Meeting with Senator Tim Scott," White House, September 13, 2017, trumpwhitehouse.archives.gov/briefings -statements/statement-president-donald-j-trumps-meeting-senator-tim-scott/.

15. Caitlin Byrd, "After Sen. Tim Scott Meets with Trump, White House Calls Him 'Tom Scott' in Photo Caption," *Post and Courier*, September 14, 2020, www.postandcourier.com/politics/after-sen-tim-scott-meets-with-trump -white-house-calls-him-tom-scott-in-photo/article_f9251092-98c1-11e7-a1ac-b 716e585bcd1.html.

16. Scott, *Opportunity Knocks*, 7

17. "Press Gaggle by President Trump en Route Washington, D.C.," White House, September 14, 2017, https://trumpwhitehouse.archives.gov/briefings -statements/press-gaggle-president-trump-en-route-washington-d-c/.

18. Adam S. Wallwork and Linda B. Schakel, "Primer on Qualified Opportunity Zones," *Tax Notes*, May 31, 2018, retrieved from Ballard Spahr, www.ballardspahr.com/-/media/files/alerts/2018-06-18-primer-on-qualified -opportunity-zones.pdf.

19. "President Trump and Republican Lawmakers Celebrate Passage of Tax Reform," CSPAN, December 20, 2017, video, www.c-span.org/video/?438843 -1/president-republican-lawmakers-hail-passage-tax-reform-bill.

20. Tim Scott (@SenatorTim Scott), Twitter, December 20, 2017, 4:23 p.m., https://twitter.com/senatortimscott/status/943592677173612545.

21. Clifton Leaf, "Q&A: Sean Parker on Napster, Spotify, and His Federal Tax Law Triumph," *Fortune,* May 25, 2018, https://fortune.com/2018/05 /25/sean-parker-napster-spotify/.

22. Megan Schrader (@meganschrader), Twitter, December 14, 2017, 5:06 p.m., https://twitter.com/meganschrader/status/941429128145678336?s=20.

23. Megan Schrader, "'Opportunity Zones' in GOP Tax Bill Ripe for Abuse," *Denver Post*, December 19, 2017, www.denverpost.com/2017/12/19 /opportunity-zones-in-gop-tax-bill-ripe-for-abuse/.

24. Jim Tankersley, "Tucked Into the Tax Bill, a Plan to Help Distressed America," *New York Times*, January 29, 2018, www.nytimes.com/2018/01/29 /business/tax-bill-economic-recovery-opportunity-zones.html.

CHAPTER 7: CHOOSING THE ZONES

1. "Opportunity Zone Resources," Community Development Financial Institutions Fund, US Department of the Treasury, last modified December 14, 2018, www.cdfifund.gov/opportunity-zones.

2. Eric Roper, "Tax Break for Poor Areas Boosts Mall of America District," *Star Tribune*, January 7, 2019, www.startribune.com/tax-break-for-poor-areas -boosts-mall-of-america-district/503952002/.

3. "Opportunity Zones Austin," City of Austin, www.austintexas.gov /department/opportunity-zones-austin.

4. Emily Hopkins, "This Incentive Is Supposed to Help Poor Areas. It's Aimed at Mass Ave. and Fletcher Place," *IndyStar*, November 13, 2019, www .indystar.com/story/money/2019/11/13/opportunity-zones-benefiting-wealthy -areas-indianapolis/4077033002/.

5. "Opportunity Zone Changes Sought," *Transylvania Times*, February 19, 2020, www.transylvaniatimes.com/story/2020/02/20/news/opportunity-zone-cha nges-sought-transylvania-county-nc/43846.html.

6. *Tax Cuts and Jobs Act: Conference Report (to Accompany HR 1)*, 115th Congress, 1st Session, 2017, HR Report 115-466, 538, www.congress.gov/115/crpt /hrpt466/CRPT-115hrpt466.pdf.

7. White House Opportunity and Revitalization Council, *Opportunity Zones Best Practices Report to the President*, May 2020, 6, https://opportunityzones.hud .gov/sites/opportunityzones.hud.gov/files/documents/OZ_Best_Practices_Report .pdf?utm_content=&utm_medium=email&utm_name=&utm_source=govdelivery &utm_term=.

8. Adam Looney, "Will Opportunity Zones Help Distressed Residents or Be a Tax Cut for Gentrification?" Brookings Institution, February 26, 2018, www.brookings.edu/blog/up-front/2018/02/26/will-opportunity-zones-help -distressed-residents-or-be-a-tax-cut-for-gentrification/.

9. "EIG Is Proud to Welcome Dan Gilbert as the Newest Member of Our Founders Circle," EIG, September 15, 2015, https://eig.org/news/eig-is-proud-to-welcome-the-newest-member-of-our-founders-circle.

10. Jeff Ernsthausen and Justin Elliot, "How a Tax Break to Help the Poor Went to NBA Owner Dan Gilbert," ProPublica, October 24, 2019, www.propublica.org/article/how-a-tax-break-to-help-the-poor-went-to-nba-owner-dan-gilbert.

11. "The Truth About Opportunity Zones," ROCK Family of Companies, www.oppzonefacts.com/.

12. Bob Sanders, "A Broken Tax Break?" *New Hampshire Business Review*, December 5, 2019, www.nhbr.com/a-broken-tax-break/.

13. Justin Elliott, Jeff Ernsthausen, and Jeff Vinik, "A Trump Tax Break to Help the Poor Went to a Rich GOP Donor's Superyacht Marina," ProPublica, November 14, 2019, www.propublica.org/article/superyacht-marina-west-palm-beach-opportunity-zone-trump-tax-break-to-help-the-poor-went-to-a-rich-gop-donor.

14. "OZ Due Diligence: A Closer Look at ProPublica's West Palm Beach Story," EIG, November 21, 2019, https://eig.org/news/oz-due-diligence-west-palm-beach-story.

15. Jeff Ernsthausen and Justin Elliot, "An Opportunity Zone Group Called Our Story About a Yacht Club Getting Tax Breaks 'Lurid.' We Respond," ProPublica, November 27, 2019, www.propublica.org/article/an-opportunity-zone-group-called-our-story-about-a-yacht-club-getting-tax-breaks-lurid-we-respond.

16. Zac Anderson, "Rick Scott Defends Opportunity Zone Tax Breaks That Benefited Wealthy Donors," *Herald Tribune*, November 15, 2019, www.heraldtribune.com/news/20191115/rick-scott-defends-opportunity-zone-tax-breaks-that-benefited-wealthy-donors.

17. Colin Wolf, "Thanks to Rick Scott, Trump's Tax Break for Poor People Went to Florida's Billionaires Instead," *Orlando Weekly*, November 14, 2019, www.orlandoweekly.com/Blogs/archives/2019/11/14/thanks-to-rick-scott-trumps-tax-break-for-poor-people-went-to-floridas-billionaires-instead.

18. "Tesla Gigafactory," Tesla Inc., www.tesla.com/gigafactory.

19. Nathaniel Popper, "A Cryptocurrency Millionaire Wants to Build a Utopia in Nevada," *New York Times*, November 1, 2018, www.nytimes.com/2018/11/01/technology/nevada-bitcoin-blockchain-society.html.

20. Storey County Board of Commissioners, April 17, 2018, audio recording (Gilman comments at 55:40), www.savestoreycounty.org/archive/2018/2018_0417/2018_0417.mp3.

21. Brian Sandoval, letter to Steven Mnuchin, May 8, 2018, retrieved from Eric Lipton (@EricLiptonNYT), Twitter, October 26, 2019, 9:45 a.m., https://twitter.com/EricLiptonNYT/status/1188134579598745601?s=20.

22. "Treasury Secretary Mnuchin's Calendar," US Department of the Treasury, April 2018, https://home.treasury.gov/system/files/236/Secretary-Mnuchin-Calendar-April-2018-%20June-2018-FINAL.pdf.

23. Mirielle Khory, email to Tamera L. Ripperda et al., May 16, 2018, www.novoco.com/sites/default/files/atoms/files/memo_irs_concerns_with_the_nevada_issue_051619.pdf.

24. Storey County Board of Commissioners, audio recording (Gilman's comments at 51:40), June 19, 2018, www.savestoreycounty.org/archive/2018/2018_0619/2018_0619_1.mp3.

25. Damian Paletta, "After Nevada GOP Push, Treasury Changed Lucrative Policy Benefiting One County," *Washington Post*, June 22, 2018, www.washingtonpost.com/business/economy/after-nevada-gop-push-treasury-quietly-changed-policy-benefiting-one-county/2018/06/22/d142acfc-74c5-11e8-b4b7-308400242c2e_story.html.

26. Eric Lipton and Jesse Drucker, "Symbol of '80s Greed Stands to Profit from Trump Tax Break for Poor Areas," *New York Times*, last modified February 19, 2020, www.nytimes.com/2019/10/26/business/michael-milken-trump-opportunity-zones.html.

27. Shawn Simmons, "New York Times Misses Real Story," Michael Milken, January 30, 2020, www.mikemilken.com/onlinefactsheet-correcting-NYT.pdf.

28. Michael Milken, "No One Is Safe from Biased Reporting," *Wall Street Journal*, January 30, 2020, www.wsj.com/articles/no-one-is-safe-from-biased-reporting-11580428578.

29. "Tahoe-Reno Industrial Center: Oasis in the Desert," *Area Development*, September 2010, www.areadevelopment.com/stateResources/nevada/tahoe-reno-industrial-center3002.shtml,

30. Caleb Melby, "Amazon Says It Won't Use Opportunity Zone Tax Break in New York City," Bloomberg, January 30, 2019, www.bloomberg.com/news/articles/2019-01-31/amazon-says-it-won-t-use-opportunity-zone-tax-break-in-queens.

31. 787 Eleventh Avenue (website), https://787eleventh.com; Jeff Cox, "Bill Ackman Is Moving His Office to Hell's Kitchen," CNBC, November 2, 2016, www.cnbc.com/2016/11/02/hedge-fund-manager-bill-ackman-is-moving-his-pershing-square-capital-office-to-hells-kitchen.html.

32. Steve Glickman and John Lettieri, letter to Governor Edmund G. Brown, March 9, 2018, https://eig.org/wp-content/uploads/2018/03/EIG-Comment-Letter-re-CA-Opportunity-Zones.pdf.

33. Brett Theodos et al., "Opportunity Zones: Maximizing Return on Public Investment," Urban Institute, www.urban.org/policy-centers/metropolitan-housing-and-communities-policy-center/projects/opportunity-zones-maximizing-return-public-investment.

34. Kenan Fikri and John Lettieri, *The State of Socioeconomic Need and Community Change in Opportunity Zones*, EIG, December 2018, https://eig.org/wp-content/uploads/2018/12/OZ-Whitepaper-FINAL.pdf.

35. Hilary Gelfond and Adam Looney, "Learning from Opportunity Zones: How to Improve Place-Based Policies," Brookings Institution, October 19, 2018, www.brookings.edu/research/learning-from-opportunity-zones-how-to-improve-place-based-policies/.

36. "Opportunity Zones: The Map Comes into Focus," EIG, June 15, 2018, https://eig.org/news/opportunity-zones-map-comes-focus.

37. "Opportunity Zones Resources," CDFI Fund, US Department of the Treasury, updated December 14, 2018, www.cdfifund.gov/opportunity-zones; Council of Economic Advisers, *The Impact of Opportunity Zones: An Initial Assessment*, White House, August 2020, https://trumpwhitehouse.archives.gov/wp-content/uploads/2020/08/The-Impact-of-Opportunity-Zones-An-Initial-Assessment.pdf.

38. Noah Buhayar and Lydia O'Neal, "A Trump Tax Break Kicked Off a Race to Redraw U.S. Census Maps," Bloomberg, February 25, 2021, www.bloomberg.com/news/features/2021-02-25/trump-s-opportunity-zone-tax-break-started-a-race-to-redraw-census-maps.

39. IRS, Investing in Qualified Opportunity Funds, 26 CFR Part 1 (2019), US Department of the Treasury, www.irs.gov/pub/irs-drop/td-9889.pdf.

40. "A Conversation with Steven Mnuchin, Secretary, US Department of the Treasury," Milken Institute, April 8, 2019, video, https://milkeninstitute.org/videos/part-1-navigating-uncertain-world-david-petraeus-part-2-conversation-steven-mnuchin.

41. Karen Sowell, letter to IRS, January 19, 2019, 15–16, https://archive.nysba.org/WorkArea/DownloadAsset.aspx?id=90150.

42. IRS, Investing in Qualified Opportunity Funds, 273.

43. IRS, Extension of Relief for Qualified Opportunity Funds and Investors Affected by Ongoing Coronavirus Disease 2019 Pandemic, Notice 2021-10, www.irs.gov/pub/irs-drop/n-21-10.pdf.

44. National Housing Conference et al., letter to IRS, December 24, 2018, www.documentcloud.org/documents/6745416-National-and-State-Housing -Organizations.html.

45. IRS, Investing in Qualified Opportunity Funds, 128.

CHAPTER 8: DON'T BLAME THE PLAYERS, BLAME THE GAME

1. Gabriella Paiella, "A Nostalgic Look Back at Scaramucci's 11 Days in Of-fice," The Cut, July 31, 2017, www.thecut.com/2017/07/scaramuccis-10-days-in -office-look-back.html.

2. Ryan Lizza, "Anthony Scaramucci Called Me to Unload About White House Leakers, Reince Priebus, and Steve Bannon," *New Yorker*, July 27, 2017, www.newyorker.com/news/ryan-lizza/anthony-scaramucci-called-me-to-unload -about-white-house-leakers-reince-priebus-and-steve-bannon.

3. "Anthony Scaramucci's Firm to Launch Multi-Billion-Dollar Opportu-nity Zone Fund," The Real Deal, November 19, 2018, https://therealdeal.com /2018/11/10/anthony-scaramuccis-firm-to-launch-multi-billion-dollar-oppor tunity-zone-fund/.

4. "Private Placement Memorandum," SkyBridge Opportunity Zone Real Estate Investment Trust, August 1, 2020, www.sozreit.com/sozreit/private-placement -memorandum.

5. Noah Buhayar, "Scaramucci Pitches 'Swank' Hotel for Tax Cut Aimed at Poor Areas," Bloomberg, December 12, 2018, www.bloomberg.com/news/articles /2018-12-12/scaramucci-pitches-swank-hotel-for-tax-cut-aimed-at-poor-areas.

6. "SkyBridge Launches New Fund to Invest in Low Income Commu-nities," Fox Business, January 5, 2019, video, https://video.foxbusiness.com /v/5986151256001/#sp=show-clips.

7. "Virgin Hotels Takes on New Orleans," Newswire, January 24, 2017, www .prnewswire.com/news-releases/virgin-hotels-takes-on-new-orleans-300395661.html.

8. "Virgin Hotels Takes on New Orleans."

9. "Caliber Opportunity Zone Presentation at the 2019 SALT Conference," CaliberCos Inc., www.caliberco.com/caliber-opportunity-zone-presentation -at-the-2019-salt-conference/.

10. "HUD Secretary Ben Carson Speaks at the 2019 SALT Conference," Fox Business, video, www.facebook.com/watch/live/?v=842916792741749&ref =watch_permalink.

11. "Opportunity Zones: How the Public and Private Sectors Came Together to Address the Uneven Recovery," SALT, video, July 8, 2019, www

.youtube.com/watch?v=W44zcoY927U&list=PLYBGAbTYD63a2jBcWt
Prv4Dx-3CI2hXZK&index=5.

12. "Donor Lookup: Michael Novogradac," Opensecrets.org, The Center
for Responsive Politics, www.opensecrets.org/search?order=desc&q=novogradac
+&sort=D&type=donors.

13. "Opportunity Zones Working Group," Novogradac, www.novoco.com
/resource-centers/opportunity-zones-resource-center/working-group/oppor
tunity-zones-working-group.

14. Opportunity Zones Resource Center, *Opportunity Zones Working Group*,
Novogradac, www.novoco.com/resource-centers/opportunity-zones-resource-center
/working-group/opportunity-zones-working-group.

15. Mary Burke Baker and Olivia S. Byrne, "Opportunity Zones—
A Golden Opportunity?" K&L Gates, March 14, 2018, www.klgates.com
/opportunity-zones---a-golden-opportunity-03-14-2018/.

16. Julia Manchester, "Mnuchin Predicts $100B in Cap Investment from
New Opportunity Zones," *The Hill*, September 28, 2018, https://thehill.com
/hilltv/rising/408980-mnuchin-predicts-100b-in-cap-investment-from-new
-opportunity-zones.

17. US Department of the Treasury, "Treasury Releases Proposed Regulations on Opportunity Zones Designed to Incentivize Investment in American Communities," press release, October 19, 2018, https://home.treasury.gov
/news/press-releases/sm530.

18. Rem Rieder, "Trump's Unsupported Claim About Opportunity Zone
Investments," FactCheck.org, June 24, 2020, www.factcheck.org/2020/06
/trumps-unsupported-claim-about-opportunity-zone-investments/.

19. "Executive Order on Establishing the White House Opportunity and
Revitalization Council," White House, December 12, 2018, trumpwhitehouse
.archives.gov/presidential-actions/executive-order-establishing-white-house
-opportunity-revitalization-council/.

20. Ben Carson, "Speech at Charleston Opportunity Zones Summit," US
Department of Housing and Urban Development, July 17, 2020, https://
archives.hud.gov/remarks/carson/speeches/2020-07-17.cfm.

21. Donald Trump, "Remarks by President Trump in State of the Union
Address," White House, February 4, 2020, trumpwhitehouse.archives.gov
/briefings-statements/remarks-president-trump-state-union-address-3/.

22. Bernard Condon, "Trump's Story About Veteran's Comeback Was
Not Quite True," WCPO 9 News, February 13, 2020, www.wcpo.com

/news/local-news/hamilton-county/cincinnati/trumps-story-about-veterans
-comeback-was-not-quite-true.

23. "Tony Rankin Was Given a Second Chance at Life Thanks to Our Pro-Growth Economic Policies," Donald J. Trump, October 5, 2020, video, https://youtu.be/dUuaTnRBUlU.

24. "2018 Kemp Leadership Award Dinner Honoring Sean Parker," Jack Kemp Foundation, last modified March 6, 2019, www.jackkempfoundation.org/post/2018-kemp-leadership-award-dinner-honoring-sean-parker.

25. Glenn Kessler, "Trump's Claim That He'd Done More for Black Americans Than Any President Since Lincoln," *Washington Post*, June 5, 2020, www.washingtonpost.com/politics/2020/06/05/trumps-claim-that-hes-done-more-blacks-than-any-president-since-lincoln/.

26. Donald Trump, "Remarks by President Trump in Press Conference," White House, September 7, 2020, trumpwhitehouse.archives.gov/briefings-statements/remarks-president-trump-press-conference-september-7-2020/.

27. "Executive Order 13946 of August 24, 2020, Targeting Opportunity Zones and Other Distressed Communities for Federal Site Locations," 85 FR 52879, trumpwhitehouse.archives.gov/presidential-actions/executive-order-targeting-opportunity-zones-distressed-communities-federal-site-locations/.

28. Caleb Melby and David Kocieniewski, "Kushners' Beachfront Strip Eligible for Trump's Poor-Area Tax Perks," *Bloomberg Businessweek*, December 6, 2018, www.bloomberg.com/news/features/2018-12-06/kushners-new-jersey-buying-spree-eligible-for-trump-tax-perks.

29. Stephen Braun, Jeff Horwitz, and Bernard Condon, "Ivanka, Kushner Could Profit from Tax Break They Pushed," Associated Press, December 12, 2018, https://apnews.com/article/37b731bd1cc443fa953b112b7afe879a.

30. *Certificate of Divestiture for Jared C. Kushner*, OGE-2020-023 (Washington, DC: Office of Government Ethics, 2020), retrieved from Citizens for Responsibility and Ethics in Washington, www.citizensforethics.org/wp-content/uploads/legacy/2020/03/Kushner-Jared-OGE-2020-023.pdf.

31. Nathan Vardi, "Financial Technology Startup Cadre Lays Off 25% of Its Employees," *Forbes*, May 11, 2020, www.forbes.com/sites/nathanvardi/2020/05/11/financial-technology-startup-cadre-lays-off-25-of-its-employees/#48eed0737c6e.

32. Brian Schwartz, "Jared Kushner Decides Not to Divest from Real Estate Tech Start-Up He Co-Founded—for Now," CNBC, July 15, 2020, www.cnbc.com/2020/07/15/jared-kushner-decides-not-to-divest-from-real-estate-tech-startup-he-co-founded.html.

33. Paul Vigna, "'Billions' Recap, Season 5, Episode 4: Bobby Axelrod Wants to Do Some Good—But Who Does He Really Want to Help?" *Wall Street Journal*, May 24, 2020, www.wsj.com/articles/billions-recap-season-5-episode-4-bobby -axelrod-wants-to-do-some-goodbut-who-does-he-really-want-to-help -11590372060.

34. Anousha Sakoui, "Lions Gate's $100 Million Yonkers Deal Highlights New Tax Break," Bloomberg, September 6, 2019, www.bloomberg.com/news /articles/2019-09-06/lions-gate-s-100-million-yonkers-deal-highlights-new-tax-break.

35. Ro Khanna (@RoKhanna), Twitter, August 31, 2019, 8:19 p.m., https: //twitter.com/RoKhanna/status/1167955088851136513.

36. Charlamagne tha God (@cthagod), "Spent my day with a few good men," Instagram, May 22, 2019, www.instagram.com/p/BxyIjKwAMyb/?utm _source=ig_embed.

37. Keith Larsen, "Scaramucci's $3B Opportunity Zone Fund Is Now $300M," The Real Deal, October 24, 2019, https://therealdeal.com/national/2019/10/24 /scaramucci-slashes-his-sights-on-his-opportunity-zone-fund/.

38. Skybridge Opportunity Zone Real Estate Investment Trust, Inc., *Fourth Quarter 2020 Investor Letter*, Skybridge, www.sozreit.com/sozreit/soz-quarterly -letter-class-o.

CHAPTER 9: SO WHAT HAPPENED ON THE GROUND?

1. Michael Novogradac, "Novogradac-Tracked OZ Investment Exceeds $15 Billion as QOFs Surpass 1,000 Mark," April 21, 2021, www.novoco.com/notes -from-novogradac/novogradac-tracked-oz-investment-exceeds-16-billion-qofs -surpass-1000-mark.

2. "Opportunity Zone Fund Directory," National Council of State Housing Agencies, accessed December 17, 2020, www.ncsha.org/resource/opportunity -zone-fund-directory/.

3. Noah Buhayar, "Trump Tax Break's Hidden Frenzy: Corporate Giants Are Rushing In," Bloomberg, December 12, 2019, www.bloomberg.com/news /features/2019-12-12/filing-frenzy-shows-companies-lining-up-for-poor-area -tax-breaks.

4. Council of Economic Advisers, *The Impact of Opportunity Zones: An Initial Assessment*, White House, August 2020, https://trumpwhitehouse.archives .gov/wp-content/uploads/2020/08/The-Impact-of-Opportunity-Zones-An-Initial -Assessment.pdf.

5. KPMG, "VC Investment in U.S. in 2019—2nd Highest on Record," press release, January 15, 2020, https://home.kpmg/us/en/home/media/press -releases/2020/01/venture-capital-investment-in-us-in-2019-hits-136-5-billion -second-highest-on-record-kpmg-report.html.

6. Brett Theodos et al., *An Early Assessment of Opportunity Zones for Equitable Development Projects: Nine Observations on the Use of the Incentive to Date*, Urban Institute, June 2020, www.urban.org/sites/default/files/publication/102 348/early-assessment-of-opportunity-zones-for-equitable-development -projects.pdf.

7. Patrick Kennedy and Harrison Wheeler, "Neighborhood-Level Investment from the U.S. Opportunity Zone Program: Early Evidence," April 12, 2021, unpublished manuscript, https://sites.google.com/view/patrick-kennedy/research.

8. Jennifer Vasiloff, *Testimony of Jennifer A. Vasiloff to Subcommittee on Economic Growth, Tax, and Capital Access*, US House Committee on Small Business, October 17, 2019, https://smallbusiness.house.gov/uploadedfiles/10 -17-19_ms._vasiloff_testimony.pdf.

CHAPTER 10: PORTLAND: TAX BREAKLANDIA

1. Hilary Gelfond and Adam Looney, "Learning from Opportunity Zones," 5.

2. Nick Batz, email to Chris Harder, January 8, 2018.

3. Nick Batz, email to Jason Lewis-Berry, February 2, 2018.

4. Nik Blosser, email to Jason Lewis-Berry, February 3, 2018.

5. "Oregon Goes Big on New Trump Tax Break," *Oregonian/OregonLive*, February 9, 2019, www.oregonlive.com/politics/2019/02/oregon-goes-big-on-new -trump-tax-break.html.

6. "Portland, OR Demographics," AreaVibes, www.areavibes.com/portland -or/demographics/.

7. "150 Best Places to Live in the U.S. in 2020–21," *U.S. News & World Report*, https://realestate.usnews.com/places/rankings/best-places-to-live.

8. Joe Roberts, "U.S. Cities with the Most Bicycle Commuters per Capita," Move.org, July 29, 2019, www.move.org/cities-most-bicycle-commuters/.

9. M. Ian Colville, "The 20 Best Performing Opportunity Zones for Real Estate Investors," Bigger Pockets, www.biggerpockets.com/blog/best-perfor ming-opportunity-zones-real-estate-investing.

10. *Sortis OZ Fund I*, Sortis Holdings, April 2019, https://sortisfinancial .com/wp-content/themes/sortis/assets/fund-docs/fund-oz/Sortis-OZ.pdf.

11. Noah Buhayar and Lauren Leatherby, "Welcome to Tax Break-landia," *Bloomberg Businessweek*, January 2019, www.bloomberg.com/graphics /2019-portland-opportunity-zones/.

12. "Design Commission Approves 3rd & Taylor Office," Next Portland, October 13, 2016, www.nextportland.com/2016/10/13/3rd-taylor-approved/.

13. Jon Bell, "NW Natural Signs HQ Lease," October 13, 2017, www.biz journals.com/portland/news/2017/10/13/nw-natural-signs-hq-lease-in-one -of-downtowns.html; Jim Redden, "NW Natural to Move Downtown," *Portland Tribune*, October 13, 2017, https://pamplinmedia.com/pt/9-news /375381-260640-nw-natural-to-move-downtown.

14. AB PR QOZB I Property LLC, "Business Entity Data," Oregon Secretary of State Corporation Division, September 25, 2019, http://egov .sos.state.or.us/br/pkg_web_name_srch_inq.show_detl?p_be_rsn=2083987& p_srce=BR_INQ&p_print=FALSE.

15. Jeff Hamann, "Portland Office Development Changes Hands," Commercial Property Executive, October 23, 2019, www.cpexecutive.com/post /portland-office-development-changes-hands/.

16. Northwest Natural Gas Company, "Annual Report (Form 10-K) (2018) (Item 2. Properties)," US Securities and Exchange Commission, www .sec.gov/Archives/edgar/data/73020/000173399819000004/form10-k2018 .htm#s5FB708AD4D38556CB23B01F79D1DE05B.

17. Internal Revenue Service, US Department of the Treasury, "Investing in Qualified Opportunity Funds," *Federal Register* 85, no. 8 (January 2020): 1908, www.govinfo.gov/content/pkg/FR-2020-01-13/pdf/2019-27846.pdf.

18. Jon Bell, "The Goodman Family's Booming Downtown Portfolio," *Portland Business Journal*, June 28, 2019, www.bizjournals.com/portland /news/2019/06/28/the-goodman-familys-booming-downtown-portfolio.html.

19. Bertoni, "An Unlikely Group of Billionaires."

20. Oregon Community Capital Inc., "Business Entity Data," Oregon Secretary of State Corporation Division, July 5, 2018, http://egov.sos.state .or.us/br/pkg_web_name_srch_inq.show_detl?p_be_rsn=1989958&p_srce =BR_INQ&p_print=FALSE.

21. Casey Chaffin, "Much-Loved Alder Street Food Cart Pod Serves Up Its Finale," *Oregonian/OregonLive*, June 28, 2019, www.oregonlive.com /portland/2019/06/much-loved-alder-street-food-cart-serves-up-its-finale.html.

22. BPM Real Estate Group, *Block 216—Featuring the Ritz-Carlton, Portland OR*, May 21, 2020, https://prismic-io.s3.amazonaws.com/baker-tilly-www

/45e049b2-c391-4221-b5bb-fee28c897697_Booklet_OZ_Block+216_QOF
_rs.pdf.

23. Block 216 QOF, LLC, "Notice of Exempt Offering of Securities (Form D) (July 31, 2019)," US Securities and Exchange Commission, www.sec.gov /Archives/edgar/data/0001779757/000177975719000003/xslFormDX01 /primary_doc.xml.

24. Block 216 QOF II, LLC, "Notice of Exempt Offering of Securities (Form D) (March 5, 2020)," US Securities and Exchange Commission, www.sec .gov/Archives/edgar/data/0001802919/000180291920000001/xslFormDX01 /primary_doc.xml.

25. BPM Real Estate Group, *Block 216.*

26. "Fund I: Eleven West," Cresset Diversified Real Estate, https://web .archive.org/web/20200925155254/https://cressetpartners.com/cresset -diversified-qoz/investment/eleven-west/.

27. Zach Harris, "This Portland Sex Club Offers a Pot-Friendly Patio Where You Can Smoke Naked," Merry Jane, July 11, 2019, https://merryjane.com/news /this-portland-sex-club-offers-a-pot-friendly-patio-where-you-can-smoke-naked.

28. Rockwood Community Development Corporation, "Your Little Team from the Rockwood CDC Put on a Conference Today," Facebook, March 22, 2019, www.facebook.com/RockwoodCDC/photos/your-little-team-from-the-rock wood-cdc-put-on-a-conference-today-in-bend-to-tell/2153023904777245/.

29. The Opportunity Exchange, *Oregon Opportunity Zone Initiative*, https://olis .leg.state.or.us/liz/2019R1/Downloads/CommitteeMeetingDocument/170980.

30. "See You at CES2020," Lora DiCarlo, https://loradicarlo.com/blog/ces/.

31. "Open Letter to CES," Lora DiCarlo, https://loradicarlo.com/blog /open-letter-to-ces/.

32. "Robotic Dildo Barred from Top Tech Showcase, Prompting Sexism Claims," *Guardian*, June 8, 2019, www.theguardian.com/technology/2019 /jan/08/ces-dildo-gender-sex-toy-ose-personal-massager.

33. "Oregon Property Tax Calculator," SmartAsset, https://smartasset.com /taxes/oregon-property-tax-calculator#us/growth.

34. Brenna Visser, "State of the City: From Boomtown to 'Zoom Town,'" *Bend Bulletin*, October 20, 2020, www.bendbulletin.com/localstate/state-of -the-city-from-boom-town-to-zoom-town/article_0b781176-1a3e-11eb-ae88 -cf8866bebd93.html.

35. Canyon Partners, LLC, "Canyon Partners and SKB Invest in Portland Metro Opportunity Zone," press release, August 11, 2020, www.canyon

partners.com/strategies/real-estate/press-releases/canyon-partners-and-skb
-invest-in-portland-metro-opportunity-zone-multifamily-joint-venture-secure
-loan-from-bank-ozk/.

36. "Tell Lawmakers: No Tax Subsidies for Wealthy Investors," Oregon Center for Public Policy, www.ocpp.org/no-giveaway/.

CHAPTER 11: BALTIMORE: WAITING TO BE ASKED TO THE OZ DANCE

1. Alison Knezevich, "Baltimore Population Drops Below 600,000, the Lowest Total in a Century, Census Estimates Show," *Baltimore Sun*, March 26, 2020, www.baltimoresun.com/maryland/baltimore-city/bs-md-ci-population -estimates-20200326-nebck2k2anbwrcfsbknphsfgwi-story.html.

2. Ian Duncan and Christine Zhang, "Baltimore Is Furiously Knocking Down Vacant Houses—but Barely Keeps Up as New Ones Go Empty," *Baltimore Sun*, October 18, 2019, www.baltimoresun.com/politics/bs-md-ci -vacants-demolition-progress-20191018-mw3cb5vlbjb4dmnxlbjvjg7tdy-story .html.

3. "Baltimore Homicides," *Baltimore Sun*, https://homicides.news.baltimore sun.com/?range=all.

4. Route One Apparel, "There's More Than Murder Here (Black)/Shirt," Pinterest, www.pinterest.dk/pin/478508147766745301/.

5. Paul Marx, "Rouse's Failure in Sandtown-Winchester," *Baltimore Sun*, March 13, 2015, www.baltimoresun.com/opinion/op-ed/bs-ed-sandtown-rouse -20150315-story.html.

6. Garrett Power, "Apartheid Baltimore Style: The Residential Segregation Ordinances of 1910–1913," *Maryland Law Review* 42, no. 2 (1983), https:// digitalcommons.law.umaryland.edu/mlr/vol42/iss2/4.

7. Lawrence Brown, *The Black Butterfly: The Harmful Politics of Race and Space in America* (Baltimore: Johns Hopkins University Press, 2021).

8. Brett Theodos et al., *Neighborhood Investment Flows in Baltimore with a Case Study on the East Baltimore Development Initiative*, Urban Institute, September 29, 2020, www.urban.org/research/publication/neighborhood-investment -flows-baltimore-case-study-east-baltimore-development-initiative.

9. Michael Snidal, "Hogan's Promises to Baltimore Are Only Lip Service," *Washington Post*, July 28, 2017, www.washingtonpost.com/opinions/hogans -promises-to-baltimore-are-only-lip-service/2017/07/28/7c235c86-5c47-11e7 -9b7d-14576dc0f39d_story.html.

10. *The 2016 Distressed Communities Index: An Analysis of Community Well-Being Across the United States*, EIG, February 2016, https://eig.org/wp-content/uploads/2016/02/2016-Distressed-Communities-Index-Report.pdf.

11. "Coronavirus Disease 2019 (COVID-19) Outbreak," Maryland Department of Health, https://coronavirus.maryland.gov/.

12. Mike Hellgren, "Ben Carson Booted from Baltimore Church Property; Defends Trump Tweets While Discussing City's Problems," CBS Baltimore, July 31, 2019, https://baltimore.cbslocal.com/2019/07/31/hud-secretary-ben-carson-baltimore-trump-tweets/; Peter Nicholas, "Ben Carson's Appearance in Baltimore Didn't Go as Planned," *Atlantic*, July 31, 2019, www.theatlantic.com/politics/archive/2019/07/baltimore-ben-carson-trump/595207/.

13. Maryland Economic Development Corporation, "Special Obligation Bonds (Port Covington Project) Series 2020," MuniOS, December 16, 2020, www.munios.com/munios-notice.aspx?e=2QKHG.

14. Jeff Ernsthausen and Justin Elliott, "One Trump Tax Cut Was Meant to Help the Poor. A Billionaire Ended Up Winning Big," ProPublica, June 19, 2019, www.propublica.org/article/trump-inc-podcast-one-trump-tax-cut-meant-to-help-the-poor-a-billionaire-ended-up-winning-big.

15. Ernsthausen and Elliott, "One Trump Tax Cut."

16. Marc Weller, "Port Covington Developer: Opportunity Zone Criticism 'Entirely Unfair,'" *Baltimore Sun*, June 25, 2019, www.baltimoresun.com/opinion/op-ed/bs-ed-op-0626-opportunity-zone-20190624-story.html.

17. *Port Covington: Spark Innovation. Ignite Potential*, Alexandria Real Estate Equities, Inc., https://pc.city/wp-content/uploads/Port-Covington_ARE-Leasing-Brochure.pdf.

18. Coastal Enterprises, "Woodforest National Bank Creates $20 Million Opportunity Zone Fund to Support Economic Revitalization Across Its 17-State Footprint," press release, November 25, 2019, www.ceimaine.org/news-and-events/news/2019/11/woodforest-national-bank-creates-20-million-opportunity-zone-fund-to-support-economic-revitalization-across-its-17-state-footprint/.

19. Colin Campbell, "Rebuilt After Fire, East Baltimore Senior Center Represents Hope for Neighborhood Rebirth," *Baltimore Sun*, February 5, 2016, www.baltimoresun.com/maryland/baltimore-city/bs-md-senior-center-rebuilt-20160205-story.html.

20. Donald Trump, "Remarks by President Trump at Signing of an Executive Order Establishing the White House Opportunity and Revitalization Council," White House, December 12, 2018, https://trumpwhitehouse.archives

.gov/briefings-statements/remarks-president-trump-signing-executive-order
-establishing-white-house-opportunity-revitalization-council/; "Baltimore Pastor
Thanks Trump for Launching Revitalization Council, Investing in Impoverished
Communities," CBS Baltimore, December 12, 2018, https://baltimore.cbslocal
.com/2018/12/12/trump-revitalization-council-baltimore-pastor-donte-hickman/.

21. Kevin Litten, "Jim Kraft Wants to Keep Walmart off the Pemco Site
on Eastern Avenue," *Baltimore Business Journal*, July 21, 2014, www.bizjournals
.com/baltimore/blog/real-estate/2014/07/jim-kraft-wants-to-keep-walmart-off
-the-pemco-site.html.

22. Prudential Financial Inc., "Prudential Financial Chooses Yard 56 for
Its First Opportunity Zone Investment to Drive Catalytic Revitalization in
Baltimore, Maryland," press release, January 11, 2019, https://news.pruden
tial.com/prudential-financial-chooses-yard-56-for-its-first-opportunity-zone
-investment-to-drive-catalytic-revitalization-in-baltimore-maryland.htm.

23. Blueprint Baltimore Opportunity Zone Fund, LLLP, "Notice of Exempt
Offering of Securities (Form D) (July 12, 2019)," US Securities and Exchange
Commission, www.sec.gov/Archives/edgar/data/0001781725/0001781725190
00001/xslFormDX01/primary_doc.xml.

24. Melody Simmons, "Penn Station Redevelopment Gets Opportunity
Zone Funding from Local Investor," *Baltimore Business Journal*, February 5, 2020,
www.bizjournals.com/baltimore/news/2020/02/05/penn-station-redevelopment
-gets-opportunity-zone.html.

25. Jimmy Atkinson, "Community Development in Opportunity Zones,
with Jill Homan," OpportunityDb, April 10, 2019, https//opportunitydb
.com/2019/04/jill-homan-020/.

26. Melody Simmons, "Apartment, Retail Project Planned Near UMB Adds
Hotel Component," *Baltimore Business Journal*, October 5, 2018, www.bizjournals
.com/baltimore/news/2018/10/05/apartment-retail-project-planned-near-umb
-adds.html.

27. Stephen Babcock, "Galen Robotics Investment Shows How the Opportunity Zone Program Can Fund Startups," Technically Media, November 11, 2019,
https://technical.ly/baltimore/2019/11/11/galen-robotics-verte-investment
-opportunity-zone-fund-startups/.

28. Meredith Cohn, "This Tech Company Is the First to Get a Boost from
Moving to a Baltimore Opportunity Zone. Are More Coming?" *Baltimore Sun*,
November 6, 2019, www.baltimoresun.com/business/bs-bz-opportunity-zone
-business-20191106-n7fxg3wpuvah5fyuoulf47kes4-story.html.

29. Meredith Cohn, "From Silicon Valley to Baltimore: Opportunity Zone Lures Surgical Robot Maker and Opens New Investment," *StarTribune*, November 10, 2019, www.startribune.com/from-silicon-valley-to-baltimore-opportunity -zone-lures-surgical-robot-maker-and-opens-new-investment/564687102/.

30. White House Opportunity and Revitalization Council, *Opportunity Zones Best Practices Report to the President*, US Department of Housing and Urban Development, May 2020, 31, https://opportunityzones.hud.gov/sites /opportunityzones.hud.gov/files/documents/OZ_Best_Practices_Report.pdf.

31. David Meltzer, "How Trevor Pryce Transitioned from Athlete to Animation Expert," Entrepreneur Media, March 7, 2020, 20:34, video, www.entrepreneur .com/video/346911.

32. Michael Snidal and Sandra Newman, *Missed Opportunity: The West Baltimore Opportunity Zones Story* (unpublished manuscript, February 19, 2021), www.brookings.edu/wp-content/uploads/2021/01/Snidal-Newman-Brookings -Draft-Feb-19-2021.pdf.

CHAPTER 12: NO GUARDRAILS

1. New Markets Tax Credit, 26 CFR Section 1.45D-1(2000), www.law.cornell .edu/cfr/text/26/1.45D-1.

2. Office of Senator James Lankford, "Senator Lankford Questions Mnuchin on Cooperation with OIRA on Regulation Review, Seeks Clarity on Opportunity Zones," press release, May 15, 2019, www.lankford.senate.gov /news/press-releases/senator-lankford-questions-mnuchin-on-cooperation-with -oira-on-regulation-review-seeks-clarity-on-opportunity-zones.

3. Canna-Hub, "Canna-Hub Announces Largest Cannabis Business Park in Northern California Is Designated as a Qualified Opportunity Zone," press release, January 16, 2019, www.prweb.com/releases/canna_hub_announces_largest_cannabis_business _park_in_northern_california_is_designated_as_qualified_opportunity_zone/prweb 16037717.htm.

4. Alexander Harris, "The Four D's," Self Storage Association, June 21, 2017, https://www.selfstorage.org/Blog/ArticleID/44/The-Four-D-39-s.

5. Colton Gardner, "Self Storage Industry Statistics (2020)," Neighbor, December 18, 2019, www.neighbor.com/storage-blog/self-storage-industry-statistics.

6. "Construction Spending," US Census Bureau, www.census.gov/construc tion/c30/historical_data.html.

7. Scott Meyers, "Opportunity Zones: A New Self-Storage Investment Option with Great Tax Benefits," Inside Self-Storage, April 24, 2019, www

.insideselfstorage.com/investing-and-real-estate/opportunity-zones-new-self
-storage-investment-option-great-tax-benefits.

8. Ryan Salchert, "SA's First Opportunity Zone Investor: Rules Too Tough for Rehabs," *San Antonio Business Journal*, January 30, 2019, www.bizjournals .com/sanantonio/news/2019/01/30/sas-first-opportunity-zone-investor-rules -too.html.

9. Joshua Fechter, "San Antonio Lands Texas' First 'Opportunity Zone' Investment Under Trump Tax Bill," *San Antonio Express News*, January 8, 2020, www.expressnews.com/business/local/article/San-Antonio-lands-Texas-first -opportunity-13517242.php.

10. The Storage Rebellion, www.thestoragerebellion.com/.

11. "Austin Developer to Build 152K-SF Self-Storage in Dallas Opportunity Zone," Connect Texas, November 15, 2019, www.connect.media/austin -developer-to-build-152k-sf-self-storage-in-dallas-opportunity-zone/.

12. Hampshire Christie Qualified Opportunity Fund, LLC, "Notice of Exempt Offering of Securities (Form D) (August 7, 2020)," US Securities and Exchange Commission, www.sec.gov/Archives/edgar/data/0001758589/000119 248220000652/xslFormDX01/primary_doc.xml.

13. "The Hampshire Companies to Develop Modern Self-Storage Facility in New London, Conn.," Hampshire Real Estate Companies, January 14, 2019, www.hampshirere.com/lens/2019-01-14/hampshire-companies-develop -modern-self-storage-facility-new-london-conn.

14. "United States Student Housing 2019," CBRE Group, www.cbre.us /research-and-reports/US-Student-Housing-2019.

15. "Investments," Jackson Dearborn Partners, www.jacksondearborn.com /investors/.

16. Campustown Opportunity Zone Fund II, LP, "Notice of Exempt Offering of Securities (Form D) (April 13, 2020)," US Securities and Exchange Commission, https://sec.report/Document/0001808388-20-000001/.

17. "32 E. Green St., Champaign, IL," Green Street Realty, www.green strealty.com/on-campus/new-construction/property/32-e-green-st-champaign-il.

18. Jared Hutter, "Visionary Developer Transforms OZ Student Housing," in *Opportunity Zone Expo Podcast*, podcast, audio and transcript, www .opportunityzone.com/podcast/visionary-developer-transforms-oz-student-housing/.

19. "#BLVD 404," Aptitude Development, www.aptitudere.com/properties; "Welcome to the Marshall Louisville," The Marshall Student Living, www .themarshalllouisville.com/.

20. Alpha Capital Partners, "Alpha Opportunity Zone Fund Acquires University Place in Lafayette, LA," GlobeNewswire, press release, May 13, 2019, www.globenewswire.com/news-release/2019/05/13/1822949/0/en/Alpha-Opportunity-Zone-Fund-Acquires-University-Place-in-Lafayette-LA.html.

21. Alpha Capital Partners, "Alpha Capital Partners Meets with White House Council About Investing in Lafayette, Louisiana," GlobeNewswire, press release, August 26, 2019, www.globenewswire.com/news-release/2019/08/26/1906707/0/en/Alpha-Capital-Partners-meets-with-White-House-Council-about-investing-in-Lafayette-Louisiana.html.

22. Aron Betru and Chris Lee, "Comment Letter: Internal Revenue Service Request for Comment Regarding the Opportunity Zone Proposed Regulations," Milken Institute, September 29, 2019, https://milkeninstitute.org/articles/comment-letter-internal-revenue-service-request-comment-regarding-opportunity-zone.

23. "The Biden Plan to Build Back Better by Advancing Racial Equity Across the American Economy," Biden for President, https://joebiden.com/racial-economic-equity/.

CHAPTER 13: DOING GOOD

1. Jimmy Atkinson, "Social Impact in L.A.'s Opportunity Zones, with Martin Muoto and Reid Thomas," May 6, 2020 in *Opportunity Zones Podcast*, OpportunityDb, podcast, audio and transcript, https://opportunitydb.com/2020/05/nes-sola-088/.

2. Anne Field, "Tapping Opportunity Zones, Social Impact Investor SoLa Raises Its Biggest Fund," *Forbes*, May 31, 2019, www.forbes.com/sites/annefield/2019/05/31/tapping-opportunity-zones-social-impact-investor-sola-raises-its-biggest-fund/#7c0816a03b18.

3. Catalyst Opportunity Funds, "Catalyst Opportunity Funds Invests in SoLa Impact Opportunity Zone Projects to Reenergize South Los Angeles Communities," Business Wire, press release, February 4, 2020, www.businesswire.com/news/home/20200204005741/en/Catalyst-Opportunity-Funds-Invests-SoLa-Impact-Opportunity.

4. "Senator Tim Scott's Nationwide Virtual Opportunity Zones Tour: California: Craig Bowers Interview," Senator Tim Scott, January 13, 2021, video, www.youtube.com/watch?v=nuTi_l24MmA.

5. SoLa Impact, "Oprah Winfrey Leads Several Major Philanthropists in Funding Scholarships to South LA Residents via SoLa Impact's CORE

Fund," PR Newswire, press release, July 24, 2020, www.prnewswire.com /news-releases/oprah-winfrey-leads-several-major-philanthropists-in-funding -scholarships-to-south-la-residents-via-sola-impacts-core-fund-301099543.html.

6. "Chicago's Newest Billionaire Doesn't Plan to Die One," Giving Compass, May 4, 2019, https://givingcompass.org/article/chicagos-newest-billionaire/.

7. "CBRE Announces Sale of Redevelopment Site in Los Angeles for $35 Million," CBRE Group, July 9, 2020, www.cbre.us/about/media-center/los -angeles-redevelopment-opportunity-zone.

8. "Valley House, 450 Main Street (Brookville, Ind.)," Indiana State Library, https://ulib.iupuidigital.org/digital/collection/IHAS/id/6458.

9. Nipsey Hussle, "All Money In," Genius Media Group, https://genius .com/Nipsey-hussle-all-money-in-lyrics.

10. "Our Opportunity Presents: Forbes Opportunity Zones Summit (David Gross, T.I., Charlamagne Tha God)," Vector90, June 20, 2019, video, www .youtube.com/watch?v=ObvwhkfCkrE.

11. Irma Wallace, "The Poorest ZIP Codes in America," Infographic Journal, February 20, 2019, https://infographicjournal.com/the-poorest-zip-codes-in-america/.

12. Ron Hillard, "Erie Named Worst City for African Americans," Your Erie.com, November 9, 2017, www.yourerie.com/news/local-news/erie-named -worst-city-for-african-americans/.

13. Erie Downtown Development Corporation, *Erie Refocused: City of Erie, Pennsylvania Comprehensive Plan and Community Decision-Making Guide*, March 2016, www.erieddc.org/wp-content/uploads/2019/04/Erie-Refocused-Plan-2016 -2017.pdf.

14. Brett Theodos et al., "An Early Assessment," v.

15. Jim Martin, "Thomas Hagen Is Writing Next Chapter of Erie History," GoErie.com, December 17, 2017, www.goerie.com/news/20171217/thomas -hagen-is-writing-next-chapter-of-erie-history.

16. Erie Insurance, "Erie Insurance and The Erie Community Foundation Partner with National Investor, Arctaris Impact Investors, to Infuse $40 Million into Erie Opportunity Zones," press release, June 30, 2020, www.erieinsurance .com/news-room/press-releases/2020/arctaris-impact-investors.

17. Erie Indemnity Company, "Annual Report for the Fiscal Year Ended December 31, 2019 (Form 10-K)," US Securities and Exchange Commission, https://erieindemnitycompany.gcs-web.com/static-files/3279c6eb-bc90-420f -94a9-43a708e2eb6e.

18. Jim Martin, "Erie Insurance to Give $1,000 Bonus to Employees," Go Erie.com, March 23, 2018, www.goerie.com/news/20180323/erie-insurance -to-give-1000-bonus-to-employees.

19. Kresge Foundation and Rockefeller Foundation, *Investing in Opportunity Act: Request for Letters of Inquiry*, Kresge Foundation, June 2018, https:// kresge.org/sites/default/files/library/iioa_rfp_6-11-18.pdf; "Kresge, Rockefeller's Request for LOIs for Opportunity Funds," Mission Investors Exchange, October 1, 2018, https://missioninvestors.org/news/kresge-rockefellers-request -lois-opportunity-funds.

20. Rip Rapson, "Mission, Money & Markets: 6 Takeaways from Opportunity Zones LOIs," Kresge Foundation, October 1, 2018, https://kresge.org/news -views/mission-money-markets-6-takeaways-from-opportunity-zones-lois/.

21. "Renaissance HBCU Opportunity Fund—Investors Doing Well by Doing Good," HBCU Community Development Action Coalition, November 1, 2020, www.hbcucoalition.org/post/renaissance-hbcu-opportunity-fund -investors-doing-well-by-doing-good.

22. Arctaris Impact Investors, LLC, "Arctaris Funds Broadband Fiber in Opportunity Zones to Increase Digital Equity," Business Wire, press release, February 17, 2021, www.businesswire.com/news/home/20210217005595/en/Arctaris -Funds-Broadband-Fiber-in-Opportunity-Zones-to-Increase-Digital-Equity.

23. Cory Booker, letter to Steven Mnuchin, June 8, 2018, www.novoco .com/sites/default/files/atoms/files/booker_letter_oz_060818.pdf.

24. "The OZ Reporting Framework," OZ Framework, US Impact Investment Alliance et al., https://ozframework.org/about-index.

25. "Opportunity Zone Community Impact Assessment Tool," Urban Institute, www.urban.org/oztool.

26. Nena Perry-Brown, "DC Launches Local Opportunity Zone Tax Benefit Regulatory Process," Urban Turf, November 2, 2020, https://dc.urban turf.com/articles/blog/dc-launches-local-opportunity-zone-tax-benefit -regulatory-process/17478.

27. "Introducing IRR with Howard W. Buffett," NES Financial, February 10, 2020, https://nesfinancial.com/meet-oz-webinar-speaker-opportunity -zones-qa-with-global-impacts-president-howard-w-buffett-part-ii/.

28. Howard W. Buffett, Robert T. Lalka, and Mark M. Newberg, "Opportunity Zones Aren't a Program—They're a Market," *Fortune*, October 3, 2019, https://fortune.com/2019/10/03/opportunity-zones-market-investment/.

CHAPTER 14: THE BOTTOM LINE

1. "Invest in Qualified Opportunity Zones With Cresset Diversified," Cresset Partners, www.cressetdiversified.com/#investments.

2. David Slade, "Developments Spurred by Opportunity Zones Tax Breaks Rising in SC, Amid Controversy," *Post and Courier*, last modified November 10, 2020, www.postandcourier.com/business/real_estate/developments-spurred -by-opportunity-zone-tax-breaks-rising-in-sc-amid-controversy/article _f45ff19c-0f95-11ea-945c-b384f5c03727.html.

3. David Slade, "Donald Trump Jr., the Former Charleston Naval Hospital, and a Settlement Costing County Taxpayers $33 Million," *Post and Courier*, October 15, 2017 (updated November 10, 2020), www.postandcourier.com/news/donald -trump-jr-the-former-charleston-naval-hospital-and-a-settlement-costing-county -taxpayers-33/article_5f6774fc-a944-11e7-8989-3b1854cfba2f.html.

4. Bertoni, "An Unlikely Group of Billionaires."

5. Rickey Ciapha Dennis Jr., "Coronavirus Delays Redevelopment of North Charleston's Historic Chicora School Until 2021," *Post and Courier*, last modified September 14, 2020, www.postandcourier.com/news/coronavirus -delays-redevelopment-of-north-charlestons-historic-chicora-school-until -2021/article_90e3954a-c5d6-11ea-82d4-3fd87112fed6.html.

6. Jiafeng Chen et al., *The (Non-) Effect of Opportunity Zones on Housing Prices*, Social Sciences Research Network, September 14, 2020, https://papers .ssrn.com/sol3/papers.cfm?abstract_id=3664961.

7. Council of Economic Advisers, *The Impact of Opportunity Zones.*

8. Alan Sage, Mike Langen, and Alex van de Minne, *Where Is the Opportunity in Opportunity Zones?* Brookings Institution, February 19, 2021, www .brookings.edu/wp-content/uploads/2021/01/Sage-et-al.pdf.

9. Rachel M. B. Atkins et al., *What Is the Impact of Opportunity Zones on Employment?* (unpublished manuscript, January 26, 2021), www.brookings.edu /wp-content/uploads/2021/01/Atkins-et-al_JPubE_Effect_of_Opportunity _Zones__employment_outcomes-2.pdf; Matthew Freedman, Shantanu Khanna, and David Neumark, *The Impacts of Opportunity Zones on Zone Residents* (unpublished manuscript, February 2021), www.brookings.edu/wp-content /uploads/2021/01/Neumark-et-al.pdf.

10. Alina Arefeva et al., *Job Growth from Opportunity Zones* (unpublished manuscript, February 19, 2021), www.brookings.edu/wp-content/uploads/2021/01 /Arefeva-Davis-Ghent-Park-2020-Job-Growth-from-Opportunity-Zones.pdf.

11. EIG, "EIG Calls on Congress to Build on Early Progress, Enact Strong Reporting Requirements and OZ Policy Improvements," press release, August 24, 2020, https://eig.org/news/following-new-wh-oz-report.

12. Kenan Fikri, John Lettieri, and Daniel Newman, *Opportunity Zones: State of the Market Place*, EIG, February 2021, https://eig.org/wp-content /uploads/2021/02/OZ-State-of-the-Marketplace.pdf.

13. Sahil Kapur and Laura Davison, "Kamala Harris Calls for Full Repeal of Trump's 2007 Tax Law," Bloomberg, May 6, 2019, www.bloomberg.com/news /articles/2019-05-07/kamala-harris-calls-for-full-repeal-of-trump-s-2017-tax-law.

14. Mrinal Gokhale, "Kamala Harris Talks Small Business Recovery During Milwaukee Visit," *Milwaukee Courier*, September 12, 2020, https://milwaukee courieronline.com/index.php/2020/09/12/kamala-harris-talks-small-business -recovery-during-milwaukee-visit/.

15. Office of Representative Alma Adams, "Adams, Clyburn, and Clay Introduce Opportunity Zone Reform Act," press release, November 13, 2019, https://adams.house.gov/media-center/press-releases/adams-clyburn-and-clay -introduce-opportunity-zone-reform-act.

16. "Wyden Introduces Legislation to Reform Opportunity Zone Program," US Senate Committee on Finance, November 6, 2019, www.finance.senate.gov /ranking-members-news/wyden-introduces-legislation-to-reform-opportunity -zone-program-.

17. Boston University, *Menino Survey of Mayors: 2019 Results*, www.survey ofmayors.com/reports/Menino-Survey-of-Mayors-2019-Final-Report.pdf.

18. Naomi Smith, *Opportunity Zones: Assessing the Benefits of Empowerment for African Americans*, Congressional Black Caucus Foundation, www.cbcfinc .org/wp-content/uploads/2020/06/CPAR-OPP-ZONES-BRIEF-0602.pdf.

19. Kelsi Maree Borland, "Why Shopoff Realty Isn't Diving Into Opportunity Zone Funds," GlobeSt.com, December 16, 2020, www.globest.com /2020/12/16/why-shopoff-realty-isnt-diving-into-opportunity-zone-funds/.

20. IRS, US Department of the Treasury, *Public Hearing on Proposed Regulations "Investing in Qualified Opportunity Funds,"* July 9, 2019, www.novoco.com /sites/default/files/atoms/files/irs_oz_hearing_transcript_070919.pdf.

Index

Credit: Jay Mallin

DAVID WESSEL is a senior fellow and director of the Hutchins Center on Fiscal and Monetary Policy at the Brookings Institution. He joined Brookings in 2014 after thirty years as a reporter, editor, and columnist at the *Wall Street Journal*. He is the author of two *New York Times* bestsellers: *In Fed We Trust: Ben Bernanke's War on the Great Panic* (2009) and *Red Ink: Inside the High-Stakes Politics of the Federal Budget* (2012). He has shared two Pulitzer Prizes, one in 1984 for a *Boston Globe* series on the persistence of racism in Boston and the other in 2003 for a *Wall Street Journal* series on corporate wrongdoing. He appears often on National Public Radio's *Morning Edition* and tweets frequently at @davidmwessel. For more about David or to contact him, see www.davidwessel.net.

PublicAffairs is a publishing house founded in 1997. It is a tribute to the standards, values, and flair of three persons who have served as mentors to countless reporters, writers, editors, and book people of all kinds, including me.

I. F. STONE, proprietor of *I. F. Stone's Weekly*, combined a commitment to the First Amendment with entrepreneurial zeal and reporting skill and became one of the great independent journalists in American history. At the age of eighty, Izzy published *The Trial of Socrates*, which was a national bestseller. He wrote the book after he taught himself ancient Greek.

BENJAMIN C. BRADLEE was for nearly thirty years the charismatic editorial leader of *The Washington Post*. It was Ben who gave the *Post* the range and courage to pursue such historic issues as Watergate. He supported his reporters with a tenacity that made them fearless and it is no accident that so many became authors of influential, best-selling books.

ROBERT L. BERNSTEIN, the chief executive of Random House for more than a quarter century, guided one of the nation's premier publishing houses. Bob was personally responsible for many books of political dissent and argument that challenged tyranny around the globe. He is also the founder and longtime chair of Human Rights Watch, one of the most respected human rights organizations in the world.

· · ·

For fifty years, the banner of Public Affairs Press was carried by its owner Morris B. Schnapper, who published Gandhi, Nasser, Toynbee, Truman, and about 1,500 other authors. In 1983, Schnapper was described by *The Washington Post* as "a redoubtable gadfly." His legacy will endure in the books to come.

Peter Osnos, *Founder*